D0039254

DATE DUE

Br   n

DEMCO, INC. 38-2931

Bride Again

By Beth Reed Ramirez

Northern Plains Public Library
Ault Colorado

New Horizon Press
Far Hills, NJ

Copyright © 2006 by Beth Reed Ramirez

All rights reserved. No portion of this book may be reproduced or transmitted in any form whatsoever, including electronic, mechanical or any information storage or retrieval system, except as may be expressly permitted in the 1976 Copyright Act or in writing from the publisher. Requests for permission should be addressed to:

New Horizon Press
P.O. Box 669
Far Hills, NJ 07931

Beth Reed Ramirez
Bride Again: An A to Z Guide

Cover Design: Norma Rahn
Interior Design: Eileen Turano
Author Photo: Shelly Kincaid

Library of Congress Control Number: 2005924251

ISBN: 0-88282-267-5
New Horizon Press

Manufactured in Canada

20010   2009   2008   2007   2006 / 5   4   3   2   1

Table of Contents

Acknowledgments

This book is a result of my own "second-time bride" experiences and the ensuing years I spent creating and publishing the national bridal magazine *Bride Again* and its latest offspring, www.brideagain.com. This means that without my second husband, Kelly Ramirez, this book would have never been written. So, a special heartfelt "thank you" to my husband for supporting all of my endeavors.

I'd also like to thank Leann Kirkham whose guidance and ability gave me the courage to take on this project.

To Joan Dunphy at New Horizon Press, I thank you for believing in me and in this book. I truly appreciate this opportunity you have given me.

I want to express my appreciation to my good friend Peggy Post who helped me first with *Bride Again* magazine and then continued to cheer me on throughout the writing of this book.

A sincere debt of gratitude is owed to Susan Wilkens of The Second Wives Club, who assisted me in contacting dozens of women who were eager to share their stories of finding love a second time around.

To all the women who shared their stories and their hearts, I can't thank you enough. We learn by what others have experienced before us. Your hopes, dreams, fears, challenges and successed are universally shared by all second-time brides. Sometimes just knowing that you're not alone is all it takes to get through the many hurbdles that a second marriage can bring. But with the trials come the many triumphs. The one resounding story shared by all second-time brides with whom I had the privilege to speak is that finding love again and being a bride again is what truly matters. Everything else, including the inevitable challenges, pales in comparison.

Author's Note

This book focuses on the theme of brides who are remarrying and is based on my professional and personal experience as well as extensive personal interviews. Fictitious identities and names have been given to some characters in this book in order to protect privacy. Some characters may be composites. In some cases for the purposes of simplifying usage, the pronouns *his* and *her* are used interchangeably.

Introduction

In 1996, I made the big decision to remarry. When I began making plans for the wedding, I immediately went out to my local grocery store and purchased an armload of bridal magazines.

After searching relentlessly through them all, I discovered, much to my dismay, that they offered very little for the soon-to-be-forty, not-a-size-four second-time bride like me.

I needed help in finding a stunning, yet age-appropriate wedding dress and picking a wedding date that didn't conflict with my daughter's visitation schedule with her father. I also needed advice on what to do because my daughter and my fiancé's daughter looked forward to being in the wedding, but his son responded with "You want me to do *what?*"

Then there were all those issues regarding prenuptial agreements, his house, my house, child support coming in, family support going out, who was going to pay for the wedding, and what to do with bridesmaids who were matrons. These were hardly the types of topics covered in bridal magazines published for the average twenty-six-year-old first-time bride!

That's when I said to myself, "There really ought to be a bridal magazine designed specifically for the second-time bride, a magazine that addresses all the issues that are solely unique to the woman who is planning to remarry." So, I spent the next two years creating *Bride Again*, a national bridal magazine that was launched in 1999. It enjoyed several years on newsstands and helped thousands of women plan their weddings—until the tragic events of 9/11. In the economic problems that followed, advertising dried up. We had to cease print with the winter 2002 issue.

Since that time, I have continued to answer the many questions asked by second-time brides on our Web site, www.brideagain.com. Not surprisingly, the most commonly asked question has always been and continues to be, "Can I really wear white?" This is followed by, "Is it okay to let my son walk me down the aisle?" Well, these questions and many more are answered within these pages. You'll find helpful advice on everything from whom to tell first, wording the invitation, planning your ceremony, and the appropriateness of a bridal shower to a step-by-step guide for drafting a prenuptial agreement, changing your name, discovering your honeymoon personality, and combining your two families after you have tied the knot. If you're already happily married and thinking about renewing your vows, there's a chapter for you as well. Hopefully, if you're a second-time bride, you'll have cause to hold onto this book and use it again when you renew your vows in fifteen or twenty years.

It is my desire that this book will inform, advise and guide you through your wedding day and also give you the tools necessary to handle some tough problems and help you make your remarriage strong, healthy and successful.

Bride Again

Chapter One

Getting Remarried

I'm Going to the Chapel and I'm Gonna Get Remarried

*F*irst Time Bride: Twenty-something-year-old blushing bride who graduated college in the last few years and is beginning her career. She has stars in her eyes and can't wait for her big day. She's got a large, formal wedding planned and she believes she's marrying the man of her dreams, and they'll live happily ever after. Do you remember when you were her?

Second Time Bride: Thirty-something-year-old bride who vaguely remembers her college days. She may be an entrepreneur, a member of the legal, mental, or physical health professions and has already begun climbing the corporate ladder. Some are stay-at-home moms. Others have or are reentering the workforce. She's got her eyes wide open and is looking forward to celebrating her second chance at happily ever after. She's planned an intimate, informal wedding and she's marrying a man with whom she can grow emotionally and build a mutually rewarding satisfying life. You *are* her.

CONFLICTING FEELINGS?

You are actually getting remarried? I'll bet just the thought of it makes you smile. And then frown. How do I know this? Because I know your feelings are a bit conflicted. I too was a bride again. Moreover, I can see it on your face. You're excited and thrilled to be in love again. When you were younger and naive would you have ever thought that could happen more than once in a lifetime? All those warm, fuzzy feelings of falling in love, looking into his eyes and knowing that he loves you just as much. But then, a flicker of fear and concern comes over you; it becomes a flame, and I see you frowning. After all, let's be honest, there are so many more emotional aspects that come into play when you are remarrying than when you married the first time around.

Linda, a recent second time bride, talks about the guilt: "I took a vow in front of God, my friends and family to love and honor and cherish forever. I broke that vow; I got a divorce. I asked myself, 'What right do I have to take that very same vow *again?*' I also felt that I did not deserve a big celebration. However my fiancé felt differently. He felt we were committing to a lifetime in which we would support and encourage each other. He wanted to take those vows with me, and he wanted a big celebration of our love and dedication. Thank goodness I listened to him."

FEAR OF FAILURE

Let's face that first fear head on. You've already been married, and you thought it would be forever. But it wasn't. Your dreams turned into a nightmare. You and your husband "failed" that marriage. Could it happen again? Actually, yes. Remarriages are not a passport to eternal happiness. There are no guarantees in life; you know that quite well by now. But be realistic. You're older now. Definitely wiser. You've lived through turmoil and you have grown. All those tough lessons learned in your first marriage, the battle of divorce or the bereavement of losing a spouse have made you the stronger woman that you are today. And that's just half of the equation. Your fiancé has also lived through a variety of experiences himself. He is older, wiser and has more experience. This means that together you have so much more to offer as a couple than you and your first husband did all those years ago. You both know not to sweat the small stuff. You know liking his mother isn't a major priority. You only have to see her on holidays anyway. He knows that when your teenage daughter slams the door, she'll get over it because he has children too. He is able to smile and console him when your eight-year-old son says he wants his daddy and mommy to get back together, because he has heard the same from his own family. Both of you know the realities of marriage and you understand that every battle doesn't have to be won in order to win the war.

WHAT ABOUT THE KIDS?

Then there's that nagging worry about telling the kids. How are they going to take the news that you and "daddy" are never going to get back together? This is always a child's dream, even if your child is now an adult or it's been ten years since your divorce. The hope of reconciliation never dies. Well, that is, until you remarry. Then that dream gets dashed on the rocks. This alone can be very devastating to a child. There are other worries too: Do your kids even like your fiancé? Will they learn to love him as you do? How will your children adjust to becoming part of a stepfamily? These are all valid concerns that are addressed later in this book. But let me tell you this much now: the children will all adjust, each in his own way and each in his own time. As the wedding draws nearer and your fears swim to the surface, keep this in mind: the love you share with your fiancé and the strength of your relationship with him will be the guiding force that will bind your families together. There is nothing better that you can give to your children than the example of a good, strong, loving relationship.

DEALING WITH YOUR EX-HUSBAND

Some ex-husbands are joyful when ex-wives remarry—no alimony. Other ex-husbands find the thought of their ex remarrying a very tough pill to swallow, even if he got remarried first. Eventually, they get over it. So take a deep breath and be mature about the announcement. Even if you're bitter, remember, the best revenge is living well. Just make sure you are the one to tell your ex first. Don't let it come from your child. And, in most cases, the sooner you tell him, the better.

FEELINGS OF DISLOYALTY

Of course, if you are remarrying after the death of a beloved spouse rather than after a difficult, or even friendly (if there really is such a thing) divorce, then you are probably experiencing some feelings of disloyalty and even guilt. You may be feeling like you have "given up" or "given in," or that you don't really deserve to be in love again. Old memories may come flooding back and you may wonder if this new love will ever be the same as your first love (which it won't: like fingerprints, no two relationships are alike).

What if it is better? What does that say about your first husband whom you loved so very much? That's where the guilt comes in. Just remember this: You were very lucky indeed to have had such a great first marriage. The death of your husband was a devastating, life-changing event. You have mourned him. You may still miss him, and that's not only okay, it is very normal.

You don't have to give his memory up. He can and will remain in your heart forever. Remaking your life without him is not being disloyal. He always will be a part of your past and an important part of who you are today. Yet amazingly, you have found love again. And he's a great guy. I bet your first husband would even like him. You know in your heart that your first husband would want you to be happy above all else. Accept his blessing. It's okay to move on.

GOING IN WITH EYES WIDE OPEN

You know what the best thing is about getting remarried? This time around you are experienced. You know more about what to expect from yourself and your partner, and you understand the less important realities of marriage. The stinky socks by the side of the bed won't be a surprise. Whose house you're going to on Christmas Eve won't start a war. The fact that he's a spender and you're a saver just means you'll have two separate checking accounts. And you're both okay with that. Happily you both are more accepting and tolerant. With this trip to the altar, you aren't marrying a young man who you hope in time will mature; you are actually marrying a mature man. What a blessing! His character is pretty much set by this stage of the game. As is yours. You are both going in with your eyes wide open, and you both love what you have and want to build together.

JUST ANOTHER ORDINARY DAY?

With the experience you've acquired, you also know that while you are planning an elegant wedding ceremony and reception, it's really just another day marking an event on the timeline of your life. It may be an extraordinary day in the fact that you have found love again after all you have experienced, but the frills of the wedding itself are not what are most important to you. Of course, you want a beautiful wedding. Of course, you want great food and excellent service at the reception. Of course, you want to look absolutely stunning in your special outfit, whether it's a Vera Wang butter cream-colored gown or a pants suit. But this time your focus will be on the celebration of finding love again and making a commitment to each other. It's not "the first day of the rest of your lives" or "a new beginning," but rather the logical continuation of the rewarding mature relationship you have embarked on together.

AN EMOTIONAL ROLLER COASTER

Have you ever taken one of those tests which assigns a certain number of points for each life event you've experienced? After adding up all the points, you refer to the chart to see how stressed you are (as if you didn't already know). Well, even though your focus is upon the relationship and not the frills, a second wedding is another stress-making life event. After all, remarriage is a major lifestyle change, even if you've been living together prior to the wedding. Think about it. You have been married, lived through either a divorce or survived the death of your husband, and been a single mom or simply single again. Then you've tested the waters of dating, eventually finding a serious and lasting relationship, and now you are getting remarried. Talk about an emotional roller coaster! And the ride isn't over yet. Soon you may be a stepmother. Perhaps you will be moving from your house into his and dealing with his ex-wife when she comes to deliver or pick up their kids at the house that was once hers. That's a roller coaster with a double loop. If you have children, they too are along for the ride.

A DATE WITH A THERAPIST

We take driving lessons before getting a license; we take swim lessons before jumping into the deep end and brush up on our

Spanish before our trip to Cancun. Don't you think it might be a good idea to brush up on relationship skills before a trip down the aisle?

Marriage and relationship skills are especially important in a remarriage where past emotional baggage and many different and sometimes difficult personalities interact. Remember, new skills can be acquired and old ones can be honed. Even if you think you have learned from the past—that you're older and wiser and know all the assets and deficits of your fiancé, trust me on this one. Spending some time with a marriage and family counselor, alone as well as together as a couple, is an important step. You will learn something about yourself and about each other that you didn't know before. Whatever that something is, it will come into play later on, and you'll be glad that you learned the skills to tackle the situation.

FIRST TIME, SECOND TIME

Remember planning your first wedding? If you were like most young first-time brides, you were in your twenties and your mother did most of the planning. She helped you select the site, decide on the guest list and find the perfect dress. Either you felt you really hadn't developed your own sense of style yet and it was easier to let your mom handle everything, or you knew exactly what you wanted and had continual arguments with your mother over every little detail, ending most days in tears. Perhaps your fiancé gave his opinion when asked. His main task was showing up on the big day. However, according to surveys conducted by BrideAgain.com, 65 percent of brides and grooms plan their second wedding together. An additional 30 percent of brides handle it themselves with some input from their fiancés, and less than 5 percent have help or assistance from their mothers. This means that your second wedding is just that: it's all yours. You can do exactly what *you* want. Well, within budget.

If your first wedding was typical, it was a formal affair with over 250 guests, most of whom were friends of your parents and included aunts and uncles you didn't even know were family. At your remarriage you and your groom may decide to invite only your nearest and dearest friends and family. You may also decide that a large extravaganza is what you've always wanted. Don't be afraid to invite too few or too many guests. While your first dress may have been a Cinderella ball gown with puff sleeves, this time you may choose an elegant designer gown that highlights your mature figure and style. According to recent statistics, a second wedding is more apt to be at an upscale hotel, a beautiful private garden or in a city hall, like Prince Charles and Camilla Parker Bowles, rather than in a house of worship. If you have bridesmaids they most probably will be matrons. Most couples spend half as much and have twice the fun.

SECOND-TIME BRIDES SPEAK OUT

Shelley tells us:

"My first wedding was in the church I grew up in. My mother planned the entire thing, even convincing me to have burgundy bridesmaid's dresses when I really wanted everything in pink. To this day, I don't own a stitch of clothing in burgundy. There's no doubt that my second wedding, which will be held near our summer cabin at the lake, will feature pink. In fact, my own dress is pale pink."

Kim confesses:

"My first wedding was so big. All I can remember of the reception is going from table to table, meeting and greeting people, many of whom are a blur to me now. What I liked best about my second wedding, which was an intimate gathering of sixty of our closest friends and immediate family, was that my husband and I were able to spend a good deal of time with each and every one of our guests. It was a true celebration."

Andrea remembers:
"My first husband didn't want a big wedding so we flew to Tahoe and got married in a small chapel with two of his friends as our attendants. I didn't even have my own best friend there. We had decided not to invite parents, but somehow his mom ended up coming. In fact, she had so much fun she stayed for the whole week! Our honeymoon consisted of four days of skiing (his favorite sport). I much prefer sunbathing (my favorite "sport"). Looking back, it's a miracle that marriage lasted as long as it did."

YOU ARE NOT ALONE

It is common knowledge that the divorce rate in America is well over 50 percent and continues to rise. Yet, because hope springs eternal, 75 percent of all divorced Americans eventually remarry, usually within only four years of their divorces. Of the 2.4 million weddings that take place each year, 46 percent represent a remarriage with 65 percent involving children from a previous marriage. That means there are over one million women every year who, like you, remarry. Although it may feel like it, you are not alone. Remarriage is much more common today than it was ten years ago. And while second weddings a decade ago were generally held as small civil services at the local courthouse or in Las Vegas over a three-day weekend, today's second weddings are just as elegant, elaborate and festive as a first wedding. And with good reason—a second-time bride has overcome many obstacles, been through the fire, and, despite it all, has found love again. What could be a better cause for celebration than that?

BEATING THE ODDS

With that said, according to the Stepfamily Association of America, an astounding 60 percent of all remarriages end in a legal divorce. Scary number, isn't it? If the second time can be "twice as nice," how can the statistics be so bleak? First of all, we come to another marriage with a lot more emotional baggage. Most have children. Some have lost or changed careers, or have had a midlife crisis. Secondly, if there are children involved we have to deal with ex-spouses, ex-in-laws who still want to see their grandchildren and perhaps debts. And last, we have endured years of hurt and disappointment. Some wounds may still be fresh. Or worse, we may carry around some anger that we can't seem to get rid of. So, yes, remarriage failure statistics are quite high. It's not something to be taken lightly. I hope you are now asking, "Are there any ways to beat the odds and make this marriage last a lifetime?" Absolutely.

FIVE WAYS TO BEAT THE ODDS

Trust: Let's start with trust. This can be a tricky one, especially if your first marriage ended because your husband ran off with his secretary, personal trainer or the babysitter. Betrayal is painful and cuts right to the heart. Even if your other marriage ended for a myriad of other reasons, trusting another human being can be difficult at best. However, to increase your chances of a successful marriage, you have to learn or be willing to trust. That means believing your new husband. If he comes home late just like your first husband did when the affair started, that doesn't mean your new husband is dancing between the sheets with someone else. When your new husband questions you about your new outfit, it doesn't mean that an argument about your spending habits is about to erupt just because that happened in your first marriage. In other words, do not bring old negative feelings into this new union. Believe the best and trust in the new love you have found together.

Communication: Wouldn't it be nice if your fiancé knew you so well that he could anticipate your every need? If he really loved you, wouldn't he know exactly what makes you happy? Well, sorry to burst your bubble, but that's just not the case. Feelings, thoughts, ideas, hopes and fears—they all need to be shared. Verbally. And not just when you're at the beginning of a relationship, but throughout the course of your lives together. Many divorced couples have told me, "Over the years we grew apart. We don't know what happened." Well, I know what happened. They stopped talking about things that were really important. Yes, they talked about the house repairs and what was for dinner that night. But they stopped talking about their dreams, feelings, fears and needs. Many couples assume they already know these things about each other. But the fact is: life changes. We continue to change and hopefully grow, and so do our dreams, needs and expectations. These are the things that keep a couple close. It's what intimacy is all about.

Passion: One of the best gifts I received when I remarried was a book called *101 Nights of Great Sex* by Laura Corn. Each page was sealed, marked "For Her" or "For Him" and contained instructions for something new, fun and exciting to do with my partner. Let me tell you, it gave new meaning to the term "Saturday Night Special." Some people call passion "fueling the fire," "keeping the flame burning" or "keeping the romance alive." Whatever you want to call this intimate connection, it needs to be at the top of your list. Underestimating the importance of sex can ruin many relationships even though two people love and care about each other. I have learned that sex is important. It ranks way up there. Good sex in a committed relationship can get you through life's small and large crises. It can be the tie that binds— the act that keeps you close together and focused on each other rather than the troubles that may surround you.

In order to build that tie, communicate your desires. Don't be afraid to experiment. Find the time. Lock your bedroom door. Do whatever it takes to keep those home fires burning and the passion building throughout the coming years of your marriage.

Money: Here is a possible scenario with which you and your partner may have to contend: He pays alimony and maybe child support to his ex-wife; you get child support from your ex-husband. He still has the settlement monies from his first marriage, and you have the inheritance funds from your parents passing years ago. You both realize that you have a financial responsibility to the children from your first marriage and his.

Money hassles in a second marriage are definitely different than the first time around. Again, talk about it with your fiancé. You both should provide full disclosure of your assets and debts. What are your expectations? Are you a spender or a saver? What does money mean to you? To your partner? Money can symbolize power, control and security. Take the time to find out what money means in your life and in his. Money may not buy happiness, but when it's in short supply, it can really make you cranky! Essentially, the more you talk about this issue now, the easier it will be on your relationship later on. You may also want to discuss pre- and post-nuptial agreements. They have become very common and often necessary in second and third marriages; don't be afraid of them.

Balance: For some of us, this is the toughest one of all. Finding balance in our lives and fitting everything in can seem almost impossible. I watched Janice, a friend of mine, remarry awhile back. She was very focused on blending the two families; she made sure they did everything together. There were plenty of family portraits, activities and events, just like one big, happy family. She purchased a dog so they could all pick out the name together. She decided to have a mutual child—one that she just knew would be the glue that would bond their two families. Guess what? Five years later, she is divorced. How can this be, you ask? Well, she was so intent on becoming the Brady Bunch that she forgot about a few very important things—things like taking time for herself and for her own biological children. She forgot to take time to be a couple with her new husband. From the very start, find your balance. Make sure you have time alone. Pamper yourself, even if it's just once a week for an hour. Read a book. Get a pedicure. Stay in touch with your friends. Enjoy a girls' night out now and then. Then, make time to be a couple— just the two of you. No children. Don't even talk about the children! Take a walk. See a movie. Go out for dinner. Watch a sunset on the beach. It really doesn't matter what you do, just that you do it as a couple. Next, spend time alone with your biological children. Think back to the things you did together after your divorce when it was just you and your kids. Maintain those traditions. Don't be like my friend and be so intent on the blending that you forget to set aside some special one-on-one time with each of your children. And last, and I mean last, spend time as a blended family. Blending literally takes years, so there's no rush. Most of the time, it's best to let things flow naturally. Make opportunities for the family to do things together, but don't force the issue.

Here's a bonus suggestion:

Learn to fight fair: I've heard that there are couples in the world that never fight, but frankly, I think that's one of those romantic myths. In real life, all couples fight. They argue about things big and small, important and mundane. Fighting is a fact of life. There are days when you'll want to do something one way, and he'll insist on another. You'll say black, and he'll say white. And on other days, he's simply going to rub you the wrong way for no apparent reason. And you're going to do likewise. What can you do about it? You can learn to fight fair.

There are four possible outcomes to every fight:

1) You do things *your* way.
2) You do things *his* way.
3) You compromise.
4) The problem goes unsolved.

Actually, all of these options occur, and it's not a problem as long as it's not always the same method in every fight and disagreement. To fight fair, first assume the best about your spouse. Believe in your heart that he wants the best for you and you for him. Believe that you both value the marriage and aren't out to get the other. Next, listen to your spouse. Really listen to what he's saying and repeat the meaning back if necessary, just to make sure that what you heard is really what he said. Be certain you understand the issue before giving your opinion. If the argument is over something that is extremely important to your spouse and it's not that big of a deal to you, give in. Pick your battles.

And last, the three *don'ts* for a fair fight:

1) Don't "sandbag." Don't bring up every past issue and hurt during an argument. Stick to the current issue.
2) Don't keep score. Don't keep a tally of how many times he's been right and you've been wrong. Fighting fair means there is no wrong or right. It means solving problems, making agreements and negotiating the best outcome. Together.
3) Don't threaten divorce. Divorce is not a desirable option and the threat of it should not be flung around lightly or in the heat of the moment. It's a bad use of heavy artillery. Don't do it.

So, let's review. It's okay to have conflicting feelings about remarriage, but face your fears. Set a date with a professional so you both can get pointers to help you beat the odds. You're now ready to announce the good news to the entire world. But first, let me tell you Rebecca's story.

Rebecca told me, "Ten days before our wedding and my fiancé's boys (ages eight and four) announced that they will not be coming to the wedding. And if they have to come, they will not eat or dance. Everyone kept telling me that they are 'just kids,' but it was really upsetting me.

"To add to this, no one from my side of the family was attending. It was understandable since we live on the East Coast and they live on the West Coast. I had assumed the main reason was financial, but my brother recently wrote me an email saying: 'You have to admit that nothing about this wedding is traditional. There is no sense of giving the bride away, no real innocence involved and you're having the ceremony in a restaurant.' He also added that I'm creating a blended family, which also isn't traditional and that I am older. I've been asking myself, 'What is that supposed to mean?' Because this celebration is not traditional it is somehow lacking and not 'real'?

"Because of the family conflict, I am choosing to focus on my extremely supportive friends and colleagues who will be attending the wedding. They are truly excited for us. To make our wedding the truly special and wonderful day my fiancé and I feel it will be, I've promised myself I will keep my eye on the fact that a week from Friday I will be on the plane with my new husband headed toward the Caribbean!"

Chances are if you are remarrying you are experiencing some of the same feelings, emotions and concerns as Rebecca. That's why you purchased this book. So take a deep breath, get cozy and let's discuss the issues, decisions and problems of being a bride again.

Chapter Two

The Announcement

Breaking the News

*F*irst **Wedding Prospective:** Bride and groom share the news with their parents first. The groom may even ask the bride's father for her hand in marriage. Then, they excitedly tell their friends and extended family. The proud parents place an announcement in the local paper for all the world to see and throw an engagement party for the happy couple. Champagne flows.

Second Wedding Prospective: Bride and groom take a deep breath and tell their children first, resulting in mixed emotions, even tears and slammed doors. Then they take an even deeper breath and tell their ex-spouses. The bride's ex-husband may be joyous (no more alimony) or angry (and withhold support in protest). The groom's ex-wife may also treat the news positively or slam down the phone. Next, they share the good news with close friends and family whose responses range from "That's wonderful!" to "Are you crazy?" No real reason for an announce-ment in the local paper or an engagement party. But still, the champagne flows.

TELL THE KIDS FIRST

Even if you really want to call your best friend or maybe your mother because you know they'll understand, don't do it. Don't tell anyone until you and your fiancé have come up with a game plan on when and where to tell the kids. If you each come to this marriage with children from a previous union, it is essential that the children be told first. Other than you and your partner, this marriage will affect the children the most. This will be a life-changing event for them too, and possibly one they are not quite ready to embrace.

The first step is to tell your children, alone, without your fiancé. Have him do the same with his kids. You want to tell your children in person, directly and clearly. If you have more than one child, tell them at the same time so that the message is the same. Some people believe that it's best to tell each child separately, but if you do that, the children who are not there at that time miss out on any questions, concerns and discussions that arise after the initial announcement. Many times those questions are ones they have, but are afraid to ask on their own. Or maybe concerns they hadn't thought of are voiced by their siblings. Not to mention that the child who is told last feels slighted and a bit left out. So tell them together if possible, knowing that you may need to follow up later with one-on-one discussions. Keep in mind that your kids probably won't be too surprised by the news if you and your fiancé have been spending time together for the past several months. Nevertheless, plan on plenty of time for questions, concerns and, yes, tears. It's a good idea to have read up on some usual concerns and voice them, allowing the children to respond.

NUCLEAR REACTIONS

Just because the news of your impending nuptials is enough to make you giddy with happiness does not mean that this is the case for your children. The most common negative feelings children experience when hearing the news of their mom's wedding are conflict and betrayal. They may like the person you are marrying and think he's a pretty cool guy, but are concerned about how this new blended family will affect their relationship with their dad. If they accept your fiancé as their stepdad, does this mean they are betraying their father? Will the new marriage affect the time they now spend with dad? Will their dad be mad at them for liking your prospective husband? And as hard as this is to say, what if your children don't really care for your fiancé? It happens. This marriage may be the very last thing that they want to see occur. At the very least, they will most likely have feelings of loss—loss of time spent alone with you, loss of the dream that you'll get back together with dad and live happily ever after, and even loss of their childhood. All of these gut reactions to your announcement may result in tears, angry outbursts or the silent treatment. But whatever the outcome, stay calm and reassure the children of your love. Let them know that you'll still spend time alone together. They are not losing you, nor will the marriage affect the time they spend with their dad. If you will be moving to another place or state, take time before this discussion to figure out how they will be able to visit their father.

Next, give them time to ask questions, state (or scream) their concerns and air their feelings. Address the issues that affect them. Questions such as, "Where will we live?" "Do we have to move into his house?" "If we move, what about my friends?" "Will I have to go to a new school?" "Will his kids have to live with us?" and "Will I have my own room?" are all bound to come up. When I remarried, my daughter loved her old bedroom and did not want to leave it. It was painted pale pink with a dark pink trim and had murals on the walls of the characters from "Beauty and the Beast," her favorite Disney movie at the time. To address her concerns we had her new room painted *exactly* like her old room, complete with "Beauty and the Beast" murals. That, coupled with the fact that the new house had a pool, totally cinched the deal for her.

Keep in mind throughout this announcement process (and it is a process, not just a one-time deal) that what is foremost in your children's mind is: "How is this going to affect *me*?" Address their concerns during the time that follows the announcement and allow them an adjustment period. Trust me, they all do adjust, eventually. Lastly, continue to keep them in the loop, updating them about the wedding plans as they progress so that they continue to feel a part of the process.

TELLING YOUR EX-HUSBAND

The sooner you tell him (after telling your own children), the better. The last thing you want is to have your children make some comment about "mommy getting married to that guy" during their next visitation. That can get really ugly. You do not want to put your children in a position of having to deal with your ex-husband's response to the news.

It's best to tell him in person, if at all possible. If not, then tell him by phone. If you are not on speaking terms, then an e-mail or brief note will have to suffice. Be direct and to the point. Again, it shouldn't come as too much of a surprise, even to him, if you and your fiancé have been spending a lot of time together in recent months. Your ex may already be remarried himself, but that doesn't necessarily mean he'll be happy to get the news. If he's been paying you spousal support, he may be glad to see that come to an end. But nonetheless, the news may still hurt his ego and pride.

If your relationship with your ex is extremely difficult and you think he'll do something like show up at the wedding and do something embarrassing or possibly keep your children from attending, then simply tell him that you will be marrying sometime in the next year and leave it at that. Later, after the wedding, you can let him know that you have been recently married, the kids had a great time and all is well. If you choose this tactic, do not tell the children the date of the wedding either, as they will inevitably tell their dad. Simply tell them the day prior to the wedding, when they are already in your home and will not be returning to dad's until after the ceremony.

At the time I remarried, my ex-husband and I had a fifty-fifty joint custody arrangement with our daughter: two weeks with me, two weeks with him. Just to find a date that would work when my daughter was already scheduled to be with us was difficult. Because my relationship with my ex was filled with conflict, we had a tough task. Also we didn't want to get married on the first Saturday following her scheduled Friday arrival (in case there was a problem with dropping her off). After subtracting all holidays, birthdays and past anniversaries, my fiancé and I were left with only two possible wedding dates! It might take more juggling this second time around to find the right date for your wedding, but try to be flexible and patient because, oh, is it worth it!

TELLING YOUR PARENTS

The first time around, this is who you told first, right? Maybe your first husband even did it the old-fashioned way and asked your father for your hand in marriage. Although this time you are not asking for permission or approval, you probably still want your parents' blessing. If your parents like your fiancé, tell them together, in person, if possible. If not, tell them together by phone. If you know that they do not like him or may be disappointed that you are remarrying, then do your partner a favor and tell your parents alone. Be direct, answer their questions and concerns, but keep in mind that whether they are supportive of this new union or not, you are now a mature woman and you are happy and secure with your decision.

If your fiancé's parents and your parents have not met, consider having them do so before the wedding so they can get to know each other. You may want to have everyone over for cocktails and dinner at your house, or as in my case, select a neutral location to meet. We chose a popular Sunday brunch to get together for the first time, with lots of activity to act as a buffer. It also guaranteed that the gathering would only last an hour and a half. Since his mother smoked and my mom hated smoking, we ate on an outdoor patio at the restaurant. My seven-year-old daughter overindulged on mini bagels and chocolate mousse, promptly putting an end to our brunch by throwing up. Yes, a fun time was had by all, and that made our wedding day much more comfortable for everyone.

TELLING YOUR EX-HUSBAND'S PARENTS

How you choose to tell your children's other set of grandparents will depend on your relationship with them and the relationship they have with your children. If they live far away or have little or no contact with your children, you may have no need to tell them of your plans. But if they are still active grandparents picking up your son after school on Thursdays and cheering him on at all of his soccer games, you will need to talk with them shortly after sharing the news with your ex. Again, in person is best. If that's not possible, then by phone. Be direct and answer the question they are yearning to ask: "Will I still get to see my grandkids?" Unless you are moving to another state or have other plans to change locales, assure them that you hope they'll still be active, involved grandparents.

FRIENDS, CO-WORKERS AND EXTENDED FAMILY

One would think that telling your friends would be easy and that the news would be met with hugs and happy wishes. Hopefully it will be that way for you, but for some it is not. Don't fret if your news is met with a chorus of "What in the heck are you thinking?" or worse yet, a muted "That's nice." Most likely, your friends, who have seen you through your divorce or the grief of losing your husband, will be truly happy for you and supportive of your decision. Telling friends, colleagues and extended family can be done in person, by phone, via e-mail, at the water cooler or by word-of-mouth.

THE WEDDING WEB SITE

A popular vehicle for sharing the news of your upcoming nuptials is the wedding Web site. There are many Internet sites which offer you the opportunity to build your own personal Web site so that you can easily spread the news and keep friends and family who may live far away updated on the wedding plans. Packages range from $54 to $89 for a six- to twelve-month period. Some good sites are www.weddingwindow.com, which was featured on ABC's "The View," www.weddingwebb.com and www.ewedding.com. Each offers an array of features such as unlimited photos, an interactive guestbook, maps to the wedding and reception sites, travel information, a calendar of events, and links to your registries. Some even allow you to upload a personal video, handle RSVPs online and add your favorite music. Special touches include a page for dedications, the story of how you and your fiancé met, the proposal details and a personal greeting to your Web site visitors. A wedding Web site is a good way to share your wedding plans with those who are unable to attend in person as well as those who are computer savvy and will utilize it for its functional features. You may even want to try a wedding "blog" (short for Web log). A blog is basically an online diary of your on-going wedding plans complete with details, thoughts, feelings and challenges. Blogs can be set up through Google, which sends out "spiders" twenty-four hours per day to hunt through your site in order to place appropriate advertisements on it. You and your partner are then paid according to the number of clicks onto your Web site. Whether you choose to have a standard wedding website and/or blog, be aware that whatever you post on the Internet is public domain; there are no secrets in cyberspace!

FORMAL AND INFORMAL ANNOUNCEMENTS

Many years ago there was a mandate in the Catholic church that stated a couple must announce three times in public their intentions to marry in case of any objections in the community. These were called Marriage Banns and were actually printed notices that were generally posted about town or read by the priest in church for the three consecutive Sundays prior to the wedding. This was done as a safeguard to both parties, giving the local parishioners plenty of time to object to the upcoming nuptials. Grounds for objection included bigamy, terminal illness or the inability to bear children. If there were no objections, the wedding plans would commence.

Today, this tradition has evolved into the posted engagement announcement. Although this is very common practice for first-time brides, only a handful of second- or third-time brides feel it necessary to do so. However, if you are one of those brides interested in having an engagement announcement printed in your local newspaper, by all means, go for it. Trust me, you won't be breaking any social taboos. If you decide to go this route, then you will want to include this information: your full names, occupations, wedding location, honeymoon destination and the city where you plan to reside. You can skip your parents' names, as they aren't hosting the wedding, as well as your alma mater since you probably graduated from college eons ago and it's no longer vital or relevant information. Include a casual photo of the two of you. If there's room, the newspaper will generally print it along with the announcement.

ENGAGEMENT RINGS

Although some couples who remarry do not have a formal engagement nor does the prospective bride wear an engagement ring, if you are planning on both, here are some good guidelines to observe:

Rule #1: Do not wear an engagement ring until both of you are legally divorced. Even if you have been separated from your husband for a million years and are just awaiting the legal documents, do not wear an engagement ring. Technically and legally, you are still married. So, I repeat, do not wear an engagement ring until the ink has dried on the dotted line of your divorce papers. You cannot be engaged to one man when you are still married to the other.

Rule #2: Do not wear your engagement ring until you have made the announcement to your children, ex-spouse and parents. Then wear it with pride. After a manicure, of course.

Rule #3: Do not wear the wedding ring from your first marriage—not even if you are a widow. Not even if you plan to wear it on your right hand. Save it for your child or have the ring made into some other type of jewelry such as earrings or a necklace. But don't wear your remade first ring in the wedding either. Wedding rings are personal and highly symbolic. Don't mix the old with the new.

The wedding ring: a never-ending circle symbolizing love and eternity with a hole in the center signifying the door to a new life.

Originally hand-woven out of reeds and grasses in ancient Egyptian civilization, wedding rings rarely lasted more than a year. They were then made out of leather, bone or ivory until the Romans began to make them out of iron. This added to the ring the symbol of strength and enduring love. Later, in Italy, silver wedding rings became the fashion, while in Ireland it was bad luck to wear any type of wedding ring other than one made of gold. Today's rings are generally made of silver, gold or white gold and now growing in popularity, platinum. Platinum is pure (95 percent as compared to gold at 75 percent), does not tarnish and is hypoallergenic. It is thirty-five times more rare than gold and more durable than any other jewelry metal. Ironically enough, platinum is used in pacemakers—truly a life saving metal.

Today's second-time brides have many options in choosing a ring. According to a *Bride Again* magazine survey of encore brides, 63 percent will choose a gold wedding ring, 5 percent will select silver and 32 percent will opt for platinum. The majority will make the traditional purchase of a diamond, one-half carat or larger, while some will go with a simple band or other gemstone. When selecting gemstones, a second-time bride tends to select her birthstone, the gemstone that represents the month she and her fiancé met, the month of the wedding itself, or one that carries a special meaning for them. For example, some women choose an emerald, because it represents rebirth, abundant life and rejuvenation—all characteristics that one hopes for in a second marriage. Rubies, on the other hand, represent opulence, passion and excitement. Again, positive qualities desired in a second marriage. There's also topaz, which symbolizes beauty and long life, and sapphires, which are symbolic of wisdom and strength. All are popular choices among encore brides.

If you're thinking of having the stones reset from your old wedding ring into your new ring, don't do it. While it's fine to save your ring for your child or reset the stones for earrings or a pendant for yourself, it's simply bad form to use any part of the old ring in the creation of a new wedding ring. A new beginning and relationship deserve a new symbol of your union.

PRIORITIES FIRST

Remember, before you get all excited and babble your good news to all the world, take care of priorities. Don't wear a ring or make any announcements until you are a free woman and your fiancé is a free man. When those two major priorities are taken care of, make the announcement to your children first, then your ex-spouse, your parents, his parents, your friends and finally, extended family members.

Of course, having talked to a variety of couples, I have heard many different ideas about how to disclose your marriage:

Sheri's Story

"My second husband and I have been married for almost a year now. We both have children from our previous marriages. His ex-wife had a daughter from her previous marriage, whom my husband adopted. She is now twenty-one. He came to this marriage with her, as well as two sons, ages eight and sixteen. As for me, I have a seven-year-old son from my first marriage.

"First of all, we told our two youngest sons together. They had pretty much bonded and already referred to each other as 'brothers,' so they were quite excited about the news. My husband told his sixteen-year-old son alone, one-on-one, because we knew he was having a hard time dealing with our relationship. His twenty-one-year-old daughter lives out of state, so we gave her the news by phone. She was thrilled, as she had predicted that we would marry ever since we started dating.

"My ex-husband lives out of state, so I called and told him over the phone. He was happy for me and thought it would be good for our son. My husband told his ex-wife in person. All in all, with one notable exception, we were happy and relieved about the positive reactions we received."

Amber's Story

"My husband, Greg, and I lived together before we were married. Since his daughter was only three years old at the time, there was really no need to tell her since she was really too young to understand. Greg shares custody, so she is in our home often. We still haven't told her and are waiting until we think the time is right. Plus, we're just not sure how best to do it. I know this sounds strange, but we didn't tell his ex-wife either. We still haven't. She is extremely irrational and we just don't know how she'll react. There are already issues of parent alienation, and we don't want to make things worse.

"Obviously, this means we didn't have a traditional or even informal wedding. We chose to elope instead and only told our closest friend. We went to Walt Disney World and were married outdoors. It was fun. Greg's parents were our witnesses. Although they kind of invited themselves along, Greg thought it would be good for them to be there so they could see his love and commitment to me. But, his parents still aren't really over his divorce. To this day, they continue to bring up his ex-wife, which really hurts and offends me.

"I was married before, but didn't have any children with my ex-husband. I didn't tell him either, since there was no real reason to do so. However, I never realized that remarrying carried so much baggage. Greg's ex-wife acts very negatively towards me and is like a big, dark cloud hanging over our lives."

Jennifer's Story

"I am thirty-one and the man I'm marrying, David, is forty-two. I don't have any kids from my previous marriage, but David has three: Mary, thirteen, Angela, ten, and David, seven. We've been together for almost three years, and I have known his kids for two and a half years. We had a very good relationship until David announced we were getting married. Since that time, the kids have been anxious about how things are going to change, and we have encountered more than a few challenges. I felt very confident that the kids liked me before we got engaged, but since then I have seen the kids struggle with loyalty issues. David read a book on helping children cope with divorce issues and thought he was handling it sensitively. However, when he told the kids we were getting married, his oldest blurted out: "You are kidding me! She's like half your age!" Surprisingly, the kids were shocked and were not expecting it, even though they'd had months to get used to the idea of having me in their lives.

"Our family and friends are very excited for us and very supportive. David's divorce was very messy—they went to trial on custody issues, and the relationship is still very contentious today. I met David after he filed, and throughout the process of his divorce, we learned who our true friends are. We have nurtured those relationships and let the others go.

"Luckily, I have a great relationship with my ex-husband. We settled our divorce amicably without any attorneys and we remain friends today. My dad even hunts with him. He remarried a friend of his from high school. They have a child and another one on the way. We live in different states, so I told him via e-mail. My ex is happy for us and very supportive. On the other hand, when David announced our marriage to his ex, it did not go over well. He sent her an e-mail during a long weekend when the kids were with us, hoping she would deal with it privately. She makes it well known that she hates us and speaks negatively about us every chance she gets, often in front of the kids. With the wedding approaching, she has become worse. About a month ago, she filed a petition to adjust David's parenting time. He has fought hard to maintain a stable relationship with his children by insisting on shared custody. She is now trying to reduce that time. It's very sad for the kids."

Ideally, your story will be like Sheri's, and when you tell your ex about your remarriage, he will be genuinely happy for you. And unlike Amber, hopefully your fiancé's ex-wife will react more reasonably. Some women will relate most to Jennifer, who felt she had a great relationship with her fiancé's kids until the news hit them and the reality of gaining a stepmom sunk in. If the outcome of your announcement is a negative one, seek professional help in handling or solving the issues, especially if there are children involved. But, have hope and be positive. Many of the encore brides I've talked to over the years have wonderful, rewarding second marriages—and one of the fun parts should be planning the details of your wedding ceremony. So let's begin…

Chapter Three

The Ceremony

My Big Fat Second Wedding

*F*irst **Wedding:** A large, formal church wedding where daddy gives away the blushing bride. The flower girl and ring bearer are nieces, nephews or the children of close friends. All of the parents' friends are there, perhaps even including people the bride and groom have never met.

Second Wedding: A small, intimate affair held in a romantic place, a beautiful garden or a beach at sunset. There are tons of kids everywhere, including yours and his. And only the people who are near and dear to the couple's heart have been invited.

The biggest issue facing you now is deciding on the kind of wedding you want. Chances are, if you had a large wedding the first time around, you'll opt for a small intimate event this time. And if you eloped last time, you'll be dreaming of the wedding you never had, but always desired. Both choices are equally good, provided you can afford them. Since the cost of this wedding is the responsibility of you and your fiancé, rather than your parents, the financial ramifications should be considered carefully.

First of all, you'll need to discuss the budget. The average second wedding costs about $12,500, about half the cost of a first wedding. Of course, it can be done for much less and much more. Ask yourselves how much you can really afford and how much you really want to spend. Even if you can afford to spend a million dollars, you may simply want a small wedding with only your immediate family and closest friends followed by a reception of cake and champagne. As second-time bride Jennifer reflected: "For us, the second wedding is far less about the details of the wedding and more about celebrating the love we share and the strength of our relationship. I am happy to be starting a marriage with this man. When I was planning my first wedding, I cared too much about the actual wedding day." The focus of second weddings is generally less about the fanfare and more about the celebration. You can celebrate big or small; it's up to you, your fiancé and your checking account.

Once you've agreed upon a realistic budget, stick to it. Next, talk about the overall type of wedding you both envision including the size, tone and style. What do you see? Perhaps a traditional church wedding? Or maybe a small chapel? Under the shade of an oak tree? Barefoot on the beach? Next to a waterfall? This time can—and should—be different, so let your imagination run wild.

LOCATION, LOCATION, LOCATION

When it comes to real estate, it's all about the location. When it comes to your wedding venue, it's still all about the location. Pick a site that is meaningful to you and your partner. Perhaps it is the place you met, a favorite getaway or the quaint bed and breakfast where he proposed. Maybe it's your church or your own backyard. If you're looking for something out of the ordinary, take a peek at this list and see if something catches your eye or sparks your imagination.

Dozens of Wedding Locations from A to Z
(Well, almost!)

Alaskan Glacier
  (It can be done!)
Aquarium
Beach
Bed & Breakfast
Botanical Garden
Butterfly Pavilion
Castle
Chapel
College Campus
Covered Bridge
  (a la Bridges of
  Madison County)
Country Club
Desert (think Palm Springs)
Dude Ranch
Estate
Equestrian Center
Fairgrounds
Faculty House
Garden (public or private)
Gazebo
Golf Course
Governor's Mansion
Harbor Cruise
Historic Landmark
Home (yours or a friend's)
Home Plate
  (baseball fans)
Hot Air Balloon
Hotel
Lakeside
Lighthouse
Mission
Mountain Cabin
Museum
National Park
Penthouse
Planetarium
Poolside
Restaurant
Riverboat
Theme Park
Southern Plantation
Victorian Mansion
Winery
Yacht
Zoo

Maybe you'd like to exchange your vows at a famous landmark such as the Empire State Building, Niagara Falls or

Chicago's Navy Pier. There's also the Seattle Space Needle, the United Nations Building or Exposition Park with the Golden Gate Bridge as your backdrop. Let your imagination wander and select a site that showcases your sense of style and individuality.

If you have your heart set on an unusual location, remember to ask yourself these questions: Is it easy for the guests to get to? Is there enough parking? Are restrooms available and convenient? Will the guests have to walk through a wet meadow to reach the gazebo? If it's hot and humid, will there be shade? What is the back-up plan in case of rain? Sometimes the idea of exchanging vows next to a babbling brook is more romantic in theory than in reality, so do your homework and plan ahead.

FORMAL, SEMIFORMAL OR INFORMAL?

I am often asked the difference between a formal, semi-formal and informal wedding. The basic differences lie in the ceremony location, time of day, day of week, number of guests and type of reception. Here's a quick overview:

The Formal Wedding

A formal wedding ceremony typically is held in a house of worship with between four and ten attendants. The guest list burgeons with more than 150 people. The upscale hotel or country club reception features a sit-down meal and a live band or orchestra. The groom's attire is black tie and the bride dons a formal ball gown. Invitations are engraved and addressed by a calligrapher. Transportation is by limousine. Generally held in the evening (with a Saturday night being the most formal), about 38 percent of second-time brides choose to have a formal or semiformal wedding. These are usually women who missed out on a big wedding the first time around or are marrying a man who has not been married previously.

The Semiformal Wedding

This ceremony generally takes place in a house of worship, country club or hotel, with the number of attendants varying from two to six. The guest list is comprised of 100 to 150 people. A disc jockey usually supplies the music, and the meal is served buffet style. The groom wears a tuxedo or formal suit, and the bride chooses a long gown. Invitations are handled by a local printer and are addressed by a calligrapher or a friend with excellent penmanship. Limousine rental is optional. These weddings are most often held in the evening or afternoon.

The Informal Wedding

At an informal wedding, the ceremony is usually held in a location other than a house of worship. The attendants range in number from one to three, and the intimate guest list is limited to seventy-five to one hundred people. The reception is held in a home, restaurant or garden-style setting with a buffet, appetizers or afternoon tea. Music is provided by a single musician, such as a harpist or violinist, or from a collection of your favorite CDs playing in the background. Invitations are ordered through your local stationery store or online and hand addressed, hopefully with good penmanship. If the wedding is very small and informal, a phone call will suffice in lieu of a printed invitation. The groom wears anything from a business suit to shorts and a linen shirt, depending upon the wedding's location. The bride wears a simple long or tea-length dress, suit, cocktail dress or, in the case of the beach wedding, a light, flowing sundress. Over 60 percent of second-time brides have informal weddings.

When planning your wedding and keeping within a budget, keep in mind that the *day* of the week in which you choose to marry will significantly impact the cost. For example, a wedding on a Saturday night, even if you are aiming for informal, will still cost you more in room rental fees than, say, a wedding on a Sunday afternoon. In addition to the room rental fees, the *time* of day has an impact as well. An evening wedding signifies that a dinner will be served, whereas a Saturday afternoon or Sunday morning affair translates into a champagne brunch, afternoon tea or simply cake, punch and coffee.

THE GUEST LIST

The number of guests you invite will depend on the type of wedding you have chosen as well as your budget. This time, your parents are not issuing the invitations. The guest list is at your discretion. You are no longer obligated to include long-lost aunts or uncles, your parents' colleagues or distant cousins. If you were like most first-time brides during that three year span before and after your own wedding, you were also a bridesmaid in four or five of your friends' weddings. This meant you needed to invite each one of them and their families, since they did the same for you. Well, no more tit for tat. No more pleasing of mom and pop and all their friends and relatives. Simply invite those who are near and dear to you.

I hope this goes without saying, but just in case you are wondering: no, it is *not* okay to invite ex-spouses. I don't care how friendly you are now or how well you think your fiancé and he get along, do not invite your ex or your fiancé's ex to your wedding. Your wedding day is a new beginning for you and your fiancé and should not include the shadow of an ex-spouse. Even if you think you will feel comfortable with your ex present, trust me, there will be plenty of guests who will be highly uncomfortable. This includes those who had to listen to you rant and rave when you were going through your divorce. It's also not fair to your children, who will certainly feel odd watching their dad watch you marry another man.

With that said, there are some people from your previous life that you may want to invite. Perhaps you have remained close to your ex-sister-in-law. You still have lunch with her every Thursday, and she and her husband go camping with you and your fiancé. Put them on the guest list. Let's say your ex-husband's parents still take your children overnight and attend their school plays and baseball games. You may want to put them on the guest list too, even if they decide not to come.

INCLUDING YOUR CHILDREN IN THE CEREMONY

Although divorced Catholics cannot remarry in the church, those who are widowed or have had their marriages annulled need to help their children adjust as much as parents from any other faith.

"When children from previous relationships aren't recognized in some formal way, you can see the disappointment in their faces," writes Father Dennis Van Thuyne, a Pennsylvania Catholic priest. "They feel left out, abandoned. But when children are publicly recognized, you can tell from the excitement in their faces that they are having a positive emotional experience. And because marriage is a public sacrament, it is appropriate that wedding guests bear witness to the couple's commitment to take care of their children."

Including your children in the wedding ceremony is one of the best things you can do to begin the process of blending your two families. However, each and every child is unique. Each child will have a different reaction when mom says, "I'd like you to be in my wedding." My advice to you: sit down with your children and discuss their level of interest in participating in the wedding. Some kids love the limelight, while others are quite shy. Some will simply refuse to be in the wedding at all. If your child doesn't want to be in the wedding for whatever reason, that's okay. Respect and support his decision. But also allow him time to change his mind. When my fiancé asked his son to be his best man, his son's response was, "I'm pretty uncomfortable with this whole thing, so I have to think about it." It was three months later, after he'd had time to get used to the idea of his dad getting remarried and realized that his participation wouldn't offend his mother, when he finally agreed to be the best man.

If your children are eager to be in the wedding, offer suggestions of what they might do and let them choose the role that they'd like to play. There are many options available, and one will surely be a perfect fit.

ATTENDANTS

Your children may want to act as bridesmaids, junior bridesmaids, flower girls, groomsmen, ushers, junior ushers, ring bearers, or even as maid of honor or best man. As a general rule of thumb, flower girls and ring bearers are between three and seven years of age. Junior ushers and junior bridesmaids are between the ages of eight and fourteen. Anything older and they take on the role of bridesmaid, maid of honor, groomsman or best man. Whatever their ages, there is a place for them in the bridal party, if that is what you and your children desire. This is the most common way of including them in your wedding.

FOR THE SHY CHILD

If your child is shy or uninterested in being a member of the bridal party, ask him if he would consider reading a poem, playing a musical instrument or singing a song. Some children enjoy handling the guest book, distributing the programs or greeting the guests as they arrive. Others like to distribute the little packets of rice or bottles of bubbles for the recessional, be a part of the receiving line or have a specially decorated seat up near the front. You can also ask your children to come forward for a special blessing after you and your fiancé have exchanged your vows.

FAMILY UNITY CANDLE

In this ceremony, the bride first lights the groom's candle. Then, together, they light a larger single unity candle symbolizing their union as man and wife. Next, the children come forward and add their separate candles to the flame of the unity candle, signifying the creation of a new family. Linda, a second-time bride, and her fiancé, Rich, altered this ceremony to fit their needs. First, Linda's father lit her candle. Then Rich's parents lit his candle. Together, Rich and Linda took their candles and lit the children's candles. Then, collectively, they walked up to the unity candle and lit it. Turning, they each blew out their own candle. Meanwhile, the song "God Bless Our Love" played in the background. The pastor concluded the candle ceremony with a message on blending families. According to Linda, there wasn't a dry eye in the house.

ROSE UNITY CEREMONY

What better gift to bestow upon your fiancé and children than a single, long-stemmed red rose, which has long symbolized true love? In this ceremony, which follows the pronouncement of the new couple as husband and wife, the groom presents his new wife with a red rose. She, in turn, presents her new husband with a red rose. This is the first gift that they give to each other as man and wife. Next, each child receives a rose from the bride and groom as a symbol that the union includes them and a new family has been formed. A special prayer or blessing from the pastor marks the end of the rose unity ceremony.

HAWAIIAN SAND CEREMONY

Similar to the unity candle and rose ceremonies, the sand is used to symbolize the uniting of the bride and groom, first, and the family, second. Two vials of sand, which represent the couple's separate lives, are poured together into a larger glass container or vase. The flowing sand symbolizes that the couple is becoming one. Next, the children add their own vials of sand to the unity vase, signifying the formation of a new family. The minister can give the children a blessing at this time or talk about the importance of each family member's love, commitment and respect for the newly blended family. The ceremony ends with the following message: "As these grains of sand are poured into the unity vase, the individual vials will no longer exist but be joined together as one. Just as these grains of sand can never be separated, so it will be in your marriage and your new family." This vase makes for a memorable keepsake and is especially appropriate for beach weddings, where the sand can be taken directly from beneath your feet.

FAMILY MEDALLION CEREMONY

One unique and meaningful way to include your children in the wedding ceremony is the Family Medallion Ceremony. Developed by Dr. Roger Coleman of Clergy Services, Inc. in 1987, the medallion features three interlocking rings. The first two rings represent the marriage union, while the third symbolizes the importance of children within the family. Like the wedding rings exchanged between the bride and groom, the family medallion is presented to the children during the ceremony, after the bride and groom have been pronounced man and wife. Entitled "Celebrating the New Family," this special presentation is very touching and an excellent way to include children of any age. It includes an introduction, selected readings, recognition of the children, presentation of the medallion, a prayer for the new family and finally, an introduction of the new family to the guests.

While traditionally performed as part of the wedding ceremony, it can also be incorporated into the reception. Faith, a recent second-time bride from Virginia, and her new husband presented the medallion necklace to her twelve-year-old daughter at the reception as part of the toasts. Faith felt that the wedding ceremony should only include her and her fiancé. But she wanted to do something meaningful for her daughter, something that expressed her joy that they were now a family of three. Her daughter was surprised and overjoyed, as were the guests who toasted the new family.

The family medallion comes as a necklace, ring or lapel pin and can be engraved by your local jeweler with the wedding date or your child's name. It does not represent any specific religion and is designed to accommodate all faiths. It can be used in a traditional wedding, a simple civil ceremony or at the reception. For more details, visit the Family Medallion Web site at www.familymedallion.com.

CHINESE TEA CEREMONY

You may also want to take a look at other cultures and traditions and incorporate them into your own ceremony. For example, an integral part of a Chinese wedding is the Chinese Tea Ceremony in which the couple pays respect to their families. The couple starts by serving tea to the bride's parents and grandparents and then the groom's parents and grandparents. You can alter this tradition by serving each other and then serving your children.

"GIVING AWAY" THE BRIDE

The tradition of the father giving away the bride dates back to the days when a woman was considered a man's property. A father owned his daughter and literally gave her to the husband. Today, giving away the bride symbolizes the father's support of his daughter's union with her new husband. However, as a second-time bride, you've already been given away, and face it, that can and should only be done once. Still, it's nice to be escorted, and having your father or stepfather escort you is perfectly acceptable. However, there are far more appropriate questions the clergy can ask rather than "Who gives this bride in marriage?" Options include:

"Who presents this couple?"
"Who supports this union/family/marriage?"
"Who blesses this union/family/marriage?"

These questions can be answered by whoever escorts you down the aisle or even in unison by your guests. Some second-time brides walk in with their fiancé by their side or meet him halfway up the aisle. You may have your son escort you if he is old enough and agrees to do so, but under no circumstances should he be asked to "give you away." Your son has already faced many losses. He has lost his father by death or divorce, he's lost his time with you when you were a single mom, and he is now going to feel as if he's losing you to your new husband. Be very careful about this issue of having a child walk you down the aisle. While it may appear sweet or cute, it carries a heavy emotional load. And last but not least, many second-time brides choose to walk confidently down the aisle alone.

WRITING YOUR OWN WEDDING VOWS
Traditionally, wedding vows read something like this: "I, Susie, take you, Henry, to be my lawfully wedded husband, to love and to cherish, from this day forward, for better or for worse, for richer, for poorer, in sickness and in health, until death do us part." Aside from a few modifications, this vow is most likely the one you recited during your first wedding. Now, however, you know exactly what marriage means, and you may want to express your commitment in your own words. You want

your vows to be a meaningful reflection of the deep feelings you have for each other.

For some, writing comes easy. But for most of us, while we like the idea of writing our own vows, it actually terrifies us, resulting in writer's block the minute we sit down with pen in hand. Here's an easy way to get started: make a list of all of the qualities you love about your fiancé. Write down the feelings that he stirs in you, recollections of when you first met and what it means to become his wife. Consider using words such as admire, cherish, inspire, lifetime, soul mate, passion, value and never-ending. Once you have the list, it's easy to arrange the thoughts into vows or promises.

Let's say your list includes faithfulness, honesty, love, supportiveness, stability, happiness, generosity and a great sense of humor. You can start out by saying: "I am proud to marry you this day and become your wife. I am thankful that I can always count on you in good times and in bad. Your sense of humor and great generosity fill my heart with love and laughter. I admire and respect your honesty and ability to stand your ground and hold to your beliefs. I feel as if I have finally found my true soul mate. Today, I promise to give myself to you wholly and completely, to support your hopes and dreams, as you have always supported mine. I promise to be honest and faithful to you and our marriage all the days of our lives."

Any vows that come from your heart and express the feelings you have for each other will be more touching and meaningful than standard vows. There's a great Web site (www.brilliantweddingpages.com) that offers sample wedding vows, gives tips on how to write your vows together or separately and even offers a vow-writing worksheet. So now there's no excuse. If you want to speak to each other from your hearts, you have the tools to make it happen.

Once you have written your vows, do your best to commit them to memory, or at least read them aloud enough times that you are completely comfortable saying them. Then write them down on a 3" x 5" index card and use it. Do not count on your memory on your wedding day. Even though you've memorized your vows, there's still the possibility that you will get nervous and end up drawing a blank. As Rebecca, a recent second-time bride, recounted: "I was so nervous, the whole ceremony was a blur. All I can really remember is seeing Rick, who was looking at me so intently, with tears in his eyes."

SPECIAL READINGS

Another way to personalize your ceremony is to select special passages that you can read yourself or have read by a friend, family or member of the bridal party. Some great places to find readings for the wedding ceremony are in the Bible, *The Prophet* by Kahlil Gibran, works from Shakespeare, or Web sites such as www.todays-weddings.com.

Starting with the Bible, there are many inspiring verses from which to choose:

"Love is patient, love is kind. It does not envy, it does not boast, it is not proud. It is not rude, it is not self-seeking, it is not easily angered, and it keeps no record of wrongs. Love does not delight in evil, but rejoices in the truth. It always protects, always trusts, always hopes, and always perseveres. Love never fails. And now these three remain: faith, hope and love. But the greatest of these is love."

(1 Corinthians 13:4-7 and 13)

"Two are better than one, because they have a good return for their work: If one falls down, the other can help him up. But pity the man who falls and has no one to help him up!

Also, if two lie down together, they will keep warm. But how can one keep warm alone? Though one may be overpowered, two can defend themselves. A cord of three strands is not easily broken."

(Ecclesiastes 4:9-12)

"There is a time for everything and a season for every activity under heaven: a time to be born and a time to die, a time to plant and a time to uproot, a time to kill and a time to heal, a time to tear down and a time to build, a time to weep and a time to laugh, a time to mourn and a time to dance, a time to scatter stones and a time to gather stones together, a time to embrace and a time to refrain, a time to search and a time to give up, a time to keep and a time to throw away, a time to tear and a time to mend, a time to be silent and a time to speak, a time to love and a time to hate, a time for war and a time for peace. He has made everything beautiful in its time."

(Ecclesiastes 3:1-8 and 11)

"May the Lord bless and keep you, may the Lord make His face shine upon you, and be gracious to you; May the Lord turn His face toward you and give you peace."

(Numbers 6:24-26)

"A wife of noble character, who can find? She is worth far more than rubies. Her husband has full confidence in her and lacks nothing of value. She brings him good, not harm, all the days of her life. Her children arise and call her blessed; her husband also, and he praises her: 'Many women do noble things, but you surpass them all.'"

(Proverbs 31:10-12 and 28-29)

A favorite reading of mine comes from the book *The Prophet* by Kahlil Gilbran and is called "What of Marriage?" It goes like this:

"You were born together, and together you shall be forevermore. You shall be together when the white wings of death scatter your days. Aye, you will be together even in the silent memory of God. But let there be spaces in your togetherness. And let the winds of the heavens dance between you. Love one another, but make not a bond of love. Let it rather be a moving sea between the shores of your souls. Fill each other's cup, but drink not from the same cup. Give one another of your bread but not from the same loaf. Sing and dance together and be joyous, but let each one of you be alone, even as the strings of a lute are alone though they quiver with the same music. Give your hearts, but not into each other's keeping. For only the hand of Life can contain your hearts. And stand together yet not too near together: For the pillars of the temple stand apart, and the oak tree and the cypress grow not in each other's shadow."

Another great choice is James Dillet Freeman's "Blessing for a Marriage":

"May your marriage bring you all the exquisite excitements a marriage should bring, and may life grant you also patience, tolerance, and understanding. May you always need one another—not so much to fill your emptiness as to help you know your fullness. A mountain needs a valley to be complete; the valley does not make the mountain less, but more; and the valley is more a valley because it has a mountain towering over it. So let it be with you and you.

May you need one another, but not out of weakness. May you want one another, but not out of lack. May you entice one another, but not compel one another. May you embrace one another, but not encircle one another. May you succeed in all the important ways with one another, and not fail in the little graces. May you look for things to praise, often say, "I love you!" and take no notice of small faults. If you have quarrels that push you apart, may both of you have the good sense enough to take the first step back. May you enter into the mystery, which is the awareness of one another's presence—no more physical than spiritual, warm and near when you are side-by-side, and warm and near when you are in separate rooms or even distant cities. May you have happiness, and may you find it making one another happy. May you have love, and may you find it loving one another."

The Apaches share a marriage blessing that begins: "Now you will feel no rain, for each of you will be the shelter for each other. Now you will feel no cold, for each of you will be warmth for the other. Now you are two persons, but there is only one life before you. Go now to your dwelling place to enter into the days of your life together. And may your days be good and long upon the earth." It continues with: "Treat yourselves and each other with respect, and remind yourselves often of what you brought together. Give the highest priority to the tenderness, gentleness and kindness that your connection deserves. When frustration, difficulty and fear assail your relationship—as they threaten all relationships at one time or another—remember to focus on what is right between you, not only the part that seems wrong. In this way, you can ride out the storms when clouds hide the face of the sun in your lives—remembering that even if you lose sight of it for a moment, the sun is still there." It then ends with,

"And if each of you takes responsibility for the quality of your life together, it will be marked by abundance and delight." I say AMEN to that!

For those of you who love Shakespeare, you may want to use these lines from *Romeo and Juliet*: "My bounty is as boundless as the sea / My love as deep, the more I give to thee / The more I have, for both are infinite." A much more unknown author and clergyman from the 1880s, Harriet Beecher Stowe's brother, Henry Ward Beecher, appropriately compares young love with mature love: "Young love is as a flame; very pretty, often very hot and fierce, but still only light and flickering. The love of the older and disciplined heart is as coals, deep burning, unquenchable."

For these readings and many, many others, check out www.todays-weddings.com. I'm confident that you'll find the perfect verse to express your love and commitment.

SELECTING CLERGY

If you are a member of a church or synagogue, you'll probably want to choose a clergy member of your faith. Of course, if you're like me, it was actually one of my first unexpected hurdles. I had been a member of my church for many years. My daughter went to the church's adjacent school, and I created the summer Sunday school program. However, when my pastor felt our wedding site was too far away for him to handle the ceremony, I was saddened, but calmly asked him for a referral in Palm Springs. This ended up being the proverbial "blessing in disguise," as the pastor in Palm Springs who married us did an outstanding job. He even married us on his birthday, and to this day, he remains a good friend of ours. So, start with your own clergy. If that person can't marry you for whatever reason, ask for a referral.

Referrals can also come from other wedding professionals involved in your wedding such as the florist, photographer or caterer. If you are renting a wedding facility, they can usually provide you with a list of local clergy members. You can contact your county courthouse for a list of judges, or go to your local university or college for a chaplain. The Internet can be a great resource, as well as local advertisements in regional and national bridal publications.

After your initial phone calls, you and your fiancé will want to schedule a time to meet with the clergyman in person to see if you feel happy and comfortable with his views. You want someone who will tell your story—who understands you and your fiancé, and is clear about the type of ceremony you want performed.

Many clergy members do not have a set fee for performing wedding ceremonies, and some will tell you to pay whatever you think is fair. Additionally, fees can vary by geographical region, faith and even size or location of the wedding. But generally, you should expect to pay anywhere from $200 to $500 for this service. When paying your clergy, ask if the check should be made out to him or the church. If you know the person well, you might consider giving them a personal and more distinctive gift rather than cash. Also, if performing the ceremony will require an overnight stay at a hotel, be sure to pay for the clergy's expenses in addition to the negotiated fee.

BLENDING YOUR FAITHS INTO THE CEREMONY

Interfaith marriages are nothing new, but coming up with new ways to blend them into your wedding ceremony can be a bit difficult at best. For Christians, the Bible warns us not to marry someone with whom we are "unevenly yoked." Essentially, this means that the more differences a couple has, the more difficult the marriage might be. However, in this day and age of multicultural neighborhoods, the Internet and easy travel, the world has become a very small place. The chances of falling in

love with someone outside of your religion or culture are actually
quite high. When you were young and first married, religion may
not have played a big part in your life or in your ceremony. Now
perhaps you have children. You've all been attending the same
church, synagogue or temple for years, and you want to continue
their religious training. What was not an issue in your first
wedding may very well be "the big issue" in your second. But not
to worry, many couples of different faiths choose to continue
their own traditions and follow their own beliefs while respecting
their partners'. If this applies to you, there are ways you can
blend both faiths into your wedding ceremony.

First of all, discuss which rituals and traditions you and the
man you are marrying would each like to have incorporated into
the wedding. Then find an officiant who will perform the
ceremony. In the case of a Christian-Jewish ceremony, this will
be a rabbi and a priest or pastor. In most instances, clergy are
happy to design a ceremony for you that includes and respects
the rituals and traditions of each of your faiths.

According to Reverend Deborah Steen and Rabbi Roger
Ross, who are interfaith clergy in New York, a second wedding
ceremony should reflect the beliefs and customs of the individual
bride and groom; things they truly wish to say. In an interfaith
marriage, this might include certain prayers, readings or cultural
traditions from each religion. For example, a Chinese wedding
may include a Blessing of the Ancestors as part of the unity
candle ceremony, or a Celtic ceremony can include the wrapping
and blessing of hands (hand fasting) right before the vows. The
old Sicilian custom of kissing the wedding ring before the groom
places it on the bride's finger can also be included. All of these
traditions make for very personal touches. A blending of faiths in
a ceremony can be richly rewarding to both you and your
partner, as well as to the guests. Speaking of the guests, you may
want to consider including a brief description of the rituals and

traditions in the program so that they will understand more clearly the importance of each ritual as it is performed.

On the other hand, each religion has its own rules and regulations, some of which may not allow the ceremonies of two faiths in one wedding. Or, the two religions may have conflicting beliefs. For example, Muslims consider praying to the trinity a violation of their belief in one God. Christians may wish to have a Saturday wedding, while according to Jewish tradition, weddings are not to be held on the Sabbath. In some of these cases, you will need to consider having two separate ceremonies and one reception.

SEATING AT THE
FORMAL OR SEMI-FORMAL CEREMONY

When a second wedding is formal or semi-formal, seating is much like that of a first wedding. Generally, the parents, family and friends of the bride sit on the left, and the parents, family and friends of the groom sit on the right.

The stickiness comes in when it's time to decide where to place parents who are divorced and remarried. Your mother gets the best seat in the house, which if you are being married in a church or synagogue is on the aisle in the front pew on the left. If she has remarried, her husband sits with her. If she has not remarried, another family member or friend may sit with her. If she and your father get along, assuming he has remarried, he and his wife can also sit in the front pew. If your parents are divorced and hate each other and things could get ugly, your mom still gets the place of honor up front. Next, her family takes the seats behind her, along with any children you may have that are not in the bridal party. Then, your dad and his wife can take seats in the third or fourth row back. The more animosity, the more desirable it is to have space between which can be easily "buffered" with family members or close friends. If your mother, or any parent, is deceased, some have started a lovely tradition of placing a single rose on a seat in honor and remembrance of the person.

When seating parents, your fiancé's parents get seated first (after all other guests have arrived and been seated), then your parents. If your dad has remarried, your stepmother gets escorted to her seat, and your dad follows behind. The same goes for your mother. If she has remarried, she is escorted, and her husband follows behind. In some second weddings, I have also seen the groom escort his mother to her seat, which is a very sweet touch. The mother of the bride is always seated last, signifying the official beginning of the wedding. Any guest arriving after that time is considered late and is to be seated from the side aisle rather than the center aisle.

Two things to keep in mind: Make sure your ushers or close friends acting in that capacity know about the seating arrangements if you have a complicated family. Instruct them where and how people should be seated. This will help avoid any hurt or uncomfortable feelings. Secondly, the best seats at a wedding are on the aisle, because those seated there can see the bride. This means it's better to have more rows with fewer seats than more seats with fewer rows.

THE WEDDING PLANNER

For a remarriage, it's usually not your mother's responsibility to help you plan your wedding. Therefore, you may want to hire the services of a professional wedding planner or bridal consultant. Here are ten great reasons to use the services of a bridal consultant:

1. The consultant can reduce the stress of planning everything on your own and be a calming force, taking on your worries and concerns.

2. She or he will save you time, which you probably don't have much of since you may have children, a career and a hectic life.

3. She can cut your costs because she has access to vendors you may never have heard about and is aware of the best services at the lowest costs.

4. She generally has a team of experts on hand—travel agents, floral designers, musicians, photographers and other wedding vendors.

5. She can get you good service. All of her contacts are tried and true, hand-selected people and companies she has worked with many times over.

6. Bridal consultants usually try to be objective and unbiased.

7. She has legal knowledge about hotel contracts, marriage license requirements and other vendor documents.

8. She is up-to-date on today's trends. From apparel to food and flowers, weddings change with the times and a consultant follows these changes closely.

9. She can offer expert advice. She has planned hundreds of weddings and has the experience to make your wedding even better than if you were to plan it on your own.

10. Many wedding planners also help you with the little "extras." She will give referrals to good manicurist, a local spa or makeup artist. Some even assist with vow writing.

Best of all, unlike the scenario of the movie "The Wedding Planner" starring Jennifer Lopez, you do not need to have a lot of money to enlist the assistance of a coordinator. The majority of planners either charge a percentage of the total cost of the wedding or a flat or hourly fee. Generally speaking, the amount of time, money and stress a wedding planner can save you is well worth every penny. (I mean dollar.)

How do you find a wedding coordinator? Start with The Association of Bridal Consultants by visiting www.bridalassn.com or calling (860) 355-4664. This association has been a professional organization since 1981 and has about 2,500 members in twenty-eight countries. They can refer you to a list of member bridal consultants in your locale or the one where you wedding will be held. You may also check out the advertisements and listings in your local or regional bridal publications. If you are attending a local bridal show, there are bound to be a few exhibiting there as well. And last but not least, there is also your handy Yellow Pages phone directory.

Now, what do you ask a wedding coordinator when you've got her on the phone? Here's a quick list of good queries:

* What are your services?
* How do you determine your fee?
* How many years have you been in business?
* Are you the person I will be working with the entire time, including my wedding day?
* Who can you recommend for music, videos and photographs?
* Will you give me two or three references of recent second-time brides you have worked with?
* To what professional bridal organizations do you belong?

The questions I've posed may seem a bit too aggressive or numerous, but trust me, these are the areas you need to cover. After talking with numerous bridal consultants, most were amazed at how many brides did *not* ask enough questions. If the bridal consultant is good at what she does, she will want you to know her background, level of professionalism and capabilities.

Also, each coordinator has a different niche. Some are awesome when it comes to large, spectacular weddings. Others excel at small, intimate ones. And still others specialize in destination weddings. So ask plenty of questions and find the consultant that best fits you and the wedding style you desire.

DESTINATION WEDDINGS

Want to get away from it all? Want to save money and time by combining your wedding with your honeymoon? Thinking of getting married on the beach in Jamaica or next to a waterfall in Hawaii? Having trouble with all the hassles of an interfaith or interracial wedding ceremony? Don't want to bother with family conflicts? If you answer "yes" to any of these questions, then the destination wedding may be for you.

Destination weddings are very popular with second-time brides who desire a small, informal and intimate ceremony in a resort setting. They can be uncomplicated, relatively stress-free and easy to arrange.

According to Linda Pasadava of A Vow Exchange in Kauai, Hawaii, 55 percent of the clients she has worked with over the past two years have been second-time brides. According to Linda, if you opt for a destination wedding, a wedding planner is crucial for two reasons. One: you will be dealing with an unfamiliar area. You won't know the local vendors or what things actually look like as opposed to the way you've seen the place pictured in a brochure or on an Internet site. Two: you will be far from home. You don't have ease of access to the vendors and may be dealing with different time zones and long distance phone calls.

A typical destination second wedding in Kauai could take place on one of their fifty-seven miles of beaches, in a secluded garden, or by a waterfall in the mountains with only the couple's children, immediate family and closest friends in attendance. Linda offers this advice to brides considering a destination wedding: "Select a wedding planner and let her know the type of location you desire, rather than selecting a hotel and being assigned a hotel employee who handles weddings. With a wedding planner you will receive better personal attention and a more creative and unique ceremony. You also won't be using a hotel employee who may have to attend to many other ceremonies going on the same day." She also notes two additional benefits of a destination wedding. First, incorporating the traditions and cultures of the destination make for a unique and memorable ceremony. Second, the opportunity to return to the same place for future anniversaries and vow renewals makes it even more special.

Another important thing to keep in mind when planning a destination wedding is to plan early. This way you can arrange for the best airfare rates and travel schedules, while allowing guests time to budget for the trip. You may even want to consider booking in the off-season for lower hotel rates and smaller crowds. Remember, you'll need to inquire about the state or country's process for obtaining a marriage license.

Upon your return from your destination wedding, you may want to host a reception for friends and family who missed out on the ceremony. At the party you can show a video of the ceremony or display a photo album or collage of snapshots taken during the wedding and honeymoon.

Here are some stories from encore brides that will both give you suggestions and get you thinking:

Linda's Story

"My first wedding took place when I was just twenty years old. I was actually the last of my crowd to marry and was feeling a bit desperate. I literally married the boy next door who was my eighth grade crush. We were married for twenty-five years, but we had little in common and didn't get along for many years. I stayed married because of the kids. Eventually, I decided to end it. I didn't ask for alimony, because I didn't want things to get ugly over money or material goods. I wanted my daughters to remember the years we had shared together rather than a bitter divorce. In fact, while planning my second wedding with Rich, my thoughts were mostly of my daughters. I wanted them to be comfortable with the idea of my remarrying, and I wanted them to be a part of the ceremony and celebration. Although one daughter was angry at first, she later accepted my new-found happiness, and both were my bridesmaids along with three of my friends.

"My first hurdle was finding a church where we could hold the ceremony. I was raised Catholic, but I am now an Assembly of God member. My pastor would not perform the ceremony because I had been divorced. It was important to both my fiancé and me that we were married in a proper church. We eventually found a wonderful minister who was happy to perform the ceremony.

"Music is very much a part of our lives, so I spent a good deal of time finding the perfect music. At first, I wanted a very small, private wedding with only our immediate family present. I really didn't want a big 'to-do.' However, my fiancé wanted a large wedding. He said a second wedding was a celebration of love and creating a new family together. It was more than just the two of us; we were uniting our families and that deserved a big celebration. So we started our guest list. I kept wanting to cut it down because I was worried about what people might think. After awhile I realized, 'What the heck, who cares what others think?' So we went ahead and invited about 150 guests.

"The only other hurdle we had was deciding who

would give me away. At forty-nine years of age, the thought of being 'given away' was ridiculous! So again we threw away the rulebook and did what we wanted. The bridesmaids, who included my daughters, walked in first. The groomsmen, including my fiancé's son, came next. And last, Rich came back down the aisle and escorted me to the altar himself. It couldn't have been more perfect. Our wedding was fabulous!"

Sheri's Story

"My first wedding was huge. We had about 400 guests and it was very formal. It was held in the church where I grew up, so all my family and friends were there. I had ten bridesmaids.

"For my second wedding, we decided to be married in an aviation museum. The man I was going to marry was a military pilot, so he wore his dress blues. I wore a simple silk gown which had spaghetti straps and no train. My fiancé's brother was his best man and my brother was a groomsman. My seven-year-old son and my fiancé's eight-year-old son were the ring bearers. My fiancé's sister was my maid of honor and his twenty-one-year-old daughter was a bridesmaid. My ten-year-old niece was a junior bridesmaid and her seven-year-old sister was the flower girl. In all, we had eight members in the bridal party, which sounds large, but not compared to my first wedding, where there were twenty."

Cara's Story

"There were several reasons why my fiancé and I chose a destination wedding. First of all, I had been a wedding coordinator years ago. I knew some of the difficulties couples encountered when making the endless decisions it took just to make the simplest of ceremonies work. Plus, my fiancé was not a religious man. He was spiritual, but not a member of a church, so we didn't want a traditional church wedding. And last, we really didn't want to take on the expense of a wedding.

"We started fantasizing about a small, simple, private, casual ceremony and a tropical, luxurious, adventurous honeymoon. We wanted to be barefoot on a beach at sunset. Other than that, my only requirements were that we write our own vows and that I be a June bride.

We looked at brochures and write-ups of places ranging from the Caribbean to the South Pacific. We settled on Yasawa, a small island in Fiji. It was a wonderful choice. When we arrived at the resort, we were treated like royalty. Everything was in place…except for the actual wedding date. I had our titanium wedding bands engraved with the month and the year, leaving the day open. Once the weather cooperated (it rains a lot in Fiji) and we decided on the exact date, something odd happened: the resort coordinator asked if we would allow the other guests to attend! It's a small resort, no more than twenty-four guests at any given time. Apparently, several of them had asked to come. We were amazed that they wanted to take time away from their own vacations, anniversary trips or honeymoons to witness our vows. We were humbled. So, we quickly sent out invitations to all—and all attended.

The day of the ceremony was even better than we imagined. We enjoyed a relaxing breakfast and a walk on the beach. Then, while I got ready, my fiancé went sailing. The entire resort seemed involved in the preparation. Some people gathered flowers from the jungle and laid them on the sand where the ceremony would take place. Others set out chairs and wove flowers into the ceremonial arch. Everyone was busy, yet smiling and relaxed.

On the day we had chosen, I dressed in an ivory tank swimsuit with an ivory silk sarong and my fiancé was clad in comfortable linen shorts and a crisp white linen shirt— both of us were barefoot. The sun was just above the water, which was gently breaking on the shore near where we were standing. The local minister spoke of spiritual union and honor. Then we recited the vows we had memorized. We exchanged rings and sealed our union with a kiss.

After the ceremony, Fijian warriors carried each of us on a hibiscus-covered throne to the honeymoon burre where musicians played and the guests joined us for champagne and cake. It was a fabulous wedding."

Whether you marry in a museum like Sheri, have your fiancé escort you down the aisle like Linda, or like Cara choose to marry barefoot on the beach at sunset in a destination wedding, your second wedding is yours and yours alone. Take the time to talk with your partner to really discover which type of wedding ceremony will best express your love and joy at finding love again. Whether big or small, at home or in a far away locale, this wedding and the future you and the man you marry will build together is a cause for celebration. Celebrate it with all your heart.

Chapter Four

Themes for Weddings and Receptions

Eat, Drink and Be Remarried

*F*irst **Wedding:** Hassling with parents over costs and guest lists, continuous fussing over the menu, agonizing over the band, perfecting the art of the first dance, fretting over who should be the bridesmaids and groomsmen, going all out for the extravagant reception and fifty-pound wedding photo album and locating the perfect little party favor.

Second Wedding: You and your husband-to-be are the only ones who must agree on style, budget and location. Who has time to argue between this month's PTA fundraiser and next month's business trip?

The average second-time bride who is in her late thirties has planned or hosted numerous parties and soirees. This means I am not going to bore you with chitchat about how to find a caterer, how to set up the reception room or how much champagne to pour. Nor will I tell you how to find a good disc jockey, florist or photographer. Since you've been married before, I'm guessing that you have attended a lot of weddings and other special events. So let's concentrate on ideas for a fun or personal reception, alternatives to the usual guest book and tips on where to seat his divorced parents. I bet you're thinking about finding toasts and music selections that are appropriate and applicable to this wedding. Also, I'm going to make a variety of suggestions on how to hold on to some fun traditions while tossing others to the wind. And last, if you have children or are acquiring stepchildren, you need ideas on how to keep the kids happy and occupied while you dance the night away. So let's get started.

Luckily, if your ceremony and reception are in the same location, half your work is already done. However, if you are exchanging vows in a chapel or house of worship and then hosting the reception at another site, you need to locate that ideal venue you're dreaming of. Start by looking at the list suggested for ceremony sites in Chapter Three. Keep in mind that you will want to select a place that is within twenty to thirty minutes of the ceremony site, making it convenient for your guests to get there. Some interesting locales are an art gallery, museum, inn or unique restaurant.

THEMES

Consider a themed reception. Themes can be tied to the time of year, reception location, specific holiday or you and your partner's favorite pastime. They can be fun, festive and more unique than the traditional wedding reception, which is usually comprised of a sit-down dinner or buffet and dancing. The following are some favorites you may want to consider.

Winter White

Second-time brides often choose winter weddings for a variety of reasons. Some simply love that time of year. Some want to take advantage of lower prices offered in the off-season. Others like the option of winter wedding gowns, because for a more mature figure they can be so much more flattering than the spaghetti strap sheath or barely-there fashions. In addition, first-time brides often choose June. Second-time brides choose a contrasting season so new memories won't mingle with the old.

Additionally, the winter white wedding can be quite dramatic. Imagine walking into a reception room decorated in pure white with just a splash of powder blue or silver for accent. White flowers adorn centerpieces and rose petals lie scattered on the floor like snow. Sheer, iridescent fabric overlays drape the tables, with a handful of rhinestones tossed on top to catch the light of the flickering white taper candles. An ice sculpture stands in the center of the room, surrounded by shiny glass stones and artificial frost. It can be completely breathtaking. For this theme, make sure you have plenty of good lighting, including up-lit walls, tons of candles, lots of glass and tiny glass chips for reflection. This is also a great time to project your new monogram on the wall, the dance floor or on the pool.

And your dress! If you're uncomfortable with your arms, as many women over forty are, you can choose a long-sleeved gown, a white faux fur jacket or caplet, a white cashmere coat, or a flowing white velvet cape. Also consider a fur-trimmed gown with matching hand muff. If you have bridesmaids, they will enjoy the luxurious feel of a faux fur wrap. Add rhinestone jewelry, a sparkling tiara or hair combs and a pure white bouquet for a look that is absolutely stunning. Your fiancé can select from either a white or black tuxedo or suit. I prefer the black as a complete contrast to your winter white ensemble. If you're having a flower girl, have her drop artificial snowflakes or white rose petals from her basket. Your ring bearer can carry a white teddy bear with the ring tied securely around the bear's neck.

Your wedding cake will be white, of course, sparkling with frost and topped with a silver or crystal snowflake. Wedding favor options could include a snow globe, white chocolate snowflake, or traditional white Jordan almonds tied up in sheer white tulle with blue or silver ribbon. Use your invitation to complete this theme. Select a winter scene, silver snowflake or snow-covered tree and fill the envelope with snowflake confetti.

Autumn Colors

Brenda, a recent second-time bride, selected an autumn theme for her wedding. It was her favorite time of year, and she fulfilled her dream to have the wedding and reception outdoors with the turning of the fall leaves in full view. The crisp chill in the air and the crunch of the leaves underfoot brought feelings of anticipation to the guests. It was absolutely spectacular. Fall is a time of harvest and bounty, a time to gather all that is precious and hold it close to your heart. What better time than fall to celebrate your wedding?

To make this theme work, build your wedding and reception around the warm color palette of fall. Picture the rich autumn colors of red, orange, russet, toasted brown, burnt yellow, burgundy, ocher, mustard and gold. Select a few of your favorites from this list and use a variety of them for your tablecloths, napkins, overlays, and chair covers. Choose fall flowers, such as yellow chrysanthemums, sunburnt orange calla lilies or terra cotta-colored roses, for your centerpieces. Use collections of eucalyptus branches, seeded plants or clumps of wheat tied in ribbon and surround them with dozens of votive candles for a nice warm glow. Toss acorns or colorful silk fall leaves on the tables. Another great idea for an autumn centerpiece is to group together fall fruits and vegetables, including artichokes, pears, figs, squash, persimmons and apples. Tuck in your favorite fall flowers among the fruits and vegetables and the look is pure autumn.

A dress in a creamy or champagne color and your fiancé in his favorite shade of brown would complete the picture. Bridesmaids in a mixture of fall shades in muted tones are lovely. They could carry bouquets of rust-colored roses, yellow and orange marigolds, red dahlias or deep burgundy hydrangeas. Orchids of all different colors are available, including shades of orange, yellow and brown to make a glowing look. Tie your bouquets in a dark, rich-colored ribbon for contrast. Surround your wedding cake with silk fall leaves or flowers and top with a cornucopia or golden maple leaf.

Wedding favors can include votive candles in fall colors, frames decorated with leaves or acorns, or foil-wrapped chocolate maple leaves. Your invitation can feature fall leaves, an overflowing cornucopia or a small acorn charm tied with sheer rust colored ribbon.

Christmas Themes

The added bonus of a Christmas wedding is that, many times, the reception site is already decorated for Christmas, and you can take advantage of the holiday look. If the decorating is left up to you, you might include a large decorated Christmas tree, mistletoe, sprigs of holly and plenty of red poinsettias. Red, green and white tablecloths and overlays on your banquet tables are a festive touch. Add tons of miniature white lights or candles in red, green and white. Your centerpieces can be wrapped "presents," miniature Christmas trees or large glass bowls filled with bright ornaments. Or consider large glass hurricanes with red candles encircled by Christmas wreaths.

Your dress might be an opulent fabric, such as velvet, or

traditional satin or silk in a shade of deep evergreen, burgundy or gold. A rich tartan is also perfect for a Christmas wedding. If you have bridesmaids, they should select dresses in a color that will compliment your gown. For example, if you chose evergreen, have them wear burgundy or gold. Your fiancé will look handsome in a tuxedo with a vest to match your dress. A bouquet of white chrysanthemums, holly and ivy, along with jewelry such as emeralds or rubies, completes the look of Christmas.

In addition to your wedding cake, you might add trays of Christmas cookies and a punchbowl filled with eggnog. You can even set aside a kids' table where they can decorate their own Christmas cookies or build a gingerbread house. For background music, select your favorite Christmas songs or hire a handbell choir to perform for you and your guests.

Wonderful wedding favors with a Christmas motif include mistletoe, Christmas ornaments or candy canes. Your invitations might feature silver bells, a Christmas wreath, holly or a sleigh with a bride and groom in fur coats and muffs.

Valentine's Day

Valentine's Day is the one day of the year reserved exclusively for lovers. It lends itself to a very romantic theme.

Too much red might be a bit overwhelming, so think pure white or pink with red as your accent color. For a Valentine's Day wedding and reception, long-stemmed red roses are particularly apt. Fill your reception room with white tablecloths and sheer red overlays. Display centerpieces of red roses with a touch of white for accent. Add flickering red candles in silver candelabras (think "Phantom of the Opera") and toss confetti hearts on the tables. Write a love quote and place in frames.

Envision this: your dress is white and flowing with a sweetheart neckline. Of course, you're wearing the infamous Tiffany heart necklace and perhaps a red velvet cape or scarf trailing down your back. In your hands, you're carrying a heart-shaped bouquet of red or tiny pink roses with strands of pearls or flowing ribbons. Your fiancé is a perfect match for you in a black tuxedo with a red rose boutonniere. Dress bridesmaids in red and have them carry pure white bouquets.

Your cake could be a heart-shaped creamy white confection with fresh red rose petals at the base. A crystal heart or clear acrylic heart-shaped frame holding a photo of you and your fiancé would make the perfect cake topper.

Wedding favor choices include conversation hearts, miniature books of love poems, champagne flutes, Hershey's kisses, long-stemmed red silk roses, Godiva chocolate truffles and heart-shaped picture frames. Try modeling your invitations after the original valentines of the 1800s using lace, pressed flowers, perfumed paper, ribbons and pearls. Or select one with a famous love sonnet by Shakespeare or two intertwined hearts. Calligraphy is a perfect choice for the Valentine's Day wedding invitation.

Beach Locale

If you live near the coast, a beach-themed wedding is romantic and beautiful. Or, if you live near an aquarium, consider hosting your reception there. Blue, white and silver make apropos colors for this theme. White tablecloths with navy overlays and white chair covers tied with silver sashes set the mood. Glass hurricanes filled with sand, seashells and water topped with floating candles surrounded by starfish at the base are ideal centerpieces. Or have a little fun and place small round aquariums filled with colorful fish on each table.

For unique touches, Marley Majcher, owner of The Party Goddess event planning company, offers the following helpful tips: take a large glass cylinder, fill it with water, and completely submerge a bit of sand or sea glass along with a large rock or striking orchid. Then, add some Chinese Fighting Fish. She also suggests taking a regular hair band, gluing on seashells or a starfish and using them as your napkin rings. Add a calypso or steel drum band for more authenticity.

Place seating cards in a wooden box filled with sand and shells atop fishing netting and cover your wedding cake in white chocolate seashells and strands of pearls.

Be imaginative in your style of dress: Consider a linen sundress, a strapless mermaid dress or one that softly billows in the breeze. Dresses with pearls sewn onto the bodice or hem are also perfect for a beach wedding. Choosing a dress in a pale aqua, light blue or sea green color accents the beach setting. Your fiancé would look very appropriate in a linen suit or even linen button-down shirt and shorts if your wedding is casual. Bridesmaids look fabulous in navy blue, aqua or shimmering green with each dress style different and appropriate to their figures and tastes. Carry a bouquet of flowers featuring the tranquil colors of the sea: calla lilies tied with ribbon and pearls, pincushion protea, or large Gerber daisies. Another great touch for your bridesmaids or guests is to carry lanterns filled with sand, manzanita branches and seashells.

Favor selections might include chocolate seashells wrapped in silver foil, sunscreen, sand buckets and shovels, miniature sandcastles, sand dollar ornaments and beach balls. Select invitations featuring surf and sand, seashells, dolphins, palm trees or sandcastles. You may even want to consider sending your invitation as a message in a bottle.

Tying the Nautical Knot

A wedding ceremony on a yacht or harbor cruise or in a nautical museum or seafood restaurant with a nautical theme can be lovely. In addition to white, go with the bold primary colors of blue, red and yellow. You can add gold or brass accents if you wish. Your banquet tables can be set with white and navy-striped tablecloths topped with brass lanterns, hurricane lamps, lighthouses or life buoys for centerpieces. If you love to sail, a large single sailboat or collection of several smaller boats nestled in fishing net makes a great centerpiece. Even an array of small votive candles tucked in a tray of sand, seashells and sea glass can be the perfect touch. Secure your napkins with rope and place sailors' knots on the chair backs. Rather than numbering your tables, name them with nautical terms or use colorful sailing flags.

Choose an outfit that is casual and crisp. Perhaps you can include a striped cape in one of the primary colors. Your fiancé could complement you in a navy blue or seersucker suit. A blue blazer would also be appropriate for this theme. Outfit your bridesmaids in navy or yellow. For a nautical theme, think bold stripes and block shapes rather than round. If you have a ring bearer and flower girl, they will look adorable in navy blue and white sailor suits.

A seafood menu fits the theme and could include shrimp, crab, lobster, salmon, ahi tuna and swordfish. An added touch would be to tie sailors' rope with a square knot around the base of your cake and top with an anchor.

Fun wedding favors could include toy sailboats, books on tying sailors' knots, or small colorful yachting flags. Look for invitations with anchors, sailboats or sailors' knots, and use a term like, "Tying the Knot," "Setting Sail" or "Anchors Away."

Victorian Charm

This theme works best in a Victorian bed-and-breakfast, rose garden, or your very own backyard. The reception can be held in the afternoon, with a high tea menu of scones and small heart-shaped finger sandwiches made of egg salad, watercress and cucumber with dill. Some fitting menu items are shortbread and meringue cookies, fruit tarts and a tray of fresh fruit. Add a nice variety of English teas served in unmatched teapots and teacups, and your guests will feel like they've been transported to another time and place. A gazebo with climbing roses is an ideal focal point and a perfect place to showcase your wedding cake and take photos. White lattice or wrought iron arches covered with climbing roses also work well as decoration along the sides of the reception area or a dramatic entrance.

Your tables could feature lace overlays, topiaries or large cabbage rose centerpieces. Flowered china dinner plates, cups and saucers and serving dishes set the perfect table. Scatter rose petals, dried lavender or fresh lilacs on each table.

A harpist playing music by Handel, Bach, Brahms, Mendelssohn and Mozart will set the mood. A horse and carriage makes for great photos and provides entertaining rides for the guests.

Victorian-era garments featured high necks, long sleeves and plenty of lace and ribbon. This style will work for both you and your attendants, if you have them. Hats, parasols, small beaded purses and cameo brooches add a distinctive Victorian flair. Choose a posy, nosegay, tussie mussy or flower ball of cabbage roses held with a loop of ribbon as your bouquet. Your fiancé can wear either a frock coat or paisley vest with dark grey trousers.

In addition to a tiered wedding cake, you could follow the Victorian tradition of the bridesmaid's cake. This smaller cake contains charms that hold a special meaning for the bridesmaids who find them in their slices of cake. The ring charm means she will be the next to marry. The anchor symbolizes adventure. The horseshoe and clove both represent good luck, and the fleur-de-lis signifies blossoming love. But woe to the bridesmaid who receives the thimble, as it means she will become an old maid.

Wedding favors such as music boxes, topiary plants, sachets of lavender or Victorian fans fit the theme perfectly. Invitations should include lace, a Victorian fan, a garden gazebo or cabbage roses. Be sure to tuck dried lavender into each envelope or spray them with rose water.

A Golf Course Setting

This was how I celebrated my second wedding and reception. We were married on the golf course adjacent to the infamous eighteenth green of the Dinah Shore Classic at the Mission Hills Country Club in Palm Springs, California. A white lattice arch covered with hundreds of salmon-colored roses acted as the altar where we exchanged our vows. My then seventy-four-year-old father drove me to the ceremony site in a bright, shiny red golf cart. Afterward, to the delight of our guests, my new husband and I sped away in the same cart.

The reception was held in the country club, with sweeping views of the golf course. The tables were set with white cloths and dark green overlays. Our centerpieces contained more of the same salmon-colored roses that adorned the ceremonial arch and bridesmaids' bouquets. They were displayed in round moss-covered wooden baskets that special guests took home as gifts at the end of the evening. Décor was already in place: framed prints and watercolors on the walls depicting famous golf resorts around the world, golf memorabilia and, obviously, the breathtaking view of the golf course itself.

Our sit-down dinner had synchronized service. For a table of six, three waiters come out, each holding two silver-domed dinner plates. At the exact same time, they each set down the first plate; then they rotated, and at exactly the same time, they each set down the other plate. It was poetry in motion. Beverages included champagne and the Arnold Palmer, a well-known signature drink for golfers.

My dress was a creamy white silk shantung gown with an off-the-shoulder neckline—long and form-fitting. I wore a veil that flowed down my back and framed my face. My boss told me I looked like a Barbie doll. I took that as a compliment. My husband looked extremely handsome in a grey tuxedo. My matron of honor and single bridesmaid wore deep salmon-colored dresses in a style and fabric similar to the silk shantung I wore. My daughter, at age eight, looked very sweet in her fluffy white dress and tiny veil.

Par for the course, our wedding favor was a golf ball bearing our names and wedding date. Several guests were seen putting them in their mouths when it came time for photos. Our invitations, which featured a watercolor scene of a golf course, completed the theme.

The Black & White Affair

Are you one of those second-time brides who came from the era of the pastel bridesmaids' dresses with pumps dyed to match? This time around you might prefer the elegant sophistication of the dramatic black and white wedding and reception. If you love a formal look and think there's nothing better than a man in a black tuxedo, this is the theme for you. The bride, groom, wedding party and even the guests wear only black and white. When using this theme, pick either black or white as the main color for decorations. Don't try for equal parts black and equal parts white. Then choose one accent color, such as a deep crimson. Use it in your wedding bouquet, boutonnieres, linens and centerpieces. This is a very dressy, classy and formal look and is ideal for the mature bride and groom.

The dinner tables can be decorated with black tablecloths with white shimmering overlays or black and white striped linens for a bold look. If your accent is crimson, floral centerpieces could include flowers such as roses, amaryllis, anthuriums or ranunculus. Or you may want to choose large candelabras and crimson candles.

A traditional white gown with long white or black opera gloves would be perfect. Outfit your fiancé in a black tuxedo and your bridesmaids in white or black dresses of varying styles. Pearls or diamonds are lovely jewelry for the black and white wedding, as are pearl-studded hair combs and rhinestone tiaras. If you have a ring bearer, he might carry a white pillow tied with a large black satin ribbon.

For wedding favors take a look at single red roses, candies in black velvet pouches, champagne flutes, or miniature black top hats filled with black and white mints. Issue invitations on heavy stock with black ink for a formal look and introduce the theme with the words "Black and White Wedding."

PLANNING POINTERS

When planning a themed wedding and reception, take the advice of Marley Majcher of The Party Goddess. She instructs her clients to pick one focal point, build from that main idea and be as specific as possible. Let's say you want a garden wedding. Decide if you have a garden on a warm summer night with the smell of jasmine in the air, a Garden of Eden, a tropical garden or a rose garden in mind. Clarify in your own mind what you want and be specific with your vendors so that they understand your vision and can help you create exactly what you want for your reception. Write down ideas for each category of the reception such as food, centerpieces, flowers and wedding favors. Find a common focus for your theme and let the ideas and thoughts flow, even if that focus is only a specific color. Use it in your invitations, linens, bouquets, centerpieces and bridesmaids' dresses. When making your lists, try not to leave out anything. Write down whatever comes to mind. Afterward, you can go back and cross out those things you definitely don't like or don't want to use. As Marley says, "Finding out what you *don't* like is just as important as what you *do* like." Share your ideas with friends and family and let them add their suggestions to your list.

SMALL CEREMONY WITH LARGE RECEPTION

Many encore brides wonder if it is okay to have a small ceremony with just the immediate family followed by a full-scale reception with numerous extended family and friends. The answer is yes. It is appropriate to have a small ceremony and a larger reception, but you may *not* have a large ceremony followed by a small reception. If a person is invited to your wedding, he or she should automatically be invited to your reception. Inviting someone to watch as you exchange your vows and then excluding him or her from the reception, regardless of the reason, is simply in bad taste. Don't even consider it.

If you have a destination wedding planned, but still want to celebrate upon your return, a reception is definitely an option. For this type of reception, you can wear your wedding dress if you like, though don't insist that your bridesmaids do the same. A nice touch is to show a video of your ceremony and vow exchange and a collage of photographs or wedding album so that your guests "experience" the wedding as well.

ALTERNATIVES TO THE GUEST BOOK
OR "SIGN HERE PLEASE"

Some second-time brides forgo the guest book. They feel it's unnecessary, because they have only a few guests or figure it will most likely just end up in a drawer somewhere. However, if you would like to try something different here are some great ideas:

A framed photograph where guests sign their good-luck wishes directly onto the matting with special pens makes a lovely remembrance. The photo can be of the two of you, the whole family or a favorite romantic scene. Afterward, cover the photograph in glass so it's suitable for hanging. It still brings a smile to my face every time I pass by ours. I just love to reread all the loving messages from our friends and family.

Another interesting keepsake is the signed tablecloth. Purchase a tablecloth that fits your dining table at home, and place the cloth on a table in your reception room near the entrance. You can have it embroidered with your names and wedding date in the center or in one of the corners, if you like. Have several permanent felt tip pens available and let your guests write as little or as much as they want; there's plenty of room for helpful marital advice and wishes for your future happiness.

A similar idea to the tablecloth and framed photo is a ceramic guest book platter, which can be heart shaped, oval or round and ordered on the Internet through The Younique Boutique in San Diego, California. The platters come in several sizes depending on your number of guests, and prices range from $78 to $108. Each one is hand-painted, personalized and arrives with its own special pen. I suggest ordering extra pens, as they always seem to disappear. The platters are imported from Italy and fired in the studio in San Diego. An additional "firing" in your home oven is required to adhere the signatures. The platter is food and dishwasher safe, although my guess is you'll be displaying it rather than eating off it. Another place to find ceramics is at your local "paint your own ceramics" store. You can select a large tray, bowl or platter and the necessary paints or pens. Each guest can sign it at the reception, and then you can carefully transport it back to the store for glazing and firing.

Another possibility for a guest book is to have a calendar made for the year of your wedding. Each month would feature a favorite photo of you and your fiancé. Ask each family member and friend to sign on the date of his or her birthday. This not only is a memento of your wedding, but an updated and current list of everyone's birthday.

Whether your guest list is small or large, an easy and inexpensive idea is to have small note cards or stationery handy for guests to write their congratulations or advice. They can then place them in a large jar or vase to be read by you and your new husband after the festivities or upon your return from your honeymoon.

A unique idea is the Wedding Puzzle. These puzzles are made from Finland Birch wood and hand cut using a personal enlarged photograph or romantic print of your choice. It can even be a photo collage up to 24" x 36". Each puzzle piece is about the size of the palm of your hand and sanded smooth, allowing your guests plenty of room to write a sentence or two in addition to their signatures. The pieces do not require a special pen nor does the ink bleed through the wood. The puzzles come with as few as twenty-five pieces or as many as 360. You can assemble and reassemble the pieces or have it professionally framed in $1/8$ inch Plexiglas at your local frame store. You can also place the pieces in a large glass bowl to be displayed on anniversaries, family gatherings or other special occasions. Like two lives merging and becoming one, so do the many puzzle pieces create one large picture. Each piece is a memento of your past or present.

A good way to display this unique guest book is on a large table at your reception. Place several pens there. Display it image-side up so guests can select the images they want or place it image-side down for a bit of mystery. You can also place the pieces in a large glass bowl or white wicker basket and let the children distribute them to each guest along with a pen. At the end of the reception, have a friend or one of the kids put the puzzle together, letting the guests see the final image before they leave.

Puzzles such as this are made by MGC in Connecticut and can be ordered online. Prices range from $75 for twenty-five pieces, $255 for one hundred pieces and $475 for 190 pieces.

Larger sizes up to 360 pieces are available by quote. Orders must be placed two to three weeks in advance, and there are extra charges for scanning and shipping. Several brides who have used these puzzles for their guest books have told me they were big hits.

Another great option is the "Our Life Together" photo quilt, which can also be ordered from the Younique Boutique. Each handmade 53" x 70" throw quilt holds a single 5" x 7" photo in the center or up to forty-five $3\frac{1}{2}$" x $4\frac{1}{2}$" photos placed strategically on each of the $7\frac{1}{2}$ inch squares that make up the quilt. Guests sign the quilt with a permanent felt marker, and there is space for up to 150 signatures. Photos can be color, black & white or sepia. The quilt is handmade by quilters in Missouri with 100 percent natural cotton fabric. It is then sent to the San Diego studio where the photos are printed onto the quilt using a commercial heat press. The quilts must be professionally dry-cleaned. Photos can be mailed or e-mailed and each personalized quilt only takes about two to three weeks to complete. You won't be able to decide if you should put it on your bed or display it on a wall.

SEATING ARRANGEMENTS

While many encore brides do not have seat assignments at their receptions, if there are more than twenty-five or thirty guests or there are some sticky family dynamics going on, seating cards can be a great help. Placing divorced family members on opposite sides of the room is usually a good idea. For example, your mother and her husband may be seated on the left hand side of the dance floor, while your dad and his girlfriend can sit on the other side. Generally, the bride's parents sit with their close friends, and the groom's parents sit with their close friends. The bridal party sits in the center of the room with you on your husband's right side facing your guests. A sweetheart table, reserved for only the bride and groom, is another possibility.

If you decide to use table cards, be creative. I recently attended my niece's wedding in South Carolina—a small, intimate affair on a southern plantation. She made photo place cards, each featuring a picture of my niece with her guest or a picture of her new husband and his guest. Mine was a photo of my niece and me at Christmastime when she was just six years old and had chocolate smeared all over her face. My seat was specified and the picture recalled that special memory, bringing a smile to my face. After each person found his or her own photo place card, it was a lot of fun checking out the other photo memories.

Some advice when choosing seating for your reception: request tables set for six guests instead of eight, as they are much more roomy and comfortable.

Remember, if for any reason you think that a difficult ex-spouse may crash your party, notify the manager and wait staff ahead of time. If possible, provide them with a photo so that they can quietly escort the person off the premises. Better safe than sorry.

TOASTS: "HERE'S TO THE BRIDE AND GROOM"

Once your guests are seated and before the meal is served, it's time to start the toasts. Have plenty of champagne ready, as well as sparkling juice or sparkling water for children and those who don't imbibe. Traditionally, the best man begins by toasting the bride and groom, followed by the maid of honor and the bride's father. Today's formal and semi-formal second weddings generally start out much the same way: first, the best man's toast, then the matron of honor and parents or stepparents. The toasts often continue with siblings, the children of the bride and the groom (if old enough), and the bride and groom themselves. At my second wedding, my husband opened with a warm welcome to all our guests. His son, who was his best man, followed by giving us our first toast. My matron of honor and best friend for twenty years gave the final toast. In more intimate and casual weddings where there are only two attendants, both may give toasts.

If you're feeling a bit uncertain about what either you or your fiancé would like to say (or if you need to advise your attendants), then let me share a bit of advice for a heartfelt and memorable wedding toast. For the best man or matron of honor: the most important thing in a toast is to personalize it. Write down theses specifics: when and where you met the bride and groom; how long you've known them; recount a favorite memory of them; share what you most admire about them, individually and together as a couple; and what you wish for them in their new future together as man and wife. Specific phrases include: "a lifetime of joy," "happiness always," "may all your dreams be fulfilled," "may you live a long and happy life together," and "may all your skies be blue." Don't forget to introduce yourself at the start of the toast.

If you and your fiancé are going to toast each other, it's the perfect time to tell each other how much you mean to one other, how happy you are to be husband and wife and how excited you are to be joining your two families together (especially if either of you have children). You might say: "I am so happy to be your wife. I love you without end, and my children adore you. My wish is that the joy of this day, our wedding day, remain with us all of our lives."

Another easy way to write a toast is to take a poem, proverb or verse and build your toast around it. If your love for each other is extremely passionate, then perhaps this African proverb would be ideal: "Our love is like the misty rain that falls softly— but floods the river." Or if every moment together is simply not enough, there is this Chinese proverb: "Rich as he is, even the emperor cannot buy back one single day." If your relationship is one of joyful playfulness, there are three proverbs that would work well. The first is an Old English prayer, "Take time to play—it is the secret of perpetual youth." The second is a Greek proverb: "The heart that loves is always young." The third is another Old English prayer, "Take time to laugh, it is the music of the soul." Many married couples seem to have a language all their own. If this is the case with you and your new husband, this Chinese proverb says it all: "Married couples who love each other tell each other a thousand things without talking." In addition, if you are making a welcome toast, then the Old English saying about friendship is always appropriate: "It is around the table that friends understand best the warmth of being together."

Things *not* to include in your toast or the toasts made by others are references to your past marriages, the "second time around," "doing it 'till you get it right" or "making a better choice this time." Avoid any negative comments, criticisms or jokes that might be in poor taste. Keep everything specific to this relationship and this marriage. It's best to stick with comments such as "Good things come to those who wait," "Ever since our paths crossed," "As we begin a new chapter in our lives," "I am so blessed to have found you," and "As we create this new family together" when toasting to a second marriage.

Once you've written and rewritten your toast until it flows, write it down on an index card. Although you will want to practice saying it aloud until its memorized, do not leave anything to chance and be prepared with the card in hand.

When giving your toast, there are also several things to keep in mind. Take a deep breath and *relax*. Don't read the toast word for word, but do refer to the card if necessary. Don't apologize for being embarrassed, uncomfortable or an inexperienced speaker. It's the feeling that counts. Speak slowly and clearly; don't rush. This is a memorable moment of the reception, the moment that actually sets the tone, so take your time and do it right.

WEDDING FEAST

When planning your reception meal, the time of day you are holding the reception is crucial. If your wedding is in the morning, you can choose from a breakfast, brunch or English tea. If it's at noon, you'll be looking at brunch, lunch or an English tea. If it's in the early afternoon, your choices include cake with champagne and punch or a selection of teas and coffees, an English high tea, or a cocktail party with hors d'oeuvres. However, if your reception takes place anytime after 5 P.M., you will need to serve dinner. So, based on your budget and the number of guests you would like to invite, select the time that works best.

If your wedding and reception take place in the morning, a breakfast menu of steaming hot coffee, cinnamon rolls, quiche Lorraine, melon and berries, mini bagels with cream cheese and smoked salmon and even a waffle or omelet bar would work perfectly.

For lunch or brunch, consider an assorted deli bar with several choices of meats and cheeses. Add a variety of salads such as cold pasta, fruit, garden, Antipasto, Caesar or Greek and everyone will be happy.

For an English high tea, you'll want ladyfingers, scones with lemon curd preserves and Devonshire cream, fruit tarts, English trifle and a variety of teas served in old-fashioned mismatched teapots and teacups.

For afternoon cocktail parties, go light on the alcohol. Serve plenty of hors d'oeuvres and appetizers. You can do this by buffet or on passed trays.

If serving dinner, there are many ways to go. You can select from a sit-down meal with synchronized service, a buffet or the ever-popular food stations. When planning your menu, think interactive. For example, if you'd like to use food stations, try something fun such as a mashed potato martini bar. At this station, your guests are given a martini glass filled with mashed potatoes. They then add on their own toppings, including cheese, bacon bits, chili, chives, mushroom gravy, and Mexican corn. Pasta bars are also fun and inexpensive. A chef stands ready with several pasta and sauce choices, such as marinara, pesto or creamy vodka. Crepe bars with fresh berries, sliced bananas and whipping cream are also very popular. If you're having a Chinese station, serve everything in small take-out boxes with chopsticks. Taco stations and seafood stations are also great choices. Build-your-own-sundae bars or hand dipping fresh strawberries in a large bowl of chocolate or tiered fountain with warm cascading milk chocolate are fun additions for dessert. Anything where your guests get to interact with each other, make choices, build something themselves and have fun doing it will result in a memorable reception.

Seasonal weddings offer a bevy of choices. If you're getting married at Christmastime, pork loin stuffed with sun-dried cranberries and walnuts is always a smash. Or try the traditional dinner of roasted turkey served with a Waldorf salad. For a Valentine's Day reception, serve plenty of champagne and chocolate. Cornish game hens in a creamy champagne sauce or a pasta dish using heart-shaped pasta also make a nice presentation.

And last, a word about cash bars. They do not belong at your wedding or any wedding. Charging someone to drink at your reception is simply tacky. Don't do it. If you can't afford a bar, don't have one. If you'd like to have something alcoholic, but don't want a full bar, consider serving only wine and domestic beer. You could open the bar only when the dancing begins. Another option is to place nice, but inexpensive bottled wine on the tables.

THE FIRST DANCE AND FAMILY DANCE

The song you choose for your first dance as husband and wife reflects your personality as a couple. My husband and I chose one of the romantic songs of the time, "Have I Told You Lately That I Love You?" written by Van Morrison (there is also a version performed by Rod Stewart). The lyrics reflect the passion, romance and wild feeling of falling in love. Other tunes such as "How Do I Live Without You?" by Michael Bolton, "Take My Breath Away" by Berlin, and "I Will Always Love You" by Whitney Houston from the movie *The Body Guard*, are also popular selections.

You and your fiancé may have a song that has touched your hearts since you first met. If you don't, search for just the right song that reflects the feelings in your heart. If you're like most second-time brides, you feel as if you have overcome much adversity to be where you are today. You have been through a divorce or suffered the loss of your spouse, and you and your fiancé have overcome numerous obstacles on the path that led you to each other. Now you want to express those intense feelings with the song you select for your first dance. Some songs which express your history and feeling might be: "Against All Odds" from the movie of the same name starring Jeff Bridges and Rachel Ward, sung by Phil Collins, "Because You Loved Me" by the talented Celine Dion, "Saving All My Love for You," another hit from Whitney Houston, or "After All," an oldie but goodie from Peter Cetera.

Other great songs for second timers are: "From This Moment" by Shania Twain, "All My Life" by Whitney Houston, "Groovy Kind of Love" by Phil Collins, and "A Moment Like This" by Kelly Clarkson of *American Idol* fame. If you're still looking for that perfect song, listen to "A Room In My Heart" or "Just Breathe," both by the beautiful Faith Hill, "Can You Feel The Love Tonight" by Elton John, or "Could I Have This Kiss Forever," a duet by Whitney Houston and Enrique Iglesias. Perhaps the haunting "Only Time" by Enya is the one for you. There are also the tried and true hits such as "Can't Take My Eyes

Off You" by Frankie Valli, "Lady in Red" by Chris DeBurgh, and "Maybe I'm Amazed" by Paul McCartney. Of course, there are my all-time favorites: "The Rose" by Bette Midler, "Falling Into You" by Celine Dion, "Forever and Always" by Shania Twain, and "I Don't Wanna Miss A Thing" by Aerosmith.

Once you have danced your first dance as husband and wife, you both may want to dance with parents. If that's too complicated, simply have your bridal party join you on the dance floor, signaling to the guests that all are welcome to join in.

THE INFAMOUS DOLLAR DANCE

Should you get paid to dance? In the traditional dollar dance, male guests pay for the honor of dancing with the bride. Denominations vary from one dollar up to $100. Pins are provided for the men to pin the money directly onto the bride's dress. My advice: Be wary of this tradition. As Peggy Post of the Emily Post Institute once told me, "While it is completely acceptable in some circles, cultures and geographical areas, it is actually frowned upon in others." A similar tradition is the money tree where guests pin envelopes of cash onto a small tree placed on a display table. Again, be careful with these traditions. If they are well known and acceptable within your community, by all means, go for it. But if you have any hesitation at all, skip these festivities altogether.

TRADITIONAL TOSSES

Feel silly having your husband lift your dress and tug at your garter in front of a roomful of people? Well, you're not alone. Although some second-time brides enjoy the fun of the garter and bouquet tosses, for many it is a tradition better left in the past. It's quite acceptable to play along or skip them entirely. Your decision will also depend on the number of single guests attending (excluding the children) and their interest in participating. However, if you decide to carry on the tradition of the bouquet toss, I suggest you toss a smaller look-alike bouquet, especially if you want to preserve your bouquet as a keepsake.

PRESERVING YOUR BOUQUET

There are several methods for preserving your bouquet for years to come. You can do what I did and have the flowers dried, pressed and then reassembled like the original. The finished product is framed and mailed to you to proudly display on your wall. Or you can have them freeze dried as a whole flower, a process that takes ten to seventeen days. They are then placed in a glass dome, shadow box or tabletop display. The entire process can take up to fourteen weeks. Prices for both options vary from as little as $99 to $750, with the average cost coming in around $425. If you'd like to preserve your bouquet, you really need to make the arrangements about two months prior to your wedding date. Ship the bouquet, along with a photo, within 24-48 hours after the wedding while it is still fresh. This probably means that you'll need to designate a friend or family member to handle the collection and shipping details of your bouquet while you are off enjoying your honeymoon. But I can assure you from personal experience, it is well worth the hassle, time and money.

CAKE CUTTING

The tradition of the wedding cake dates back to the ancient Romans, who would bake a cake of wheat or barley and break it over the bride's head as a symbol of her fertility. In time, this ritual evolved into stacking a small cluster of cakes over which the bride and groom would then have to kiss without toppling the cakes onto the floor. Myth said if the kiss was successful, they were granted a lifetime of good fortune. Eventually, this tradition resulted in the three-tiered wedding cake of today. Of course, you don't have to opt for the usual wedding cake. Many second-time brides prefer cheesecake with a selection of sauces, single cakes for each table of six or eight guests, or a mini-wedding cupcake for each and every guest.

The cake-cutting ceremony has two meanings. First, it is a sign that guests can leave the festivities. It is considered rude to leave before the cutting of the cake, so don't wait until the clock strikes midnight to cut yours. Be considerate of your guests. Secondly, the ritual of feeding one another the first piece of wedding cake symbolizes how you will share your life together—how you will take care of each other, nurture and respect each other. When you see a groom smash a piece of cake all over his new bride's face, it's a bad sign. It shows lack of respect and a possible mean streak. One of my friends, who is a marriage and family therapist, reports that many of the clients she sees are couples in which either the bride or the groom smashed cake in the other's face. Coincidence? I think not.

On a lighter note, there's the cake topper. I don't know about you, but I just can't face looking at another plastic bride and groom standing atop a cake. Neither could my sister, so she bought porcelain collectibles and painted the bride's hair with blonde streaks and the groom's hair with grey streaks to better reflect my husband and me on our wedding day. Other than the traditional bride and groom cake toppers, you may want to consider fresh flowers, seashells, your new monogram, butterflies, wedding bells, or intertwined wedding rings. Even a clear acrylic framed photo of the two of you would work well.

If you want to follow tradition, save the top tier of your cake for your first anniversary.

WEDDING FAVORS

Once upon a time, the wedding favor of choice was the little tulle packet of Jordan almonds which are both bitter and sweet, symbolizing the two sides of marriage. However, there are many other choices. Here are some of my favorites, what I like to call my Top 20:

1) Champagne splits with your own personalized label
2) Holiday ornaments
3) Aromatherapy candles
4) Golf balls imprinted with your names and wedding date
5) Cookie cutters
6) Snow globes with your picture inside
7) Miniature books of love poems
8) Fortune cookies imprinted with your own message
9) Kaleidoscopes
10) Silver heart-shaped photo frames
11) Music boxes
12) "Love Beyond Measure" measuring spoons
13) Beach balls
14) Sachets of herbs or potpourri
15) "Perfect Blend" tea bags imprinted with your names and wedding date
16) Conversation hearts
17) Seed packets
18) Bud vases
19) Topiary plants
20) Heart-shaped wine bottle stoppers

ACTIVITIES FOR YOUNG CHILDREN

Either give them a dining table of their own or do what I think works best, which is to let children eat with their parents and then run off to a special area where they can do crafts, hear some storytelling or get their faces painted. Either way, serve them their meals early on, so they don't get whiny and cranky. Be sure to include a kid-friendly menu complete with chicken fingers with dipping sauces, peanut butter and jelly sandwiches with the crust cut off, macaroni and cheese, ravioli and carrot sticks with Ranch dressing. Later on in the evening, when they are in their own play area, they can build their own sundaes, decorate cookies or enjoy their very own miniature wedding cake.

Even if you have as few as two or three children at your reception, I highly recommend that you hire a babysitter. I know it's easier and less expensive to use grandma, a friend or a favorite aunt, but trust me, these people are actually guests and want to enjoy your wedding and reception, too. So, get someone whose sole job that night is to watch and entertain the children.

Fill the kids' play area with arts, crafts and activities to keep them busy while the adults dance the night away. Fun activities include puppet shows, temporary tattoo painting and decorating hats with glitter, glue, sequins and feathers. Set up a glamour bar with dress-up clothes and costumes for both boys and girls. This works especially well if you are using a Victorian theme. If it's Christmastime, consider having Santa visit and distribute toys or let the children decorate Christmas cookies or build a gingerbread house. Get a couple of Polaroid cameras. Let the children take photos of the guests and put together a collage as their gift to you.

One final tip: If you know that the night will be a long one, consider having several blankets and pillows on hand. The kids can even use them to build a fort!

Here are some stories of the unique and wonderful wedding days of some second-time brides:

Joanie's Story
     "My second wedding was actually a fairy tale wedding. It was held on the beach at the Ritz-Carlton in Laguna Beach, California. We had both the ceremony and the reception on the beach next to the surf. The ceremony site had two large

rose-colored columns facing the water. Rose petals covered the sand from where the limousine dropped me off all the way to the columns, which acted as the altar where we exchanged our vows. We were dressed formally but barefoot. In fact, we asked that all the guests remove their shoes. We even had a shoe check to avoid the confusion of lost or misplaced shoes.

"We commissioned an artist to create our wedding invitations. She hand drew and water-colored a beach scene with the columns on each invitation, glued sand from that very beach onto them, and then signed each and every one. George and I felt that the invitation would set the tone and mood of the whole wedding and reception, so we went all out. Of course, like most second-time brides, I have no idea where my keepsake invitation is located! But I know it's here some place!

"Before the ceremony started, we hosted a cocktail reception up on the bluffs overlooking the Pacific Ocean. I, of course, was getting ready at this time. However, my fiancé, George, joined in the festivities, welcoming and greeting everyone as they arrived.

"The guests were then brought down to the beach ceremony site by golf carts. Somewhere during this time, one of my fiancé's sons took off in a golf cart for a bit of fun, and it took awhile to hunt him down. Eventually we did, and the rest of the day went without a hitch. My father and my son, both barefoot, walked me down the aisle, one on each side. George and I exchanged our vows with the sun cascading on the water behind us. It was spectacular.

"My dress was made by Mona Lee, a Beverly Hills designer. It was very lacy, with lots of tiers and layers. It was a full-length gown with a v-neck and gathers at the satin bodice. There was transparent lace around my waist, so it appeared as if my tummy was bare. When my father and I stepped out of the limousine to begin our walk down the aisle of rose petals, he said to me, 'Honey, where's the rest of your dress?' It was so funny. My hair was done up in loose curls with a fabric comb and a veil falling down my back. I not only felt like a princess that day, I *looked* like a princess.

"My bridesmaids—my sister and two nieces—wore three-quarter length rose-colored dresses. My flower girl wore a sweet white dress with flowers from my bouquet floating in the netting of the dress. George wore a tuxedo with tails and, of course, was barefoot just like me.

"For the reception, we brought in a football field of sod and had it placed next to the water. We had a tent filled with tiny twinkling lights, fountains and flowers. It was stunning – a magical place where we could hear the waves crashing on the beach all night long.

"George's son was his best man, but by the time we did the toasts, his son had fallen asleep! So, George did an impromptu welcome and toast in lieu of the traditional best man's toast.

"We rented a wooden dance floor and hired a full band. Our first dance was to Elton John's "Your Song." Afterward, our parents came out on the dance floor, followed by the rest of our family and guests. We did both the garter toss and the bouquet toss. Though in all the excitement, I don't even remember who caught them! Our wedding favor was salt-water taffy, and our wedding cake was decorated with solid, white chocolate seashells.

"One of my favorite memories of that day took place early on the morning of our wedding when I went down to the hotel restaurant for breakfast. Everyone was talking about the "big production" going on down at the beach – the sod, tenting and all that. They were all wondering who was getting married and speculating that it must be some famous celebrity! Well, that "celebrity" was me!"

Marley's Story

"They say that opposites attract, and that is certainly true about my husband and me. A second marriage for both of us, I am considered the wild woman and he the conservative gentleman. To show both sides of this marriage, we actually sent out two invitations in the same large plastic frosted envelope. My invitation was hot pink and orange with a cheetah background. It was wrapped in orange fur with acid-green French ribbon. The invitation urged guests to 'Join us in the biggest rage party ever,' and my response card said, 'I'll totally be there.' On the other hand, my fiancé's traditional cream-colored, embossed invitation, 'Requesting the Honor of Your Presence,' featured a little tissue, old fashioned RSVP card and was addressed by a calligrapher.

"For the reception, we rented an old warehouse in Los Angeles in a pretty bad area of town. We had 350 guests and a ten piece band. We actually divided the room exactly in half. On my half of the warehouse, we decorated the tables in leopard print underlays with pink marabou trim and orange fur-trimmed overlays. My menu included baby cheeseburgers, macaroni and cheese and a mashed potato bar. It was total hedonism at its best.

"My husband's half of the warehouse was decorated completely in cream and with chandeliers and gold dinnerware. His menu consisted of roast beef au jus, salmon and sautéed green beans. It was very conservative and so very much him. Our guests thought it was just perfect: Two complete opposites completely in love."

Brenda's Story

"My second wedding was the best day of my life! Although we married in the fall, the temperature was about 80 degrees outside. We had the wedding and reception at home in a large covered area. We brought in tents, even though we only had about fifty guests. We chose a high English tea and served plenty of delicious sandwiches, pastries, chocolate-covered strawberries, homemade scones with fruit, butter and preserves, and a lovely selection of teas and champagne. We also included beer, as my husband is a firefighter, and the guys love a good beer.

"We placed our stereo outside, out of the view of the guests, and played music we had personally selected. Our song was "Hero" by Enrique Iglesias. Early on in our relationship, my fiancé e-mailed me a card with this song and asked if he could be my hero. Needless to say, he has been exactly that from that day on.

"My dear friend insisted on making our wedding cake, and it was incredible! It consisted of three tiers of delicate white cake with lemon filling and the most delicious butter cream frosting.

"As for my dress…I wore white! Actually, it was more of an ivory, but since my dress for my first wedding was a rose color, this felt like a white wedding dress. It was beautiful with a pearl bodice and long satin skirt. I wore my hair up with pearl strands to compliment the dress. I special ordered silk flowers so that all of my bridesmaids could keep their bouquets. In fact, all of the flowers were silk in shades of deep reds and ivories, which were perfect for an autumn wedding."

Second weddings can be unique and special. As these brides did, take the time to make yours an occasion you and your husband will always remember as symbolic of your love.

Chapter Five

Wedding Attire

Can I Really Wear White?

*F*irst **Wedding:** The young bride wears a beautiful white Cinderella ball gown with lots of tulle, taffeta and sequins. Her train is cathedral length and topped with a bow in the back. She adds a blusher veil, her mother's pearls and a lacy blue garter.

Second Wedding: The encore bride selects an elegant and sophisticated sheath dress in a butterscotch color that she knows shows off her mature and well toned figure, creamy complexion and dark hair.

"Can I really wear white?" This is the question I hear more often than any other from women getting remarried. So let's start there. Yes, you absolutely can wear white. Originally, brides simply wore their best dress of any and all colors on their wedding day. Back then, no one would even consider having a special dress made to wear for just one day. In that era there was little money to spare and clothes had to last a long time. Throughout the world and throughout history, brides have been dressed in almost every color of the rainbow. In Japan, brides wear a colorful kimono called an uchikake, which is often red. She then changes into several colorful dresses throughout the wedding and reception. In the Bible, brides wore blue, the color that signified purity. Deep jewel tones such as jade, garnet and sapphire were popular in medieval times and the Elizabethans preferred gold, sage and rose. When President Monroe's daughter married in 1821, she wore a blue dress with red embroidery. Royal British brides wore silver gowns with fur-trimmed robes.

Queen Victoria was the first to wear all white when she married Prince Albert in 1840. She started the tradition of the white wedding dress. Symbolically, Romans considered white to be a color of celebration. At the beginning of the twentieth century, white became known as a symbol of purity. Today, it represents celebration, happiness and joy. So, if you really want to wear a white wedding dress, but are concerned about what your guests might say, don't worry; wear the white dress and enjoy your day of joy and celebration.

A word of caution: stark white makes many complexions appear drawn and washed out, whereas shades of cream or ivory tend to flatter almost all complexions. My advice to you is to choose the color that looks best on you, whether that color is white, cream, butterscotch or pale pink. Other popular colors for second-time brides are champagne, bronze, platinum, pewter, bisque, maize, gold, blush, pale rose, shell pink and ecru.

A very popular way to introduce some color into your gown is to select a cream or ivory dress with colored embroidery, beading, crystals, a sash at the waist or ostrich feathers at the cuffs and collar. Many designers are using these splashes of color and embellishments in their current collections.

Perhaps you'd like to wear a color that symbolizes a certain meaning. For example, blue symbolizes integrity, honesty, loyalty and commitment. Green is harmonious, generous and the color of unconditional love. Red is bold, daring and the color of sexual expression. Yellow is soothing, warm and radiant. Orange communicates passion, vitality and enthusiasm, while purple symbolizes spiritualism, universal love and understanding.

You can also choose a dress color to match the theme or time of year of your wedding: emerald green or crimson for a Christmas wedding; taupe, gold or bronze for a fall wedding; peach or apricot for a wedding held in the spring. Summer offers the colors of periwinkle blue, maize or celadon. Or you can use your birthstone color: sapphire blue for September, aquamarine for March, emerald for May, or amethyst for February. You can wear white or choose from any color of the rainbow. Pick a flattering color that makes you feel like the most beautiful woman on earth. That's the real secret to the perfect wedding dress.

STYLE

When deciding on the style of your wedding dress, first take a look at the type of wedding you are having. Is it formal or informal? Held in the afternoon in a garden or at an upscale hotel on a Saturday night? Will it be a warm July wedding or during a light snowfall in December? The type of dress you select should fit the style, tone and location of your wedding. Here are some suggestions that can serve as simple and basic guidelines:

Formal and Semiformal:
For the Bride: a floor-length wedding gown in white or cream. If you wish you may wear a veil trailing down your back or framing your face. The only taboo for a second-time bride: abstain from wearing a blusher veil, the type that falls in front of your face. This is still reserved only for first-time brides and

continues to represent virginity. Gloves are optional but a nice touch for both day and night formal weddings.

For the Groom: Cutaway coat, striped trousers, waistcoat and white shirt for day or black tailcoat and trousers for night.

For the Bridesmaids/Matrons: Floor-length matching gowns with matching shoes for both day and night.

Informal

For the Bride: Long wedding gown or evening gown, tea-length dress, simple two-piece ensemble with long skirt and top with bolero jacket, cocktail dress, suit or dressy pant-suit for both day and night. If you're poolside, a cocktail dress is ideal. If you're on the beach, a cream-colored tank and sarong or soft billowing sundress will work too. Simple cuts and silhouettes are the cornerstones of the informal wedding dress. In fact, the options for an informal wedding are numerous and a great opportunity to think outside the box.

For the Bridesmaids/Matrons: Complimentary to whatever the bride is wearing.

For the Groom: Dark suit in winter, light suit in summer, or a tuxedo if the bride's dress is long and the wedding is at night.

SHOP 'TIL YOU DROP

Before you start shopping, look in your closet and think about the styles that work for you. Examine the outfits and colors that draw compliments from your friends and make you feel wonderful every time you wear them. By this point in your life, you most likely know the styles and colors that flatter your face and figure. You'll want to keep those styles, fabrics and colors in mind while you shop. On the other hand, be open-minded and don't be afraid to try on a few new styles. You just might be surprised at how good you look in something you might not normally select. Other things to keep in mind while shopping for that perfect wedding dress:

1) Shop early. If you want to order a dress, it may take three to six months once you've found the perfect one. Don't wait until the last minute.
2) If going to a bridal salon, make an appointment, midweek if possible. Plan on spending a couple of hours trying on dresses. Don't be in a hurry.
3) Bring along one friend and one friend only. Buying a dress by committee is simply a bad idea.
4) Wear the right undergarments. If you're looking for a strapless dress, by all means, wear a strapless bra to the salon. And wear a thong, control top pantyhose, Spanx or body shaper if you plan on wearing it on the big day.
5) Bring a hair band, clips or bobby pins to put your hair up.
6) Bring shoes with you of the same type and heel height that you will wear on your wedding day.
7) Bring several pictures of the styles you like, clipped from bridal magazines, so the salesperson can help you wade through the variety of dresses available.
8) Keep in mind that it's usually better to pick your best features and flaunt them rather than to try and hide any perceived flaws.
9) Don't count on losing that last five pounds before your big day.
10) Lie about your wedding date. There are so many horror stories out there about brides getting their dresses late, in the wrong sizes, or the wrong dresses altogether. Tell the salesclerk your wedding is one month prior to the real date. Just in case.
11) Purchase your gown by credit card to avoid unforeseen problems later.
12) Once you select your dress and go for your fittings, wear

the right shoes and undergarments. Sit down in the dress to see if it's too tight, crumples or simply looks weird. Is it too scratchy? Is the fabric too stiff? Does it wrinkle like linen? Bend over, raise your arms, do the twist. Make sure it's a comfortable fit. If the dress is tight now, it will be tight that day. Trust me.

FABRICS

You'll want to select a gown in a fabric that complements the season and location of your wedding. A velvet long-sleeved dress will look out of place in the middle of July. If your wedding takes place in the spring or summer, choose light and cool fabrics such as chiffon, cotton, linen and light silk. For the winter, try warm, heavy fabrics like velvet, satin or brocade. For fall, try silk shantung or one of the many laces available. Great fabrics for comfort and fit are silk crepe, silk organza, silk shantung, silk duponi, crepe chiffon, and empress silk. For that old-fashioned vintage look, go with one of the many types of lace, such as Alencon, Venise, Chantilly or Brussels. Remember, figure out how long you will be wearing your gown (most are worn for about six hours) and consider the weight and comfort of the fabric you select. If it feels slightly scratchy now, hours into your reception it will only get worse and you'll be miserable. And don't forget, fabrics cut on the bias will make you look more slim and trim.

A BEVY OF CHOICES

Ball Gown: The traditional Cinderella-style floor length dress with tight bodice and full skirt compliments an hourglass or small on top and heavy on bottom shape. Conversely, women who are buxom also look great in a ball gown, because the full skirt balances out the top. The key to the right fit in a ball gown is where the waistline falls. Just an inch above or below your natural waistline can make a big difference, as it's all in the proportions. With the right seamstress, the ball gown can be absolutely stunning, even if you're forty something.

Basque: Like the ball gown, this dress is fitted on top with a full skirt. However, the waist falls below your natural waistline and forms either a U- or a V-shape. It can be much more flattering than the traditional ball gown.

Sheath: Long, tea length or short, this dress closely follows the contours of your body. If you are in pretty good shape, a sheath dress flatters. Additionally, if the fabric is cut on the bias, it will glide over any lumps and bumps.

Slip Dress: Like the sheath, this dress skims the body and resembles a slip. Usually made in a silk fabric, it has spaghetti straps, can be of any length and is a bit flirty. This style is great for beach weddings, poolside ceremonies or garden weddings that take place in the summer months.

A-line: One of the most popular styles, this dress is fitted on top and flows in an A-shape to the floor. Less poufy than the ball gown, this style is one of the most flattering of all. If you feel you are a bit bottom heavy, have a small waist you want to show off, or simply appreciate simple lines, then this is the dress for you.

Empire: This floor-length dress is known for its high waistline that falls just under the breasts and flows in a straight line to the floor. It's perfect if you're small busted, have a boyish figure or are pregnant. (Tip: Thread Bridesmaid also makes gowns in maternity sizes that will work well if you're expecting a baby.)
Strapless: Teamed with a ball gown or an A-line silhouette, this style

is currently the most popular. It is ideal if you have toned arms and sculpted shoulders or are marrying in warmer climates. A dress with a halter top is also a good way to show off lean arms and a nice back. If you love the strapless look, but are uncomfortable baring all, try topping it with a sheer cropped jacket, faux fur caplet or wrap.

Off the Shoulder: This is the style I chose for my second wedding. My husband thought it was sexy and I liked it because it showed off my shoulders, but still covered that bit of my upper arms. Unfortunately at my age, arms often jiggle a bit.

Asymmetrical: For something a little different, try a dress with an asymmetrical neckline, a handkerchief hemline, one bare shoulder or an eight-point skirt. A gown that gathers at one side of the waist is also a unique option.

Drop Waist: Usually strapless, this long gown is form fitting to your fingertips and then flares out from there to the floor. You'll need a nice flat stomach and slender hips for this one.

Tiers: This gown features a form-fitting bodice with three to six tiers of fabric flowing to the floor. Tiers give an A-line dress or ball gown a bit more interest and depth. This style even looks great in tea length.

Cutout: A new trend that shows some skin at the waist, sides or back. This dress conveys a very contemporary and sexy look.

Coatdress: This looks great in satin and can be worn over a simple gown or silk taffeta pants. It can either touch the floor or be longer in back and double as a train. You'll be warm and glamorous at the same time.
Mermaid: A flattering dress for women with curves, it hugs the

body from top to knee, where it then flares out.

Cocktail: I know that the words "little black dress" are what come to mind when I say cocktail, but the bridal cocktail dress is much different from its cousin. Made in fabrics such as English net, Chantilly lace and silk satin organza, this style falls to the knee. Often coming in white or ivory, it can be strapless, A-line, tiered or asymmetrical. Watters Brides has a great selection of this style.

Tea Length: Another popular choice among second-time brides, this dress falls half way between your knees and ankles. This style works for almost all informal weddings and looks best in light, flowing fabrics.

Vintage: Many brides having Victorian themed weddings or loving the look of lace choose a vintage gown or dress.

Suit: Once upon a time, this was the uniform of the second-time bride. If you have great legs but want to cover your arms, the suit is the perfect choice. Look for embellishments, such as beading, crystals or embroidery, for a dressy, elegant and festive look.

Pantsuit: Believe it or not, I have seen some gorgeous bridal pantsuits. Usually made with embellished tops, harem or palazzo pants and in cream, champagne or ivory, this style is comfortable and a perfect match for the at-home or garden wedding.

CHOOSING STYLES FOR YOUR BODY TYPE
Thin and Tall: You are the lucky one in that you can choose just about any style. However, pick your best feature and highlight it. If you have great, toned arms, wear something strapless. Consider a dress that dips to a low V to accentuate your beautiful

back or a halter-style top to display sexy shoulders.

Thin and Short: Styles that fall straight to the floor, such as a sheath dress, look great on you and help build height. Matte fabrics look best, as well as simple, elegant styles without a lot of fussy details.

Average Height and Weight: Like the woman who is tall and thin, you can select most any style. Keep in mind that a "fit model" is usually a perfect size 8, so if this describes you, almost anything off the rack is going to suit you to a 'T'.

Full Figured and Tall: If you're full figured on top, look for a dress that molds to your form. If there's too much fabric, you can look fat, which you're not. A V-neckline is the most slimming of all and accentuates your bust line, making you look curvy but not large. Other good choices are a scoop neck or sweetheart neckline. You can even go strapless with the right strapless bra. If you're full figured on the bottom, look for fabrics that are flowing and skim your body or a dress that's cut on the bias. Select a dress that has some detail near the neckline to draw attention away from your hips. Or go with a dress that is two-toned with the darker shade on the bottom.

Full Figured and Short: Go for an A-line dress with a high neckline. Use matte fabrics, which create a slimming look and add the illusion of height.

IT'S ALL IN THE NUMBERS

If you're thirty-eight years old, you may not be looking for the same type of dress as a woman remarrying in her early thirties. Likewise, a twenty-six-year-old most likely won't be looking for the same style as a woman of fifty-nine. Of course, you may be forty-nine with the body and attitude of a thirty-five-year-old and will look great in just about any style. The point is not to worry about your age when selecting your wedding dress. Find a dress that you love—one that flatters your figure in a color that complements your complexion. As Steven Birnbaum of Birnbaum & Bullock says, "If your dress is cut to your measurements rather than by a size chart, and it's cut proportionally, you can wear any style of dress you desire. You can be a size two or a twenty-two and if the dress is cut right, it will look fabulous." He also stresses the importance of dressing to enhance rather than to camouflage. He believes that a bride is a bride no matter what her age or how many times she has been to the altar. There is a beautiful dress for every bride at every price point. His advice: know your budget. Don't let the bridal industry overwhelm you and don't settle for anything less than excellent customer service.

SIZE CHARTS

Trying on a wedding dress can be as frustrating as trying on a pair of designer jeans. First of all, the gown samples come in a size six or eight, although the average American woman is 150 pounds and a size twelve. Then to top it off, the size charts vary so widely that a dress by one designer will fit you in a size ten, while another's may fit you in a size fourteen. This means that it is essential to have your measurements taken in undergarments you'll be wearing for your wedding by a professional and then taken again to ensure a correct fit. Don't get discouraged. Just like jean designers, you'll find the wedding dress designer that makes gowns for your shape and proportions. The following are a few examples of the ways size charts vary.

From Willows & Ivy

Size	4	6	8	10	12	14	16
Bust	32	34	36	38	40	42	44
Waist	25	27	29	31	33	35	37
Hip	36	38	40	42	44	46	48

From the Jim Hjelm Couture Collection

Size	2	4	6	8	10	12	14	16
Bust	32.5	33.5	34.5	35.5	36.5	38	39.5	41
Waist	22.5	23.5	24.5	25.53	26.5	28	29.5	31
Hip	33	34	35	36	37	38.5	40	41.5

From Watters Brides

Size	2	4	6	8	10	12	14	16
Bust	34	35	36	37	38	39.5	41	43.5
Waist	26	27	28	29	30	31.5	33	35.5
Hip	36.5	37.5	38.5	39.5	40.5	42	43	44

This means that if I were to go by size chart alone and not by my specific measurements of a thirty-nine-inch bust, thirty-inch waist and thirty-eight-inch hips, I would not fit perfectly into any of these sizes! If I went with Willows & Ivy and selected the size to fit my bust, which is a size twelve, my dress would be three to five inches too large in the waist and hips. In selecting a Watters gown, I would also be a size twelve, but the bust and waist would be a bit roomy, and the hips would be four inches too big. However, in a Jim Hjelm dress, I'd be a size fourteen with the bust and hip too big and the waist so small that I probably couldn't zip it up, even with my stomach sucked in all the way. In "real" life, I wear a size six pant, a size twenty-nine jean, and a size ten dress. So how does one go about finding a wedding dress that actually fits without doing so many alterations that you lose its graceful lines? Many salons recommend that you just buy "big" and have the rest taken in to fit. This generally results in an ill-fitting dress. If you can select a dress designer whose size chart most resembles your measurements or one that works from your personal measurements rather than by size chart alone, you will get a much better fitting and flattering wedding gown.

FROM THE EXPERTS

Carmela Sutera, a New York fashion designer who has been in the bridal business since 1979, believes that just as no two women are alike, one dress does not flatter all women. Her advice: The silhouette is the key to beauty, so the dress must be appropriate to your body shape and form. She advises, "Know your body and what you look best in, whether that be a ball gown or a soft A-line. She also stresses that magazines can be deceiving. Don't be disappointed when that particular dress you love in the magazine doesn't look good on you. Keep trying on different styles, and when you find the one you *feel* great in, that's the one you'll *look* great in.

Michelle Kelly of Willows and Ivy believes that the second-time bride should throw out the rulebook and wear whatever she wants. Kelly designs simple gowns with simple cuts. Because of this, she works mainly with second-time brides, ages thirty-five to sixty-five, who are having informal or destination weddings. She has designed dresses in ivory, sage green, light lavender and even a vibrant cobalt blue with red accents. She is known for her two-piece ensembles comprised of simple floor-length skirts and strapless bodices accentuated with pearls, crystal beading or embroidery. She loves to work with silk, especially silk charmeuse, as it is very slinky and reminiscent of 1930s glamour. Kelly cautions: Don't read the articles in the bridal publications; they will only stress you out by telling you what to do and when to do it. Try to relax, have fun and do things your way.

Janell Berté, a clothes designer in Pennsylvania, reports she is seeing and using a lot of accent color, usually in sashes, beading, crystals or designs hand painted on the fabric. For encore brides, she thinks the days of the "sexy sheath" are being replaced with the romance of the strapless gown in either a ball gown, A-line or softly flowing column design. Janell meets with many brides who feel overwhelmed with too many choices and have no clear sense of direction. Her recommendations: when shopping for your dress, bring along a trusted friend who will give you her heartfelt opinion. Don't over shop. Three good salons are more than enough to find the perfect dress. She also advises that you try on dresses only within your budget. Going overboard and trying on dresses you know you can't afford will only make you miserable and frustrated.

Claire Pettibone is a designer in Los Angeles who originally started by creating a line of lingerie. She now designs wedding dresses with a vintage look that includes plenty of antique lace and embroidery. Her clientele range in ages from forty to sixty. Her advice is to select the most romantic and feminine dress you'll ever wear. She suggests looking at as many dresses as possible, taking a friend along and having *fun*. Claire encourages brides to be true to themselves and wear the dress that speaks to them.

Amy Michelson, a southern California designer, recently designed a wedding dress for a seventy-year-old woman who was remarrying. The dress was cut on the bias, strapless and made of flowing sheer chiffon. A loose, draping jacket reminiscent of the1920s topped it. According to Amy, the best style for curvy figures is the bias cut. And the key is to select a dress that is not too tight. She advises encore brides to stick with simple, clean lines and avoid overly fussy styles. And last Amy states, "Almost half of the brides today are second time brides, so be proud and enjoy the process."

MY FAVORITE DESIGNERS

Having spent five years creating and publishing *Bride Again*, I have developed a list of favorite designers who just seem to know what the second time-bride is looking for in a wedding dress. They understand the second-time bride, her body, her image, her level of sophistication, and her desire to look her absolute best on her wedding day. Here's my list in alphabetical order, as I just can't decide whom I like the most. Each one has a lovely vision for the second-time bride.

Amy Michelson
Avica   LaBelle Special Occasion
Birnbaum & Bullock   Lazaro
Carmela Sutera   Nicole Miller
Claire Pettibone   Maggie Sotero
Damianou   Martin McCrea
Daymour Couture   Mera
Ian Stewart   Marisa Bridal
Jane Booke   Mon Cheri
Janell Berté   Ramona Keveza
Jennifer Tiscornia   Stephanie Allin
Jessica McClintock   Tadashi
Jim Hjelm   Willows & Ivy

If you're looking for great styles in plus sizes up to size forty-four, good designers to check out are: Birnbaum & Bullock, Alfred Angelo, Damainou, Mon Cheri, Marisa Bridal, Ian Stewart, Jim Heljm, Jasmine, Impression Bridal, and Diva by Paloma Blanca.

BORROWING, RENTING, AND REUSING

Some may be wondering if it is okay to wear their dress from their first wedding. The answer is no, absolutely not—not even if you plan on removing the sleeves, making it shorter, dying it or whatever else you're thinking of doing to it.

However, if you don't want or can't afford the expense of a new wedding dress, you may want to consider borrowing one from a friend or renting one from a shop or boutique. Most large cities have formal gown rental shops where you can rent an expensive dress for a fraction of the original cost. They offer large selections, a full range of sizes and colors, personal fittings, and accessories such as veils, jewelry and handbags. They even have dresses for your bridesmaids and flower girl. If you are looking to cut costs, this is an easy way to do it. Besides, grooms have been renting tuxedos for ages, so why can't a bride rent her dress as well?

GOWN PRESERVATION

If you are sentimental and you've spent a good deal of money on your dress, not to mention time and tears selecting it, you may want to consider preserving the outfit. Wouldn't it be wonderful if this dress, in which you had the best day of your life, could become an heirloom and be worn by your daughter when she marries or again by you when you have your vows renewed on your tenth anniversary? Before you hang your wedding gown in the closet, consider the following important points to help preserve its beauty:

How do you want your gown cleaned? Investigate both the wet and the dry method of cleaning your gown. Often, harsh dry cleaning chemicals can ruin delicate fabrics, beading or sequins. Many gown-cleaning companies offer gentle baths for wedding gowns. Whichever method you choose, find out how much experience the company has in cleaning wedding gowns.

Does the cleaning company inspect the condition of your gown? Perhaps it needs stain removal or repair of a tear. Good cleaners will take care of your veil, headpiece and other accessories, as well as perform minor repairs such as sewing a loose button or bead.

Does the company to whom you entrust your gown test before cleaning? Resin testing determines if buttons and other gown enhancements will be damaged. Further testing will determine how a stain may react to the cleaning process.

What is the cost of inspecting, testing, repairing and cleaning the dress? Before you commit to a certain service, you will want to know the price. You should expect a figure between $150 to over $300 depending on the cleaning quality, the amount of lace, beads and sequins, and whether or not your gown has a train, long sleeves or added fabric.

Does the company require you to sign a release? Be careful of waivers, as some companies ask you to release them from any responsibility should the dress be damaged in the cleaning process. Find out what their policy is if something goes wrong.

Does the cleaning company have a refund policy that will cover the cost of your gown, as well as the fee charged for its cleaning? Settle upon a replacement value…just in case.

How does the company pack your gown after it is cleaned? Be sure the cleaner uses acid-free packing materials. If the company packs your gown in a box with viewing windows, be aware that these plastic windows emit gases, which can yellow a gown. Your dress should not be hermetically sealed, and you should be able to open the packing whenever and as many times as you wish.

After you have your dress cleaned and packed, store it in a cool, dry place. Lay it flat rather than hanging it up, as the weight of the dress can stretch or tear the fabric or seams.

YOUR MOST IMPORTANT ACCESSORY

Whether you choose to wear a ball gown, a simple sheath or a suit, the right undergarments make all the difference. Even if you're already in great physical shape, the right undergarments will enhance your natural shape and slim any perceived imperfections. There is nothing worse than having a beautiful dress and then ruining the effect with the wrong undergarments.

Let's start with the bra. On your emotional and stress-filled wedding day, what you need is *support*. A good bra gives a woman both physical and emotional fortitude. It lifts and comforts throughout the day. Look into bras that reduce if you are buxom. Some bras, called minimizers, reduce your bust measurements as much as an inch and a half. On the other hand, if you have a small cup size, choose a padded and push-up bra that provides the most cleavage and has detachable push-up pads. Consider what will enhance your dress. Do you need something more flexible with removable straps so you can create a halter or strapless look? Try on different types of bras. This is the best way to select the right one to wear under your wedding gown. Take them home, try them on and see the effect.

Corsets, cinchers and waist eliminators give that extra bit of control and take away inches. This doesn't mean you should buy a smaller sized wedding gown and depend on the undergarment to make it fit you. These types of undergarments smooth, control the midriff bulge and enhance the bust line. Whichever undergarment you select, be sure it is comfortable. You can choose from foundations, body shapers, waist nippers, control slips, bust minimizers, and long-line strapless and backless bras. Most are made of micro fiber fabrics, such as Lycra, Elastane and Spandex, for stretch, comfort and control.

To avoid panty lines, try wearing a thong panty or pantyhose. If you'll be wearing open-toed shoes or sandals, there's nothing better than a pair of Spanx. A footless, body shaping pantyhose made of nylon and Lycra by Sara Blakely, they stop below the knee so you can wear any style shoe, look slimmer, and avoid both panty lines and binding at the waist. As their tagline states, "Don't worry, we've got your butt covered."

TOPPING IT OFF

There are very few taboos in second weddings, but one of them is the blusher veil. As I mentioned earlier, this is the type of veil that falls in front of your face and is lifted by you or your husband for your first kiss. The blusher veil is still reserved for the first-time bride. It has always represented purity, concealment and innocence. It has also been thought to keep away evil spirits, and during the days when marriages were arranged, it hid the bride's face from her new husband until after the vows had been exchanged and there was no turning back. It has denoted subordination of the woman to the man with the lifting of the veil a symbol of male dominance. Veils carry heavy meaning and tradition, so be careful in the type you select if you're planning to wear one.

Although it's best to stay away from the blusher veil, there are many types of appropriate veils and other creative alternatives to accent your face, hair and dress.

Other veils you might consider are the waist-length veil, fingertip-length veil, or the elbow length veil. There is also the Spanish mantilla which drapes over both your head and shoulders and the sweep veil which reaches all the way to the hem of your dress. For a very formal wedding, there is the chapel veil which trails about one or two feet behind you or the cathedral veil which trails one to three yards behind your dress. Most second-time brides choose the elbow, waist or fingertip veil. Rather than the drama of a longer chapel- or cathedral-length veil, these veils frame the face but are not overwhelming. If you want to wear a veil, make sure it complements your dress, doesn't fall in front of your face, and flows behind your back.

If you don't want to wear a veil, there are many other choices including headbands, bun rings, hair combs, tiaras and hair clips. They come encrusted with pearls, rhinestones, beads, crystals or filigreed flowers. You can also go with simple fresh or silk flowers, a wreath or even a hat.

One of my favorite wedding headpieces comes from Winters & Rain in Rhode Island. They make wedding tiaras, headpieces, bun wraps, headbands and hair combs that can be restrung after the wedding into necklaces, bracelets or chokers. In essence, they become a favorite piece of jewelry you can wear forever or a family heirloom you can pass down through the generations. They use Swarovski crystals and freshwater cultured pearls in an amazing array of colors: white, ivory, pink, peach, lavender, platinum, coffee, bronze and peacock. You can also choose from gemstones including sapphires, emeralds, aquamarines, pink tourmalines, citrines and garnets. Since you select the stones, pearls and crystals, you create a one-of-a-kind headpiece that you will wear again and again as a necklace or bracelet in the years to come. Prices range from $200 to $375 with restringing at a standard cost of $75. I am only sorry that I didn't learn about them before my own second wedding or I would have worn one.

IF THE SHOE FITS, WEAR IT

Okay, you've found your Prince Charming, and now you need the proverbial glass slippers to complete your ensemble. The shoes you choose to wear on the day of your wedding can make the difference between dancing the night away or hoping the clock strikes midnight—fast. Keep in mind that your special day will mostly consist of standing, walking and dancing, so comfort is key.

The most important element of picking a shoe is finding the

right size. Always try shoes on at the end of the day when your feet are tired and swollen from the heat. By doing this, you will get a pretty accurate fit. Make sure your toes don't cramp in front, your heel doesn't slip, and the arch supports hit you in the right place. I'll always remember the shoes I wore to my stepdaughter's wedding. They were absolutely beautiful and matched my dress perfectly. They felt great...for the first hour. But every hour after that—and there were quite a few of them—those shoes felt excruciating. My feet were even tender to the touch the following day. It simply wasn't worth it.

The length of your dress will determine the style of your shoe. If your dress is long and your shoes won't be seen, choose a low or flat heel. However, if your dress is tea length or shorter, you'll want to stick with a low- to mid-heel. Although a nice pair of Jimmy Choo's or Manolo Blahnik's with four-inch heels may give you long, sexy looking legs, save them for your honeymoon when you're dancing on the deck of the cruise liner.

BUY THE PURSE WHILE YOU'RE AT IT

After you've found the perfect shoes, an elegant handbag is next on the list. The right bag can add the perfect finishing touch to your ensemble, whether your wedding is formal or informal. Make sure the bag you select complements your dress and shoes and can actually hold your lipstick, facial tissue, compact, blotting tissue, Tums, breath mints, miniature sewing kit with safety pins and other wedding day essentials. Handbags with pearls, sequins, crystals, beads, tassels or rosettes or one made in the same fabric as your dress are all great choices. There are fabulous bags by Nicole Miller, Sandra Leal, Tammy Darling and Lisa Brett. Your local David's Bridal or department store will also have a good selection.

BOUQUETS

What's a dress without a gorgeous bouquet to accent it? Looking back at my own second wedding photos, I am amazed at the size of the bouquet I chose. It was an enormous cascading bouquet that overpowered my dress. A small hand-tied bouquet or nosegay would have been much more appropriate. I don't know what I was thinking when I ordered it. Obviously, I didn't really think it through. Learn from my mistake and put some thought into ordering the right kind of bouquet for your dress. That way, when you look back on your wedding photos one day, you'll be happy with your choice.

There are several types of bouquets from which to choose. There's the arm bouquet, which is much like the enormous bouquet of roses that Miss America accepts. Then, there's the cascade where flowers drape from the top creating a waterfall effect. This type of bouquet looks best with a ball gown. Very popular is the hand-tied bouquet, which can be bound by beautiful cream, white or colored ribbons or raffia. It's a perfect bouquet for an outdoor or informal wedding. Another good choice is the nosegay. This bouquet is round and has closely packed blooms placed into a florist's foam-filled bouquet holder. It works well with all styles of gowns, but looks particularly good with the A-line dress. Some brides choose to hold a single flower such as a calla lily or large sunflower. Usually tied with a ribbon, this can be quite stunning and dramatic. Another popular choice is the pomander, or rose ball, often referred to as a "kissing ball." These balls can be made from most any type of flower and are held by a loop of ribbon. These are a perfect match for a Victorian or garden wedding.

Roses make a beautiful bridal bouquet and they come in every color of the rainbow. There are over 1,000 varieties from which to choose, and you can display them long stemmed, hand tied, in a florist's bouquet, as buds, or in partial or full bloom. Some last longer than others, so be sure to check with your florist. Other flowers that come in a large variety of styles and colors are orchids, dahlias, ranunculi, lilies and peonies.

When selecting flowers, it's always a good idea to select blooms that are in season. You'll find a wider variety, and the cost will be considerably less than trying to locate an exotic flower out of season. If you're marrying during a holiday such as Valentine's Day, then red roses are a natural, as are chrysanthemums at Thanksgiving, holly, seeded eucalyptus and berries at Christmas, and calla lilies during Easter. Winter weddings call for orchids and deep chocolate cosmos, autumn weddings for zinnias, asters and dahlias, while summer weddings are a time for Gerber daisies, sunflowers, calendula and stock. Spring is the perfect time for tulips, daffodils, iris and other blooming bulbs.

If you're going for a specific color such as red, try ranunculi, red roses, cockscomb, scarlet dahlias, peonies and tulips with some fully open and others still closed. For a purple bouquet, you can choose from sweetpeas, hyacinths, lisianthus, hydrangeas, heather, purple roses and violets. Yellow bouquets can contain daffodils, tulips, roses, orchids and ranunculus. If you're planning on pink, there are peonies, roses, orchids, Gerber daises and calla lilies from which to choose. For peaches and cream, look at stephanotis, Leonides roses, lily of the valley and calla lilies. For fragrance, the Star Gazer lily and Casa Blanca lilies are heavenly choices.

If you're marrying on the beach in Hawaii or in another tropical locale, a bouquet of exotic flowers, including bird of paradise, red or pink anthuriums, red ginger and orchids, is ideal. You can also follow the Hawaiian tradition and wear a fragrant tuberose or dendrobium orchid lei.

Perhaps you want your bouquet to reflect the feelings you and you fiancé have for each other. If this is the case, consider hand-selecting flowers that have a traditional meaning assigned to them. To get started, take a look at this list of blossoms and their symbolic meanings:

Flower	Meaning
Baby's breath	Everlasting love
Orchid	Love and beauty
Peony	Happy life
Phlox	United souls
Red chrysanthemum	I love you
White chrysanthemum	Truth
Clover	Good luck
Gladiolus	Sincerity
Heather	Admiration
Primrose	I can't live without you
Peach rose	Desire
Red rose	I love you
Blue hyacinth	Constancy
Red/pink hyacinth	Playfulness
White Hyacinth	Loveliness
Yellow iris	Passion
Ivy	Wedded love
Jonquil	Desire
Lily of the valley	Sweetness
Stephanotis	Happiness in marriage
Stock	Everlasting love
Sunflower	Adoration
Veronica	Fidelity
Blue violet	I'll always be true
Purple violet	Faithfulness
White violet	Take a chance
Wheat	Fertility

A few flowers to be wary of are marigolds, which myth says

symbolize cruelty and jealousy; larkspur, which symbolize fickleness; and begonias, which mean beware. Oleander is also a bad idea. Not only is it poisonous, but it also spells caution in the language of flowers. Other blooms to stay away from are the petunia, which represents anger and resentment; narcissus, which stands for egotism; and the orange blossom, which is still reserved for the first-time bride, as it represents virginity, purity and innocence.

JEWELRY

Most people think of pearls and diamonds when they think of bridal jewelry. But there are many other types of jewelry you might want to consider. If you're trying to bring a bit of color into your ensemble, select a gemstone necklace, earrings and bracelet. One second-time bride I know wore aquamarines, because aquamarine was her daughter's birthstone. Another bride wore sapphires to match the blue embroidery in her bodice, and still another selected amethyst to go with her bouquet and bridesmaids' dresses. A friend of mine who had a garden wedding wore a simple daisy chain necklace and bracelet. If you're feeling daring, forgo traditional jewelry and do what the women of India do—adorn your hands and feet with henna designs.

MAKEUP TIPS

Is your idea of makeup some mascara, a bit of eye shadow and a quick sweep of blush? Well, for your wedding, you may want just a bit more. You probably desire flawless skin, romantic eyes, soft cheeks and lipstick that will last for hours, right? The last thing you want is a shiny forehead, dark shadows or smeared mascara showing up in all your photos.

According to Lisa Joy Walton, a Los Angeles makeup artist, if you're using alpha hydroxy or retinol products, such as Renova, Roc or other similar over-the-counter products, stop using them about three or four weeks prior to your wedding date. This is for two reasons. First, these products are very drying, and makeup looks better on moist, healthy skin. Second, your dry skin will soak up the foundation, so you'll require more and it won't last as long. Also, if you are tanning at a salon, do not tan your face. That, too, can be drying. It's easy to blend your face makeup to match the skin on your chest, so don't worry that your face will appear too pale for your body.

To get that perfect bridal look you're dreaming of, start with a clean fresh face. Either have a professional facial a week out or do one yourself at home. Don't wait until the night before and end up with red, patchy skin. If you get a blemish the night before, try Clinique's Acne Solutions Spot Healing Gel with salicylic acid. Plain old toothpaste will also do in a pinch. And then there's the model's secret to fixing puffy skin under your eyes: a little dab of Preparation H before you go to bed. Yes, it sounds disgusting and smells worse, but it really does work wonders.

The next step is to moisturize your face. It will help fill and plump out the fine lines, creating a smooth canvas. Once you're ready to apply your makeup, Walton recommends doing so in natural light rather than in your bathroom.

The third step to a polished look consists of three key ingredients: concealer, foundation and powder. Start with an oil-free matte foundation that is long lasting. Match the color of the foundation to the color of your skin just below your cheekbone. Try it on the back of your hand as well and go outdoors in natural light to see the true color. The wrong color or tone can age you five to ten years, so take your time finding the right shade. Also, avoid using old makeup. All makeup has a shelf life; pigments start to break down and bacteria start to build up. Mascara is good for about three to six months; cream blush about six months to one year; and concealer, pencils, eye shadow and eye cream will last up to a full year. Foundation, lipstick and moisturizer are good for about one to one and a half years and face powder and powder blush can last as long as two years. If you need to cover dark circles under your eyes, use a foundation that is one to two shades lighter than your regular foundation. Beware, however. If the shade is too light, you'll end up with "raccoon eyes" from the flash photography. A good alternative is to use a concealer in the appropriate color. Concealers work by neutralizing what you are trying to cover up. For example, if you are trying to hide a red pimple, then the concealer should be in the counteracting color, which is green. If you're trying to offset the purple and blue tones of dark undereye circles or broken capillaries, you'll want a yellow or orange concealer. To even out a yellow birthmark or bruise, a blue concealer will work best. Once you've selected the right concealer, pat it on with your fingertip or a sponge. Swiping concealer can erase it or make it uneven. Use concealer sparingly; a little goes a long way and too much will age you. Another tip from the experts: Put a little concealer on your lids to help eye shadow last longer.

Next, set your foundation and concealer with powder. This will make your foundation last longer and keep your face from becoming shiny. Use a large brush and avoid your eye area where lines are easily emphasized by powder. Select loose powder to set and a pressed compact for touchups. Small blotting tissues will also keep shininess at bay. For those of you who refuse to wear foundation or more makeup than you're used to wearing, consider these three points: Foundation helps blush last longer, naked skin reflects the flash from cameras, and bright lights wash out color. Foundation and a little added color are necessary.

For eye shadow, think warm colors such as browns, bronzes and mauves. Go with matte rather than shimmery colors, as they can age you. Line your eyes if you like, but smudge the lines with your finger or a Q-tip to keep from looking hard or harsh. Or better yet, take Walton's advice and just dot in between each lash. Then, with an angle brush, blend for a soft line. Fill in your eyebrows with a soft eyebrow pencil or the right shade of eye shadow. (A clerk from MAC taught me that trick, and it's a much more subtle and natural look than an eyebrow pencil.)

For your lashes, Walton suggests getting them dyed about one week prior to your wedding. The cost is only about $25 and makes for much bigger, brighter eyes. Before applying mascara, always use an eyelash curler to make your eyes look larger. Then use brown or brown-black mascara for daytime weddings and black for evening weddings. Lisa Joy swears by Maybelline waterproof mascara in black, although my favorite is Lancome's Definicils Waterproof High Definition mascara. Whatever brand you choose, it's a good idea to opt for the waterproof version, as tears of joy are sure to flow at some point during the wedding or reception. She also suggests refraining from putting mascara on your bottom lashes to avoid dark shadows in your wedding photos and using a fine-toothed lash separator comb to keep lashes from clumping together. If you're going to add false eyelashes, buy the individual ones that generally have three lashes to a "clump." Attach anywhere from three to ten clumps, starting at the outside edge and working your way in.

To avoid having big, round clown cheeks, use a large soft brush when applying your blush. Smile as you apply and the color will naturally go on the apple of your cheeks. Stroke the brush lightly over your nose, chin and forehead for a sun-kissed effect. Choose sheer pinks if you are fair skinned, apricots and corals if you are medium toned, and reds or burgundies for dark or olive skin.

Lips complete the look. To make your lipstick last the night, use a lip liner not only to line your lips but to fill them in as well. Then cover with a longwearing lipstick. If you need to eat or drink while getting ready, take tiny bites of food and use a straw for drinking.

Some second-time brides seek professional assistance and have their makeup done by a consultant. They could also make an appointment at their local department store for a free application. Of course, if you do this, it's a good idea to purchase the lip liner, lipstick, and pressed powder for use throughout your wedding day. If you can afford a good makeup artist, go for it. It will be worth the money. You'll just wish you could have her at your beck and call each and every day.

BEAUTY TIPS

In the weeks before your wedding, make sure you get plenty of sleep. For better looking skin and to avoid dehydration, which results in irritability and fatigue, drink tons of water. Get your hair cut a few weeks before (rather than a few days prior) to your wedding. If you're getting married outdoors, don't forget sunscreen. And get rid of any unsightly facial hair. Tweeze eyebrows, stray chin and nose hairs, and wax your upper lip, if necessary.

FROM YOUR FINGERS TO YOUR TOES

If you have a sparkling full carat diamond wedding ring set in pure platinum, everyone will want to see it at the reception. This calls for a good manicure the day prior to your wedding. Whether you go to a professional salon or do it yourself, here are a few tips. Select pale colors like sheer ivory, beige, pink or nude. A French manicure is always in style, or be more bold and match your nail color with one of the colors in your floral bouquet. Try lavender, bright pink or even red. If you have skin with yellow undertones, select a brownish red, and for those of you with pink undertones, go with a more bluish red. For great staying power and dozens of color selections, my favorite nail polish is OPI.

Other good brands are Bobbi Brown, Essie and Lancome.

If you're wearing open-toed shoes or sandals, get a pedicure before the big day as well. One or two days prior is best for a fresh look. Bring a bottle of your own polish just in case you get a chip and need a touch-up the day of your wedding. To avoid chips altogether, pick up a bottle of Skip Chip from OPI and apply it as the final coat. Your fingers and toes will look great, even after you return from your honeymoon.

WHAT ABOUT THE REST OF THE WEDDING PARTY?
Bridesmaids/matrons

Have you ever wondered why bridesmaids are always dressed in matching gowns of the same color? Well, once upon a time, it was a common belief that if you were favored by good fortune, envious evil spirits would be drawn to you and put curses upon you. Since a bride's wedding day was to be the happiest day of her life, she was considered to be at special risk. However, if all the bridesmaids and the bride herself were dressed exactly alike, the evil spirits would be confused and unable to figure out which woman was the bride. Therefore, she would escape the curses of the evil spirits and live happily ever after. Although bride and bridesmaids no longer dress exactly alike, the tradition of bridesmaids wearing dresses of the same color and style has remained.

Today, your attendants have a wide variety of dresses from which to choose. Gone are the days of the horrendous chartreuse bridesmaid's dress. (You know, the one your best friend said was so pretty that you could shorten it after the wedding and wear it out on a date. Yeah, right.)

When selecting dresses with your bridesmaids, there's only one thing to keep in mind. Ask them to pick something that is consistent with the style of your dress and the degree of formality or informality of your wedding. Just don't expect them to wear it on a date. Give them some freedom in their selection and let them choose according to their figures. It is perfectly acceptable for each bridesmaid to wear a different style, as long as all of the dresses are complementary, the same color, and made of the same fabric. A happy bridesmaid or matron makes for an even happier bride.

Some of my favorite designers for bridesmaids' and matrons' dresses are Alfred Angelo, Barijay, Bill Levkoff, Dessy Creations, Jasmine, Jessica McClintock, Jim Hjelm, Impressions Bridal, Lazaro, and Watters & Watters. Each of these offers dresses that are simple, elegant and age appropriate. They also come in a wide variety of colors.

Flower Girl

If your daughter is like mine, she couldn't wait to be a flower girl. She loved her white tulle dress, miniature veil and shiny new shoes. Of course, the best part was the sweet little basket and the chance to toss the rose petals. After being told throughout her whole life not to throw things on the floor, here was her big chance. She took full advantage of the situation, running out of petals by the time she was halfway to the altar. When looking for your flower girl's dress, check out designs from Jessica McClintock, Just Adorables, Pure Avica, Posies, Mon Cheri, and US Angels.

The "Tweener"

If your or his daughter is too old to be a flower girl, but still too young to be a bridesmaid, then she fits into the category of junior bridesmaid. Finding her an appropriate dress can be difficult. They are either too little girly, much too sophisticated or just plain old ugly. My favorite designers are Beth Blake and Sophie Simmons of Thread Bridesmaids, although you may also find lovely dresses at Krysia Bridal or David's Bridal.

THE GROOM

Yes, yes, I know, it's all about the bride. But what about that good-looking guy of yours? Luckily for most grooms, a simple suit or tuxedo will almost always work.

The tuxedo is said to have begun at the Tuxedo Club at Delmonico's in New York City. In 1886 at the first Autumn Ball, a man by the name of Griswold Lorillard came decked out in a scarlet satin lapelled dinner jacket without tails while all other men wore the traditional white tie and tails. The new style was a hit and became known as the tuxedo. Eventually, this style came to signify high society, elegance and celebration.

For a good fitting tuxedo, Jim's Formal Wear has these suggestions: if your fiancé is tall and slim, he will look great in just about any style, but especially so in a double-breasted tuxedo. He will also look exceptional in a vest. If your fiancé is tall and husky with broad shoulders and a muscular frame, a shawl-collared tuxedo will suit him well. If he has a thick neck and wide face, he should avoid narrow ties and wing-tip shirts because they may appear as if they are choking him. A laydown collar shirt and bow tie would be a better option. For a man that is short and stocky with an athletic or muscular build, Jim's Formal Wear recommends tuxedo jackets with slim collars and pants that extend as low as possible on the foot and angle slightly in the back to elongate his legs. If you are marrying a man that is short and slim, he should look for simple breasted jackets with long lines and wide-peak lapels or a double-breasted tuxedo jacket. A vest will also look great on him.

Tuxedos come with several accessories. Your fiancé can choose suspenders, a cummerbund or vest. The rule here is that he can wear suspenders with a cummerbund but not with a vest. Both cummerbunds and vests should cover the top of his waistband for a proper fit. If your fiancé thinks he'll be removing his jacket at the reception, make sure he opts for a full-back vest.

When wearing a tuxedo, the cummerbund is to be worn with the pleats facing up. The boutonniere should be worn on the left lapel and placed slightly outward. Your fiancé should select either a boutonniere or a pocket square, but not both. His shoes and socks should match the tuxedo. That means black shoes and socks with a black tuxedo and white shoes and socks with a white tuxedo. If the jacket is any other color, go with black shoes and socks.

THE GROOM'S ATTENDANTS

Pardon the pun, but the attendants simply "follow suit" and wear what the groom is wearing. The challenging part is matching the vests or cummerbunds with the bridesmaids' dresses, bouquets and accent colors. That's where individualism can come in with a varied selection of bright or muted colors, paisleys or prints.

RING BEARER

If your or fiancé have a young son, this will be your chance to see your sweet little guy all dressed up, something that rarely happens. Little girls love to play dress up, but little boys tend to be happiest in their favorite pair of jeans. Most ring bearers in second weddings will wear a boy's suit, an Eton suit or junior tuxedo. If you're having a themed wedding, then sailor suits, kilts or military-styled uniforms are also fun choices.

REAL LIFE EXPERIENCES

Rebecca's Story

"For my second wedding, I bought a white dress at a bridal salon, but then decided I wanted something less formal and without a train. So I ended up borrowing an ivory wedding dress from a friend at work who had married a year earlier. It was from Eden Bridals and was made of flowing chiffon. The silhouette was A-line, and reminiscent of the Renaissance period. It had bell shaped sheer chiffon sleeves that were slit up to the inner elbow and flowed past my fingertips. It had an empire waist and was very flattering. The scoop neckline was trimmed with beading, as was the empire waistline. It dipped to a low V in the back, giving it a very graceful look and feel. The style was actually from their bridesmaids' collection, which made it well suited for our casual wedding. I loved it! I had a few problems getting it altered, but it all worked out in the end. Plus, the price was right!"

Linda's Story
"Finding a dress was, for me, probably the most difficult part of planning my second wedding. I was forty-nine and a big white gown and veil seemed inappropriate. I looked at dresses at every bridal salon, boutique and department store within a fifty-mile radius of my house. I tried on long gowns, suits and dresses in every style imaginable. Finally, I found a simple long ivory dress with short sleeves and a scoop neck. I knew it was "the one" the minute I put it on. I used two hair combs with silk flowers to put up my hair. I felt like a beautiful bride."

Amber's Story
"Although my husband and I eloped, I still wore a wedding dress. Designed by Watters Brides, it was made of silk satin. It was long, hung straight to the floor and had a very simple cut. It was beautiful. It was strapless and had a band that criss-crossed at the waist and then tied low in the back with long streamers that acted as a small train. I wore a veil that started at the crown of my head and fell over my shoulders. I carried a round bouquet of pink titanic roses and pink hydrangeas, which I had preserved in a dome by Keepsake

Floral. My husband looked extremely handsome in his black tux. It was everything I imagined."

Kira's Story

"Although this was my second marriage, it was my first time wearing a gown. When I was married before in our backyard, the ceremony was very low key. So this time, my fiancé told me I could have the wedding of my dreams, which I did. We were married outdoors at Lake Morey Inn in Vermont, right on the lakeshore. It was a July wedding on the most beautiful day of the summer.

"My Mori Lee dress was a white, strapless ball gown with a small train. It had silver beads on the fitted bodice and on the lower part of the dress. When I first went shopping for my dress, I was almost in tears because even though I was a size eight, the first two dresses I tried on were so small that I was sure I was going to look like a fat bride. Then, I tried on the third and final dress. It fit perfectly, as if it had been custom made just for me. The gown came with a beaded, sheer tulle shawl. I wore a silver tiara with butterflies on it and a veil that trailed down my back. I selected silver high heels, per my husband's request. Needless to say, I took them off at the reception.

"My wedding colors were white, red and silver, so I carried a bouquet of red Gerber daisies. My bridesmaids and matron each wore a red or silver dress, while the male attendants donned complementary colored vests. My husband wore a black tux with red vest to match my bouquet. It was spectacular."

Brenda's Story

"I chose an Alfred Angelo gown made of satin with a pearl-beaded bodice. I chose ivory because I am extremely fair skinned and white washes out my skin. I found the dress in a bridal salon that sells on eBay. I bought it directly through the "Buy It Now" program rather than via auction. It was a $1,000 dress that I got for only $125. I started out using eBay for the wedding decorations and just thought I'd check out the dresses. Not only did I get a great deal, but the selection was also much better than in the small town where I live. The salon shipped the gown immediately, and I had a professional seamstress do the alterations since it was a tad too big for me. When I wore it on my wedding day, I felt like a true princess, especially with my fireman hubby next to me all decked out in his Honor Guard uniform."

Like these women, you can also find the perfect attire for you and your wedding party. Start looking as soon as possible. Don't get discouraged, and don't settle. It's your day. Stamp it with your signature sense of style!

Chapter Six

The Invitation

All the Ins and Outs

*F*irst **Wedding:** Since the bride's mom and dad are paying for this extravaganza, they issue the invitation in their names, requesting the honour of the guest's presence at their daughter's wedding. It's formal. It's engraved. Usually, one will be saved and perhaps framed as a keepsake.

Second Wedding: Since the couple marrying almost always bear the financial costs of this celebration, the invitation reads something along the lines of: "We ask you to join us as we celebrate our new life together," "The children of Bob and Joan invite you to join them as they witness their parents exchange vows," or "Together, with our children, we joyously ask you to join us as we begin anew." It's most often informal. It can be printed at Kinko's. The couple will save one and place it in a drawer.

Long before the printing press and the spread of literacy, marriage announcements were made by the town crier or read aloud at a religious service. Eventually, the masses learned to read and write and were then able to emulate the wealthy and hand-write their own wedding invitations. When the printing press was invented, printed invitations largely replaced the handwritten versions.

One way to make the wedding invitation appear more special than regular correspondence was placing it in a double envelope. This also kept the inner envelope in pristine condition while the mail wound its way through the postal system, which essentially was a messenger on horseback. Upon arriving at its destination, a servant would trash the outer envelope and serve the invitation to the lady of the manor on a small silver plate. The small tissue placed on top of the engraving was meant to keep the print from smudging. The response card is a recent addition. This small card placed with the invitation helps the bride tally an accurate guest count for the caterer, ceremony site, wedding favors and other important details. It's truly a modern convenience.

Today, there are a myriad of choices of wedding invitations, but the choice you make is an important one. Your wedding invitation will be the window through which your guests get a glimpse of what your wedding style will be. From your invitation alone, your guests will know if your wedding is formal or informal—if it's a casual event in your backyard, a Victorian garden wedding, or a solemn church ceremony steeped with tradition. So think about the type of wedding you want. Consider its location, tone and style. Then select an invitation that captures the essence of your wedding day.

Let's talk about where to start. First, let's review a few printing terms so you'll know what kind of paper, type and design to look for when you start shopping around, whether you are using a stationery store, independent printer, Internet, mail order catalog, graphic designer or making them yourself at home.

Engraving: The most expensive print style is this classic look. Unless you are having a very formal wedding, you may want to pass on it. However, if expense is no problem and you want the most formal invitation of all, then choose an engraved invitation. Engraving is the process where the words are carved onto a metal plate, usually copper or steel, and then forced onto the paper to raise the type. Once a printer creates this plate for you, it is yours; you own it. Engraving works best on heavyweight papers like cardstock.

Thermography: This technique mimics the look of engraving at a much more reasonable price. If you like the formal look of engraving, but don't want to pay the higher cost, then take a look at thermography. In this process, metal or resin powder is mixed with wet ink and then heated to create raised type. The lettering has a shiny finish rather than the matte look of engraving. Smooth paper works best with this printing style.

Offset Printing: Also called lithography or flat printing, this great choice for an informal second wedding uses a rubber cylinder to press ink onto the paper. The ink simply lies flat on the surface of the paper. It is the most common style of printing chosen by second-time brides. Offset is simple. It looks nice, can be used on any type of paper and is affordable.

Home Computer Printing: If you're good on the computer and have a little artistic ability, you can easily create your wedding invitation yourself at home. Stationery and office supply stores have plenty of ready-to-go invitations or you can use a software program such as Publisher, PageMaker, Photoshop or QuarkXPress to design your own. You can also purchase less expensive software programs, including The Printshop and PrintMaster by Broderbund (both about $40) or Publisher Pro by Nova Development (about $80), which can be found at stores like Staples, Office Depot and Best Buy.

Handwritten Calligraphy: If you are planning a Victorian-themed wedding, garden wedding or if you simply love the look of calligraphy, you may want to consider hiring a calligrapher to design your invitation. At a cost of $100 to $300, you can have this unique wedding invitation created just for you. Mary Lou Johnson of M Johnson Design, whose rates start at $150 for a complete invitation suite, reports that "copperplate" is very popular right now. Not to be confused with the font by the same name, this formal style of calligraphy is done with a very fine, flexible metal nib dipped in ink. Every five to seven letters the pen must be dipped in the ink again. It is a very slow and deliberate process. Spencerian is a similar script and also quite popular. Once your invitation is designed, you take it to your local print shop and have the sample reproduced. Of course, the envelopes should be addressed in calligraphy to match. Johnson's rates for addressing envelopes range from $2 to $3.75 per set. She also paints watercolor illuminations which are absolutely stunning. Her signature grapevine motif is $3.50 each. If you've got the budget for your invitations, the age-old art of calligraphy is a classy touch.

Computerized or Digital Calligraphy: If you can't afford handwritten calligraphy, you might opt to have your envelopes done by digital calligraphy. Look for a stationery store in your area that has a calligraphy machine or go on-line to PegasusPlume.com. It's much less expensive (about $1.25 for each set of envelopes) and looks and feels similar to the handwritten kind. Pegasus Plume carries over 350 fonts from which to choose so that the envelopes will match the invitation you have already selected. They can usually have your envelopes completed in as little as three days. There is a $15 set up fee and a slight charge for ink colors other than black.

Debossing: The words are stamped from the front onto the paper without ink, leaving an indented image. Debossing works well for motifs, monograms and borders.

Embossing: The opposite of debossing, in this process the words are pressed from behind into the paper, creating a raised image. The embossed area can be inked or left plain. If left plain, this technique is called blind embossing. It looks great with a seashell or leaf motif, your new initials, or a border around the invitation.

Deckle Edge: I just love this style in which the paper has that torn, uneven, feathery edge. This works best with parchment invitations, but it can be used with a variety of other papers as well.

Die-cut: The process of cutting paper into shapes and designs composes this style. For example, if you're getting married on Valentine's Day and you want your invitation to be in the shape of a heart, then you'll want to die-cut.

Layers: Two layers are glued or tied together with ribbon in this beautiful style. The top layer can be translucent, showing the printed invitation on the second page. Conversely, the bottom layer can feature a design, image or a photograph of the two of you, with a printed overlay.

Foil Stamping: Gold, bronze or platinum foil stamped into the type, which can be shiny or matte, is ideal for a fall wedding. It can be a bit pricey, but it produces an elegant and warm effect. Foil stamping works well for simple motifs without a lot of detail.

These are the major types of printing used for wedding invitations. Let's move on to another important consideration: the paper.

Content: Paper is made of cellulose fibers, either by hand or by machine. Fine paper is handmade with 100 percent cotton fiber, although linen and flax can be used as well. Second best is machine-made paper from a combination of natural fibers and wood pulp. The paper we use everyday is machine made with wood pulp. Specialty papers, such as those made by Botanical Paperworks, include elements like small flower petals, twigs and fall leaves.

Weight: You'll also need to consider paper weight. Basically, the heavier the paper, the more expensive it will be. If you are engraving, you'll need heavyweight paper. Medium weight is good for almost all other printing styles. If you're going with offset printing, you can usually get away with a lightweight paper.

Finish: The surface of your paper can be shiny, matte, smooth, pearlized or marbleized. It can be parchment, linen or vellum. It's all just a matter of taste and your personal preference.

Color: You no longer have to pick ecru, white or cream for your invitation. Choose your favorite color, the color of your bouquet or the color of your bridesmaids' dresses. Select a color that matches the season or holiday if you're marrying in the autumn or on St. Patrick's Day. The same goes for the color of ink you select. You needn't stay with black. Pick red for passion, orange for energy, blue for loyalty, or green for abundance. Just stick with a single color, both for cost and ease of reading.

Embellishments: This is the fun part! You may love an invitation tied with a silky ribbon, adorned with beautiful antique lace or attached to a small charm. You might like one that is embossed with a motif or symbol such as a flower, fall leaf, seashell, acorn or snowflake. You may even want to consider using the oriental yin yang (meaning the balance of two forces) or Egyptian ankh (meaning life everlasting) symbols.

ALL THE LITTLE EXTRAS

If you love detail, you may want to include envelope seals boasting your new monogram, your first names, the date of wedding, two intertwined hearts, doves or other symbols of love. You can also pick a custom lining for your envelopes, choosing from a variety of prints and solids. Some second-time brides, especially those having Victorian-themed weddings, like to use old-fashioned sealing wax on the outer envelopes.

Trust me, just knowing a little bit about the options will help you in the long run. Look at samples in each of the styles, see which ones appeal to you, and consider the prices versus your budget. While you want your invitation to be special, you probably don't want to break the bank. Visit your local stationery store and browse through the many books they have on hand. If you have selected a motif, theme or color for your wedding, incorporate those into your invitation, as well as your reception décor, centerpieces and cake.

Let's say your fiancé proposed to you while on a trip to San Francisco with the Golden Gate Bridge in the background. You decide to select a bridge as your motif (which is actually ideal for a second wedding, as a bridge symbolizes a transition from one life to another or the joining of two entities). Finding an invitation on which a bridge is depicted might be difficult, but pictures of the Golden Gate Bridge are numerous. Buy one and have it scanned at a copy store. Ask your printer to incorporate this image into a single panel wedding invitation. It can be printed in color, embossed or bronze foiled. Next, print the wording onto vellum paper and tie to the panel with ribbon or raffia. Use the same image of the bridge on your program, menu cards, thank you cards and other printed items.

You can exchange your vows in San Francisco at Exposition Park with the bridge in full view or near a bridge in your hometown. Many Japanese gardens have beautiful bridges crossing over graceful koi ponds which are ideal locations for wedding ceremonies. You may want to consider purchasing a wooden bridge from a garden center or renting one from an event company. Place it in your backyard and exchange your vows while standing beside or on it. Another option is to place one in the entryway of your reception room so that all guests must walk over the bridge.

Carry the bridge motif through with your centerpieces by going to the Golden Gate Bridge's Web site and ordering some crystal bridges. Place them on blue glass or fabric to simulate the water below. Tables can be identified with the names of other famous bridges rather than by table numbers. For your cake, the Web site sells a beautiful ornament that can be used as a cake topper and a scarf that can be draped around the base. Next, use a photo of you and your fiancé from your San Francisco trip. Enlarge it and frame it. Then have the guests sign the matting as they enter the reception room. Another idea is to purchase a print of the bridge and have them sign along the white border. Utilizing either of these ideas will make for an exceptional guest book. Wedding favors can be small Golden Gate Bridge charms purchased at the many tourist boutiques in downtown San Francisco or playing cards with the Golden Gate Bridge on them, which can also be purchased online. The idea is to provide continuity in the style and tone of your wedding from the moment your guests first open their invitations until they leave the reception with their party favors.

WHAT AM I BUYING?

Most experts say that about 2 percent of your wedding budget should be used for your wedding invitation. This cost should include the invitation, reception card and response card with envelope, ceremony program, printing, calligraphy and postage.

Reception Card: You will need a separate reception card only if you are having a formal wedding, the reception is being held someplace other than the ceremony site, or all the information won't fit onto the wedding ceremony invitation.

Response Card: You can also forgo the response card with envelope and select a response postcard instead. It's less expensive and requires less postage. Also, since many guests forget to fill in their names on the response card or have illegible handwriting, you may want to number code your guest list and write the corresponding number on the back of each response card. This can help you to know who was there and assign nameless gifts.

Program: If you wish to have a ceremony program, you can usually order one to match or complement your invitation. Another idea is to make your own on your home computer. Just remember to stick with the style, colors and motif of your wedding ceremony invitation. Programs are good ideas if you have a large wedding party or are honoring someone who has passed or is unable to attend. It is also good when you are including some traditions and customs that not all your guests will understand. When creating a program, be sure to include this information:

1) Your names.
2) Date and time of your wedding.
3) Listing of events from the prelude and the processional all the way to the pronouncement of the marriage and the recessional.
4) Names of people who are reading special poems or passages, singing songs or playing musical instruments.
5) Names of the bridal party and a short sentence explaining each member's relationship to you.
6) Name of your officiant.
7) A brief, personal message from you and your fiancé.
8) A tribute to any family members who are deceased or unable to attend the ceremony.
9) Brief explanation of customs or traditions used in the ceremony.

Keep in mind, having programs is a choice some want, but many second-time brides skip them altogether, especially if their wedding is very small, intimate and informal.

WORDING YOUR INVITATION

Unlike most first weddings, second weddings are usually not paid for by the parents, nor do they issue the invitations. Since you and your fiancé are hosting this soiree, the invitation should be issued in your names.

If you are going the formal route, you will want to use the traditional wording:

The honour of your presence
is requested
at the marriage of
Ms. Cindy Nelson
to
Mr. Richard Roy

or

Ms. Cindy Roy
and
Mr. Richard Roy
request the honour of your presence

The term "request the honour of your presence" is used only if your ceremony takes place in a house of worship. If it is a formal event held at a hotel, country club or other wedding venue, then you would use the phrase "request the pleasure of your company."

If you would like to use something less formal, try one of these:

Cindy Nelson
and
Richard Roy
invite you to share in the celebration
of their marriage

Cindy Nelson
and
Richard Roy
invite you to share in their joy
as they exchange vows

Cindy and Richard
invite you
to join in the celebration
as they begin their new life together

Our joy will be more complete
if you share this special day
as we exchange our marriage vows
"Today I marry my best friend"
Cindy and Richard
invite you to join them
in celebrating their new life together

We invite you to share this day of happiness
when the two of us,
Cindy Nelson
and
Richard Roy,
begin our new life together

Love fills a lifetime
and a lifetime begins this day
when the two of us,
Cindy Nelson
and
Richard Roy,
exchange vows

Cindy and Richard
joyously invite you to
celebrate with them

*Cindy Nelson
and
Richard Roy
have chosen the first day of
their new life together.
You are invited to share in their joy
as they exchange marriage vows*

*Please join us
as we join our lives in marriage*

*It is with joy that we,
Cindy Nelson
and
Richard Roy,
invite you to share in
a celebration of love*

*It is with joyous hearts that we,
Cindy and Richard,
invite you to attend our wedding*

If you'd like to include your or his children on the wedding
invitation, you might consider:

*Together with their children,
Cindy and Richard
request the pleasure of your company
at the celebration of their marriage*

*Eric, Andrea and Kelly
invite you to join them as
they witness the vows of their parents*

Together with their families,
Cindy Nelson
and
Richard Roy
ask you to join them
as they begin their new life together

For those who pick a themed or outdoor wedding, you might try something along these lines:

Join us for a day in the country
as we celebrate our marriage
with family and friends

Please join us
where the surf meets the sand
as we exchange our wedding vows

We're finally tying the knot!
Please join us as we celebrate
our new life together
at the Sandy Shores Yacht Club

Meet us under the mistletoe
as we join our hearts as one

WHO GETS AN INVITATION?

As I mentioned earlier, ex-spouses should not be invited. Other than that caveat, invite anyone you wish. Most second-time brides and grooms include only those who are near and dear to them. Relatives rarely seen, bosses, or the best friends of their parents aren't usually invited unless you both want them at the ceremony. The average second wedding has a guest list of seventy-five people. This usually translates into less than fifty invitations, as most of the invitations cover more than one person. As a general rule, children over eighteen years of age receive their own invitations, even if they are still living at home and the parents are also on your guest list.

THE ENVELOPE, PLEASE

Addressing the outer and inner envelopes is a matter etiquette governs. A guest's full name should be placed on the outer envelope and his or her last name should be put on the inner envelope. Here are some easy guidelines:

Guest Single woman
Inner Envelope Miss or Ms. Gour
Outer Envelope Miss or Ms. Nancy Gour

Guest Single man
Inner Envelope Mr. Nelson
Outer Envelope Mr. Daniel Nelson

Guest Married couple, same name
Inner Envelope Mr. and Mrs. Jackson
Outer Envelope Mr. and Mrs. Jeremy Jackson

Guest Married couple, different names
Inner Envelope Ms. Cliff and Mr. Shaw
Outer Envelope Ms. Joan Cliff and Mr. Thomas Shaw

Guest A couple living together
Inner Envelope Miss or Ms. Reed and Mr. Bell
Outer Envelope Miss or Ms. Melissa Reed and Mr. Robert Bell

Guest Same sex couple (list alphabetically by last name)
Inner Envelope Mr. Davis   Mr. Peterson
Outer Envelope Mr. Paul Davis   Mr. Jonathan Peterson

Guest Family with children under eighteen
(list by age with oldest listed first)
Inner Envelope Mr. and Mrs. Clark Amy, Sara, and Justin
Outer Envelope Mr. and Mrs. James Clark

When writing names on invitations, don't use nicknames. With people who use nicknames such as Nick or Tom, write "Nicholas" and "Thomas." Avoid writing "and Guest." Find out the guest's name. It makes that person feel more welcome and part of the celebration. Finally, do not use computer printed labels. This is a social celebration, not a company event.

Remember to send an invitation to your parents, all members of your bridal party and your officiant if he will be staying for the reception. Save one for you and your fiancé and one for each of his and your children as keepsakes.

JUST SAY NO

How do you let your guests know that you want cash gifts or don't want any gifts at all? How do you tell them that children are not invited? Or how do you let them know where you are registered? You do it the old fashioned way—by word of mouth. Do not include any of this type of information on a wedding invitation—ever. Here is a list of things **not** to put in your wedding invitation as they are considered rude and in poor taste.

No Kids or Adults Only: If you don't want to invite children, then omit the children's names on the inner envelope. If a guest phones and asks if she can bring her kids, be direct. Tell her that although you'd love for everyone to come, it simply isn't in your budget and thank her for understanding.

No Gifts or Cash Gifts Preferred: A wedding invitation, as you probably are aware, is a request for your guests' presence, not their presents. Listing anything about gifts conveys that you are more concerned with the presents than the guest's presence. Don't do it.

Including Registry Cards: Yes, I know the stores print registry cards and give them to you, but do not include them in your invitation. Again, it is equivalent to asking for a gift. I was appalled recently when I saw the Web site of a national well-known bridal publication actually encouraging brides to include these little cards. It's just tacky. Let your family and bridal party spread the word about where you are registered.

Black Tie: Another no-no for a wedding invitation. However, it is acceptable to print "Black Tie" on the reception invitation in the lower right hand corner.

Choice of Entrée: This, too, should be left off the reception card. These are details best suited to your caterer.

Beer and Wine Will be Served or Cash Bar: Whether or not cocktails are served is not a part of a wedding or reception invitation. Don't have a cash bar. As mentioned in an earlier chapter, it isn't acceptable to invite guests to your wedding and then charge them for drinks. Don't list this item and don't do it.

E-mailing Invitations: We all love and depend on e-mail; however, your wedding day, no matter how small and casual, is too special a day to use this informal communication.

HELPFUL HINTS

Here are some helpful hints that will ensure the whole invitation process runs smoothly:

Mailing: Mail invitations about six weeks prior to the wedding. Ask that response cards be returned no later than three weeks prior to the wedding. This will give you plenty of time to call those who forget to respond and get the correct head count for your caterer.

Order extras: This is a whole lot cheaper than placing a reorder because you forgot to invite your favorite neighbor, misplaced a few invitations (yes, it's been done), or had problems with the post office. Not to mention, you'll make at least one mistake on the envelopes. Plus, you'll want to have one for a keepsake, even if it ends up in a drawer somewhere.

Use a good pen: Pick one that has black ink, doesn't smear and flows well.

Use the same type style: Don't mix and match fonts. The only exception to this rule is that it is considered acceptable to use a larger script font for your names. But please keep to the same font in the rest of the invitation.

Ink color: If you choose a color of ink other than black, use it consistently throughout your wedding festivities. If you pick red ink, let's hope there will be red roses in your bouquet, red linens on the tables and bridesmaids in red satin dresses.

Postage: Use real stamps, not metered mail. Again, this is a social event, not a company picnic. The post office almost always carries the "Love," stamps although you can choose from many others that may reflect your wedding including roses, hearts or seashells. Check the required postage amount, just in case. Take one completed invitation with all the inserts to the post office and have it weighed. Oversized envelopes and alternative containers, such as boxes, bottles and mailing tubes, can all increase postage. Even a simple invitation in a heavy card stock with several inserts can increase the amount of postage required.

Spelling: If you're going the formal route, "honor" and "favor" are always spelled "honour" and "favour" with the English "u." Spell out all numbers. For example, "Saturday, August 10, 2006" would be written "Saturday, the tenth of August, two thousand and six." Half hours are "half after four o'clock" rather than "four-thirty."

Write out all words: Nothing is abbreviated, except Mr., Miss and Mrs. All other words are spelled out. To illustrate, you would write "Street" rather than "St." or "Avenue" rather than "Ave." Spell out the word "and" rather than using the ampersand symbol. You can choose from RSVP, R.S.V. P. or R.s.v.p. All are correct and come from the French words "Respondez, s'il vous plait," or when translated in English, "respond if you please".

Addressing envelopes: Allow plenty of time for addressing the envelopes. It always takes longer than you think. Enlist the help of family, friends or your bridal party if necessary.

Inserts: Include a map and travel information for your guests.

20 Ways to Save Some Cash

1. Limit your guest list.
2. Go with offset printing or print your invitations at home on your computer.
3. Watch the size and weight of the invitation to ensure that it will not require additional postage.
4. Skip the inner envelope and tissue.
5. Shop around. Sometimes you can find the exact same invitation you fell in love with at the stationery store online for much less.

6. Address your own envelopes or enlist the help of your bridal party or best friend (only if they have good penmanship).
7. Order your invitations early so you don't pay rush charges.
8. Choose a single panel invitation. It is less expensive than an invitation with a single, double or tri-fold.
9. Select a lightweight paper.
10. Skip the reception card and put that information on the wedding ceremony invitation by including the "Reception Immediately Following."
11. Use a postcard instead of traditional response card and envelope.
12. Use a single color ink. Make it black.
13. Skip the lined envelopes.
14. Design and print your own invitations.
15. Double and triple check for mistakes with wording and spelling to avoid a complete reorder.
16. Order standard-sized invitations. Oversized and odd shaped envelopes cost more to mail.
17. Keep insertions to a minimum.
18. Make sure your address list is up to date, so you don't have to send a second invitation when the first one is returned.
19. If your wedding is small, say less than fifteen guests, consider inviting everyone with a simple phone call.
20. Use a ready-made invitation kit.

Speaking of invitation kits, there are some great ones available at stores like Staples, Michael's, Party City, Target and Office Depot. "The Invitation Kit" by Gartner Studios includes fifty invitations, fifty envelopes, fifty response cards, fifty response card envelopes, fifty translucent vellum papers, fifty seven-inch ribbons, one test sheet, and complete instructions for only about $25. They offer kits with specialty handmade papers pressed with botanicals for about $40, along with accessory kits of ribbons and self-adhesive envelope seals. They have matching programs, place cards, thank you cards, and even candy bar wrappers, votive candle wrappers and wine labels. For smaller weddings, Ampad makes a kit of ten panel invitations with ten overlays, ten ribbons, ten envelopes, and a test sheet with instructions for about $8. Talk about a great deal.

Here are some fun and interesting ideas from Marley Majcher, owner of The Party Goddess:

The Spitfire Couple: Imagine receiving a clear plastic container and inside is a cardboard box. On the lid of the box is a romantic photo of a couple dancing cheek to cheek. When you open the lid, nestled inside are miniature bride and broom figurines. All the information about the wedding is printed on the inside lid. These "box cards" are a fun, unique and dramatic way to invite your friends and family to your wedding. And they don't cost nearly as much as you'd think. They come in sizes small, medium and large and start at just $34 for eight. Postage for the small size is about $.60 and goes up to about $1 for the large size. They also have another box with a tiny champagne bottle, goblet and candle.

The Story of Our Lives: Perhaps your relationship is a love story waiting to be told. If that's the case, consider turning your invitation into a book. Done in accordion style and bound, the cover is made of cardboard and covered in a fabric reflecting the formality or informality of your wedding. You can choose something like taffeta or raw silk for something a bit formal, gingham for a picnic, a floral print for a garden wedding or lace for a Victorian theme. These little books run about $10 each and are about two by three inches in size.

Beach Weddings: If you are having a beach wedding, Majcher suggests using a large, sturdy shell and tucking your printed invitation into the shell. It can be mailed in a cardboard or clear plastic box. Or, place your invitation in a bottle and mail it as a "message in a bottle." You could even handwrite your invitation onto a coconut and mail it whole, without a container—really.

THINK OUTSIDE THE BOX

Speaking of mailing containers, it's literally time to think outside the box. As long as the container is sturdy and doesn't hold anything harmful, the post office will mail just about anything. Your invitation can be slipped into a large fortune cookie and mailed inside a plastic Chinese take-out container. You can print your invite on a compact disc and send it in a bubble envelope of any color imaginable. There are also mailing tubes of all colors that can hold your invitation. Majcher's company will even take your wedding invitation, place it inside a soup can and exchange the soup label with a mailing label. To open, the recipient will need to use a can opener! These run about $12 each and would be the talk amongst your guests. And last, don't forget about bottles. They can be used for more than a beach wedding. Bottles come in all shapes and sizes and make great mailing containers. For example, a wine bottle is ideal if you're being married at a vineyard or if you and your fiancé are wine collectors or aficionados.

WHAT'S THE MAGIC WORD?

Don't forget to order coordinating thank you cards when ordering your invitations, even if you are printing your wedding invitations at home. Do not purchase cards that have the words "Thank You" preprinted across the front. This is considered to be a tacky short cut and poor etiquette. Folded note cards are also more appropriate than a full sheet of stationery since your note will be brief. Many of your gifts will arrive by mail in the two weeks prior to your wedding. If you have your thank you cards handy, you can write them as the gifts arrive. This way, your guests will know their packages arrived safe and sound. All other gifts you receive at the wedding deserve to have a personal note of thanks within two to three weeks. Keep in mind you can always address the envelopes before the wedding to help save time. And have your fiancé help. After all, he'll be enjoying these gifts too.

Thank you notes should be handwritten, not typed or printed out on your computer. So grab a good pen, preferably in black or blue ink. Mention the actual gift. Rather than saying, "Thank you for the gift," be sure to write, "Thank you for the lovely champagne glasses." The only exception is in the case of a cash gift. It's pretty tacky to say, "Thank you for the $100" or "Hey, thanks for the big bucks!" Instead, write something like: "Thank you for your generous gift. We plan to use it to buy a new comforter for our bed." Always thank your guests for attending your wedding, and let them know how good it was to see them.

If you have an informal wedding you may want to use those little disposable cameras, which produced some great shots of your guests. Then, you can include a photo in each thank you note, provided your note card is large enough for the snapshot. A friend of mine actually took a photo of each guest posing with her and her new husband at the reception and glued it onto card stock, making her own personalized thank you cards. I still treasure mine.

Remember to send thank you cards to those who attend your showers and anyone who helps with the details of your wedding. This includes your sister-in-law who picked up the flower arrangements, your friend who sang a song during the ceremony and your niece who handled the guest book duties. Do not combine thank you cards. If you receive a shower gift and a wedding gift from a friend, then you need to send her one thank you card for the shower gift and a separate thank you card for the wedding gift. Besides, your thank you card from the shower should be sent within a week after your shower anyway. Last, keep your note brief and to the point. Do not add news of your honeymoon or ask for a lunch date. Simply be gracious and say those two magic words, "Thank You."

Some of the encore brides I've interviewed told me interesting accounts of their special invitations:

Jennifer's Story

"To find my wedding invitation, I started out by requesting a ton of those invitation catalogs that are advertised in the bridal magazines. I looked for the nicest one at the lowest price, since we were on a pretty tight budget, and I figured they would just get dumped in the trash afterward anyway. I spent about $300 on paper products, which also included napkins and books of matches with our names on them. The invitation was rectangular in shape and had a heart border indented (debossed) into the paper. The first line read, "A new day, a new life together" in red ink to match our wedding colors."

Rebecca's Story

"We bought one of those invitation kits from a craft store. The paper was handmade with small leaves and twigs in it. It had a vellum overlay with a gold ribbon. The kit came with matching RSVP cards. I printed them myself on my home computer. We used burgundy ink, which came out really nice. We bought a total of fifty invitations (one kit) and used every one. My sister-in-law did the calligraphy on the envelopes and assembled the invitations, including tying all the ribbons. The funny thing is she had previously purchased the same invitations for my surprise bridal shower. When I joyously showed her the kit I bought, not knowing she'd purchased the kit for the shower, she practically had a heart attack. Although she had already printed and assembled them, she started over and bought a new kit in a different style. That means she actually completed three sets of invitations—two for my bridal shower and one for my wedding. Then, to top it off, I asked her to address the envelopes. She graciously agreed. I guess I'm lucky to have such a nice sister-in-law!"

Elaine's Story

"We were married in Palm Springs, so we selected a cream-colored invitation with swaying palm trees against a large sun. The trees and sun were pearlized and very pale, almost cream on cream with just a hint of peach in the sun and a hint of green in the palm trees. The envelope lining was green to match the ink. We chose to use the words 'Happily we, Elaine Russell and William Stanton, have chosen this day as the first day of our new life together. We invite you to share in our joy as we exchange our vows.' We did not use a reception card, since the reception was at the same location as the wedding and there was plenty of room on the invitation to add 'Reception immediately following at the Country Club.' We had only one insert other than the response card, also printed in green ink. One side had a map on it and the other side listed accommodations for out-of-town guests with a special hotel rate we had arranged. The response card had a smaller version of the palm trees and sun on it as well. We liked the invitation because it set the stage for our 'Palm Springs Country Club' wedding. It was 'casual elegance,' as my husband likes to describe it."

Your second wedding is an event you've dream about for a long time. Like these women, taking time to choose the small details carefully can make it the special, memorable event you've envisioned.

Chapter Seven

Bridal Showers and Wedding Gifts

Gifts? For Me? Oh, You Shouldn't Have!

First Wedding: The bride takes her fiancé to several department stores. Together, they select a china pattern and register for tons of glassware, an array of pots and pans, a multitude of kitchen gadgets and the infamous blender for their new home.

Second Wedding: Guess what? Second-time brides can register too! Only most choose to register at places like REI for kayaking gear, an online wine of the month club or a home improvement store. This couple probably already has the pots and pans, sparkling stemware and a myriad of chef's delights. After all, they have been cooking up sumptuous meals for a family of five for the last ten years.

To register or not to register? The answer is yes, absolutely. It's perfectly acceptable to register for gifts for a second wedding. Not only is it acceptable, it's actually helpful to your guests. It may be even more helpful for a second wedding than for a first. For your first marriage, it was probably pretty obvious that you needed just about everything to set up housekeeping. But as a couple remarrying, how would your guests ever guess that you are suffering from the affliction I call "post divorce chaos"? You know, where he got the skillet and you got the crock-pot; he took his mom's silverware and you got the flatware; and then you took one bedroom lamp and he took the other. Because of this, your present kitchen is contemporary "mix and match," and you'd love to replace your odds and ends with mixing bowls that coordinate and stemware that totals a complete set. Wouldn't it be nice to have new bathroom towels?

On the other hand, you may have eloped for your first wedding and never had the exhilarating bridal registry experience. You have never felt the rush of the handheld scanner as your list rapidly grows from a single page to almost ten. Or, perhaps it's time to get rid of the ghosts from your previous marriage by starting fresh with items handpicked by the two of you. Many second-time brides prefer to be free of the past and all things associated with it. So, they dump everything they shared with their ex and start over. Not a bad idea. Whatever your situation, using the services of a bridal registry will allow you to select the gifts you need and desire, avoid duplicates and unnecessary exchanges and give your guests the peace of mind that their money is being well spent on items you will actually use.

Here are some suggestions for those of you who prefer no gifts. I understand. You've been married before and you don't want a lot of fuss this time around. You just want a lovely ceremony to celebrate this special day with your friends and family. As I mentioned earlier, it is considered poor etiquette to include information about gifts, wanted or not, on your wedding invitation. You can, however, share your wishes by word of mouth. Let your friends, family and bridal party spread the news. However, when it comes to gift giving, it's my experience that because your guests love you and are truly happy for you, they will want to commemorate this special day of yours with gifts.

For those of you who have decided to register, things may have changed a bit since your first registry experience. Department stores are still great places to start and will give you the opportunity to see and touch the actual items you are selecting. However, the internet has created a vast number of options. Here are several of my favorites.

REI

If you're the outdoors type, REI is Mecca—the land of milk and honey. Their bridal registry includes ski and snowboarding equipment, kayaking gear, Global Positioning Systems, watches, sunglasses, even ice tools and crampons for ice climbing. If you're into cycling, they have a great selection of helmets, rainwear, gloves, dehydration packs and bike racks for your car or garage. And get this: they offer what they call "REI Adventures." These are organized tours and trips throughout the world. For example, you can register for a nine-day Tuscany Bike Tour where you can bike through centuries-old Italian towns, rolling countrysides and winding city streets. Or you might select their fourteen-day bike tour through North Central Vietnam where you'll see miles of beautiful beaches, emerald green mountains and the French Colonial capital of Hanoi. If you prefer to hike or raft, REI offers twelve days in the Northern Lake District of Argentina and Chile. You'll get to hike, bike, raft and ride on horseback through thick green forests, flowing rivers, crystal clear lakes and snow-capped mountains. I mean, how can you beat that? Oh yes, I know how. By taking their nineteen-day Royal Trek through Nepal, home of Mt. Everest, the highest mountain in the world. Check them out at www.rei.com.

Italian Wine Merchants

If you're a wine lover like me, this is a fabulous bridal registry. Located in Union Square Park in New York City, the store offers a very sophisticated wine selection. They have wine consultants on hand to assist you with wine picks, wine cellar questions and the investment potential of your wines. Online, at www.italianwinemerchant.com, their bridal registry includes a list of red and white wine pairings, anniversary bottles for you and your husband to drink on your first, fifth, tenth or even twentieth anniversaries, wine baskets, stemware, specialty corkscrews, wine racks and gift certificates. Since you are assigned a sommelier to assist you in your registry selections, you don't need to be a wine connoisseur to take full advantage of this registry. What a great way to start a new marriage—with a well-stocked wine cellar!

Home Depot

This is a registry that will make your fiancé sit up and take notice. Here you can list practical gifts such as saws, ladders and power tools. You can select something from every department or pick one particular home improvement project and register for the things you'll need to complete it. For instance if you and you fiancé are planning to add on a patio deck in your backyard for entertaining and personal relaxation, you can go to the "Outdoor Living" page on their Web site and choose from items such as decking, exterior lights, grills, smokers and fryers. Perhaps you'd like a nice cozy hammock, porch swing or soothing cascading water fountain. A few potted plants, a couple of topiaries, some gardening tools and a compost container may help you create a wonderful setting for enjoyable summer evenings on your new patio. Visit Home Depot at www.homedepot.com and choose a gift for the home you and your fiancé are creating together.

HoneyLuna.com

Here is a registry for your honeymoon! At HoneyLuna.com you can select from honeymoon destinations in the Caribbean, South Pacific, Europe, Africa or the United States. This is how it works: the registry breaks down your honeymoon into specific items, activities and adventures. For example, let's say you'd like to take a honeymoon cruise through the Caribbean and Panama Canal. You can register for airfare (it's divided up into small amounts, the same way a department store would divide up a set of china), spa treatments, shore excursions, flower arrangements, picnic for two, bottle of champagne and a professional photograph of you while on the cruise. Perhaps you'll be honeymooning in Hawaii and would like to register for scuba diving, snorkeling at Molokini Crater, a sunset cruise, a bike trip down the Haleakala volcano, a traditional luau, a whale watching boat excursion or a couple of hours racing on wave runners. HoneyLuna.com offers a personalized consultation to discuss your preferences and will research trip options and activities you may not have considered or known about. They'll then make your basic travel arrangements, including air and hotel accommodations. Although they will not make the reservations for activities such a scuba diving or helicopter touring, they will collect the gift payments and provide a lump sum to you prior to your honeymoon. So, if you're spending most of your budget on the wedding ceremony and reception or have all the household items you need, this may be just the honeymoon ticket for you.

Though you've been married before, this doesn't mean you have everything you need for the new home you and your fiancé will live in. Your towels may be frayed, your pots may be scratched and your espresso machine may have died a slow death years ago. Great places to register for this type of stuff are Bed, Bath and Beyond, Pier 1 Imports, Crate & Barrel and Williams Sonoma.

Bed, Bath & Beyond

This store is stocked from floor to ceiling with home and bathroom accessories. For the master bath, you can choose from a huge selection of bathroom towels, shower curtains, hampers, scales, area rugs, decorative mirrors, fluffy Egyptian cotton robes and warm comfy slippers. As a new couple, you'll also want to customize your bedroom. Select from hundreds of sheets, pillows, blankets, quilts and comforters. Don't forget a couple of bed trays for some late morning breakfasts in bed. Add a few lamps, candles, frames holding your wedding pictures and vases for fresh flowers to create the perfect ambiance for the new Mr. and Mrs.

Pier 1 Imports

With over 750 stores in forty-seven states, Pier 1 offers a wide variety of imported decorative home furnishings and accessories, as well as seasonal items. Registration is easy with the handheld scanner that records your selections automatically. Since you'll be combining two households, you may need some decorative items to help blend them seamlessly together. Choose from baskets, clocks, wall prints, lamps, pillows, candles, wall sconces, sculpture, vases, jeweled boxes, table runners and wall mirrors.

Crate & Barrel

There are over fifty stores nationwide where you can register. If they don't have a location near you, you can set up your registry online or over the phone. In addition to traditional dinnerware and stemware, they offer rugs, linens, bathroom accessories, picnic baskets, ice buckets, decanters and trendy martini glasses. Check out their selection of steak knives, knife blocks, chef's knives and wooden cutting boards. They also carry tons of great furniture, wall prints and DVD organizers. My favorite gift to give from Crate & Barrel is what I call the "I scream, you scream, we all scream for ice cream" gift: an ice cream maker along with a set of eight colorful footed dessert bowls, an ice cream scooper and a book on how to make the perfect ice cream sundae. Toss in a sampling of ice cream toppings such as chocolate syrup, caramel, nuts and sprinkles, and you are good to go. Yummy! As an added bonus, Crate & Barrel's registry is updated every twenty-four hours, so you can keep close tabs on your registry.

Williams Sonoma

If you love to cook, this store is a dream come true. It carries top-of-the-line cookware and accessories not found at other stores. They have saucepans, roasting pans, crème brulee torches and ramekins, pasta machines, pasta bowls, electric woks and wine storage units. For those of you who enjoy baking, they offer cake pans in the shape of a heart, daisy, rose and even a cathedral. There are also waffle makers, panini presses, ice cream makers, and even that espresso machine you've been meaning to replace.

Wal-Mart

Believe it or not, even Wal-Mart now has its own bridal registry. A great place for electronics, you can register for digital cameras, home computers, software programs, laptops, DVD players, televisions, cordless and cellular phones, stereo systems and iPods and MP3 Players. If you're looking for more than electronics, they also carry car tires, hot tubs, music, binoculars, books, bikes and patio furniture. The registry is available both online and in-store. Also helpful are the two dozen complimentary buying guides they offer which tell you what to look for when making a new electronics purchase.

Target

This store's bridal registry lists everything from kitchen appliances to dinner plates, flatware and table linens. They carry accent rugs, lamps, window coverings, patio furniture, digital cameras, DVD and MP3 players, computers and telephones. They also have camping gear, luggage and a vast array of power tools.

One-Stop Shop

Do you need things from Bed, Bath and Beyond, Macy's, Home Depot, Gump's, Sandal's *and* Pottery Barn? Registering at two or even three locations is acceptable for a second wedding; registering at four or more is definitely overkill. However, Web sites such as WeddingChannel.com and theKnot.com make coordinating registry items from many sources simple for you. By registering with them, you receive complete access to the bridal registries of over twenty companies. In addition to the ones I've gone over, this includes places like Restoration Hardware, Macy's, Starwood Hotels, Neiman Marcus and Tiffany & Company.

DID YOU FORGET SOMETHING?

According to WeddingChannel.com, there are five items for which almost all brides, even second-timers, forget to register and later regret. The first of those items is barware. Everyone registers for wineglasses, but bypasses the margarita glasses and matching pitcher, beer mugs and highball glasses. Next on the list is everyday dinnerware. You know, nothing fancy, just the dinner plates and cereal bowls you and your new family will be eating from for the next several years. So take the time to pick out something casual, durable and kid friendly. The third item on the list surprised me—a serving platter. Apparently it's the gift of choice, the universal wedding gift, yet so few brides register for them. However, your taste and your brother-in-law's taste may be complete opposites, so help him out by registering for a platter or two that you love and will use for years to come. Home décor ranks fourth among forgotten items. This includes odds and ends like candlesticks, vases and decorative bowls. These decorative touches reflect your personality and style and will help blend your two homes into a single one. If you desire holiday décor, be sure to register for things like Christmas linens, dinner plates, cookie platters, a tree stand, tree ornaments and collectibles. These will make your first Christmas together especially memorable.

GREATER GOOD
The I Do Foundation

In conjunction with Donation Registry, Inc., a donation services company, the participating stores in this foundation have agreed to donate to charity a percentage of all purchases made by couples and guests who use their online wedding registries. There is no cost to you or your guests, and you can select from a list of charities. The stores in this program include Amazon.com, JC Penney, Mikasa.com, Ross-Simons, Cooking.com, Linens 'n Things, REI and Target. These stores contribute anywhere from three to eight percent of the total purchases from your online registries. There are charities for children, youth and families, community development, the environment, health, education and social justice. WeddingChannel.com also works in conjunction with the I Do Foundation. Rosanna McCollough, Editor-in-Chief of WeddingChannel.com, states that almost $120 million dollars were purchased on their site in 2004. Can you imagine if all brides and grooms chose to participate in the program? In case you're curious, the top five charities chosen by brides at WeddingChannel.com last year were the American Cancer Society, The Susan G. Komen Breast Cancer Foundation, St. Jude Children's Research Hospital, the American Society for the Prevention of Cruelty to Animals and the Humane Society of the United States.

JustGive.org

If you'd like your favorite charity to get more than three to eight percent of your total registry purchases and prefer no gifts anyway, then choose this registry. JustGive.org is an independent, non-profit organization that works with about 1 million charities nationwide. The group will not sell, share or disclose donor information, nor does its credit card company. All donations are tax deductible. The registry is easy to create, and you can add charities whenever you wish. Although there is no charge for creating the registry, each donor will be charged a $5 gift center service fee. It is a one-time charge and not dependant on the amount donated or the number of charities donated to. This fee is also tax deductible. There are about twenty categories of charities to select from such as animals, community, disabled, disaster relief, elderly, homeless, human rights and substance abuse. The whole process is completed online and you will receive an e-mail notifying you of each donation made in honor of your wedding.

Top 15 Registering Tips

1) Register about six months prior to your wedding. At the bare minimum, make sure it's done before your wedding invitations go in the mail.
2) Include your fiancé. This stuff will be his, too.
3) Include gift certificates. Many guests prefer this no-brainer gift.

4) Be specific. Use model numbers, colors and sizes whenever appropriate. Don't make your guests fret over which size wine goblets you want.

5) Do not register for items for your children. It's your wedding, not their birthdays.

6) Print out your registry and double check for errors.

7) Choose gifts in a wide variety of price ranges.

8) Do not include registry announcement cards in your invitations. It's tacky. You can, however, give them to your maid of honor or a family member. When guests ask where you are registered, they can give them one of the cards.

9) Select one or two big-ticket items. Your parents, a group of friends or office mates may want to chip in for one large gift rather than purchase individual gifts.

10) Register at more than one store, but no more than three.

11) Make sure at least one of your registries is online. It's the easiest way for your guests to make their selections and purchases.

12) When registering online, try to visit the store's physical location so you can see and feel the quality, or lack thereof, of the items you have selected. Colors, sizes and fabrics can look completely different on the screen than in real life.

13) Register with stores that have reasonable return and exchange policies.

14) Find out how each registry keeps track of your purchases and how often they update the databases.

15) Your chosen registries should have the capability of arranging direct shipment to your address so that your guests don't have to haul the gifts to your reception.

BRIDAL SHOWERS

An old story goes something like this: a very poor Dutch boy fell in love with a beautiful Dutch girl. Her father refused to accept him and approve of the match, so he withheld his daughter's dowry. At that time, a dowry typically consisted of land, jewelry, livestock and sometimes cash. Her friends took pity on her and collectively brought her various pots, pans, linens, bowls and other household items she would need to set up housekeeping with her new, poor husband. Thus, the tradition of "showering" a bride with gifts was born. Luckily, the father gave in and approved the marriage so there was a happy ending.

Another good story tells of a social event where the bride's friends wrapped their gifts and placed them in an inverted umbrella. They then opened the parasol and "showered" the gifts onto the bride. Hence, the symbol of an open umbrella for a bridal shower became vogue.

Today, a bridal shower gives the friends and family of the bride a chance to shower her with gifts, support, encouragement and marital advice. Even though you are a second-time bride and have had the privilege of a bridal shower in the past, you are still entitled to a second shower. Your maid or matron of honor, bridesmaids, friends or co-workers are usually the ones to host your bridal shower. Your mother, sister or other family member should not host the shower, as that is considered tacky and in poor taste. As a rule of thumb, the guests who are invited to your shower are also invited to your wedding. The only exception to this rule is if your co-workers at the office throw you a surprise (or planned) shower, you are not expected to invite the entire office. Second-time bridal showers tend to be co-ed and include the groom and his friends. Themed parties are very popular.

The Garden Party

All decorations, gifts, invitations and menu selections at this party are based on a garden theme. Held in a friend's backyard or on an outdoor patio if possible, the party area is decorated with potted plants, topiaries, picnic tables and a gazebo. You can include a park bench, birdbath or white trellis. Add some twinkle lights in the trees for ambience. Great centerpieces are glass bowls filled with water and floating gardenias, potted orchids, or geraniums nestled in watering cans. All of these decorative items can also double as the bride's gifts, each with a card attached. Smaller gifts can be placed in a broadcast spreader. Other great garden gifts are wind chimes, solar path lights, garden globes and small fountains. Purchase a make-your-own stepping stone kit and have all the guests sign it as a guest book keepsake for your garden. A seed packet works well as an invitation with wording that reads, "Friends are the flowers in the garden of life," "Love is in full bloom" or "Roses are red, Violets are blue, Jennifer's getting remarried, Really it's true!" Tablecloths should be floral. Tie each napkin with string holding a fresh flower or sprig of rosemary. A menu of tea and scones or lemonade and finger sandwiches completes this theme.

Progressive Dinner

When my next-door neighbor, Katherine, was getting remarried, we decided it would be fun to have a lot of friends participate. We decided to have cocktails at Pam and Jeff's house, (they always serve a festive bottle or two of champagne), dinner at Tracy and Tim's house (she's the best cook on the street) and finally, dessert and gifts at my house (yes, I'm the one with the sweet tooth). The other neighbors helped with the preparations, as well. It was fun to divvy up the chores among the eight couples that live on our block and enjoy each couple's specialty. We picked an Italian theme for the menu, which included the famous Italian cocktail "the limoncello," made up of fresh lemon juice, vodka and sugar; appetizers such as bruschetta, fried calamari and antipasto; and a dinner of ravioli, fettuccine and cannelloni. Dessert was tiramisu, of course, with some strawberry zabaglione and espresso-flavored cheesecake. We all enjoyed the food and each other's company, and Katherine and David got some great gifts. What a fantastic night.

Hawaiian Luau

If you're planning on a Hawaiian honeymoon, which is, by the way, the number one honeymoon destination in the United States, here is a fitting party. It works best in the summer, poolside. Decorate with tiki torches, grass skirts, hula dancers, pineapples, coconuts and hibiscus flowers. Hand each guest a silk or fresh lei as they arrive. Use a bright, printed sarong as the tablecloth for your buffet table and order a flower arrangement with birds of paradise, red ginger and exotic orchids. Ask guests to wear their favorite Hawaiian shirts or dresses, play Hawaiian music, and dance the hula. For your menu, serve a baked ham (in lieu of a roasted pig) or grilled mahi mahi, sweet potatoes and a tropical fruit salad. For dessert, display a platter of chocolate-covered macadamia nuts and serve coconut-flavored ice cream. Mai tais, pina coladas and blue Hawaiians make the perfect cocktails. Add a bowl of tropical fruit punch with floating orchids. For fun, go online, convert your guests' names into their Hawaiian names, and see who can figure them out (it's harder than it sounds). Your invitation can feature a pineapple, tiki torch or a bird of paradise.

Country Western Barbecue

If you and your fiancé are fans of country singers like Faith Hill, Randy Travis, Shania Twain and Garth Brooks, this might be the theme for you. Have your guests don their favorite pairs of cowboy boots, bolo ties and cowboy hats. Hand them bandanas as they walk in the door. Only denim is acceptable at a country western barbecue, although leather and fringe are optional. Decorate with potted cactus, rope, bales of hay, and cowboy hats turned upside down and filled with daisies. Use a "Wanted—Dead or Alive" poster for your invitation and a red-checkered tablecloth for your buffet table. Drink out of mason jars and consider renting a beer keg. For entertainment, there's the obvious county music, line dancing and game of horseshoes. Serve homemade chili, cornbread, barbecued ribs or chicken, corn on the cob, and ranch style beans. Top it all off with a big serving of hot peach cobbler a la mode.

Honeymoon Shower

Let's say you're planning on a honeymooning at a tropical resort. Guests can bring one item that you will use on the trip. This includes beach towels, sunscreen, sunglasses, novels, crossword puzzles, a travel dictionary, maps, tourist information, travel guides, luggage, travel alarm clock, disposable cameras and tickets to specific events or attractions at the destination. Or perhaps you'll be skiing in Lake Tahoe. In that case, you'll need mugs and hot chocolate mix, scarves, mittens, gloves, sunglasses, wool socks, ski lift tickets and Uggs. Use travel posters for the décor and an airline ticket jacket or postcard from the resort for your invitation. This theme also works well if you're not able to get away for a honeymoon immediately following your wedding. Guests can provide you a "stay-at-home" honeymoon with tickets to local events and attractions, a day at a spa with massages for two, a limousine ride along the coast or a gift certificate to your favorite restaurant.

Home Improvement

Are you and your fiancé moving into a house that needs a little Tender Loving Care? Then this bridal shower theme can provide you with all of the tools you will need to complete your home projects and "honey-do" lists. Gifts such as ladders, power tools, paint brushes, tool boxes and screwdrivers will help turn your home into your dream house. Gift certificates from stores such as Home Depot, Orchard Supply or ACE are ideal for guests who don't know a lot about tools or home improvement. The party room can be decorated with drop cloths, brooms, shovels, paint rollers and paint trays. Tables can be covered with tarps, using paint buckets filled with wildflowers as centerpieces. Gifts can be placed in a wheelbarrow or laid out on a tarp, and the invitations can be made out of sandpaper, wallpaper or paint sample cards. Guests can arrive attired in their old work clothes, tool belts, painters' hats or hard hats.

Christmas

If you are getting married in the months leading up to Christmas, then this can be an ideal theme. First of all, if the shower is held in December, your hostess may already have her house decorated. Of course, even if you select this theme in the middle of summer, it's easy to put up an artificial tree and grab some decorations out of the attic. Place all shower gifts under the tree. Your guests can buy you everything you will need for your first Christmas together as man and wife. Both Bronner's and ChristmasesPast.com carry a beautiful set of ornaments made specifically for the new bride and groom. Called the Old World Glass Bride's Tree Ornaments, they are handcrafted in Germany by Inge-Glas. The set contains twelve ornaments, each symbolizing something for the newlyweds. Included is a heart to symbolize true love, a fish to represent Christ's blessing, a house that stands for shelter and protection, a teapot signifying hospitality, and a bird to represent happiness and joy. For this theme, you might want to serve eggnog and sugar cookies and have a gingerbread house-decorating contest.

Have someone play Santa to distribute party favors to the guests. Play some Christmas music in the background and use Christmas cards for your invitations. Don't forget the mistletoe for a co-ed party!

Cinco de Mayo

If you love a Mexican fiesta, then Mexico's Independence Day, Cinco de Mayo, is a great theme for your bridal shower. Decorate with piñatas, potted cacti, maracas and red chili peppers. Use the red, green and white of the Mexican flag for your table linens, napkins and balloons. Drape colorful serapes as overlays for the tables, and use sombreros for your centerpieces. You can even use a giant sombrero to hold some of the smaller gifts. Place plenty of bowls filled with tortilla chips, salsa and guacamole around the room. Have guests serve themselves at a make-your-own taco bar or serve cheese enchiladas family style. Sip fruity sangria or tasty ice-cold margaritas. Don't forget the Corona or Dos XX—two of the top imported beers from Mexico. Hire a mariachi band, or play some salsa or tejano music. You might even try performing the Mexican hat dance. The invitation should feature bright, bold colors with a piñata, red chili peppers or a cactus. Ole!

The Chef's Shower

Do you love to cook but wish you had more recipes or exactly the right cookware? The chef's shower is the perfect occasion to build up your dinner menu repertoire. For this theme, invitations are sent on recipe cards. Each guest brings a favorite recipe along with whatever type of pot, pan or specialty cookware is required to produce or serve it. For example, one guest might bring her favorite bran muffin recipe with two or three non-stick muffin pans. Another might bring a casserole dish and the recipe for her famous chicken, cheese and artichoke casserole. Hopefully you know someone with a good paella recipe to go along with a large, oversized skillet. Then there's the Belgian waffle maker and package of waffle mix for the friend who really can't cook, a pasta machine and recipe for creamy fettuccini alfredo, a bundt pan a with a recipe for a lemon chiffon bundt cake and a fluted ceramic pie pan for deep dish apple pie. Wear chefs' hats, decorate tables with bouquets of kitchen utensils, and pass around an apron or cookbook, asking the guests to sign it as your keepsake.

Wine Tasting

This is perfect for a summer evening. Each guest brings a bottle of wine, and the hostess plays the part of sommelier. The bottle label is covered prior to pouring for each taste test. Wine is poured in order from the lightest white to the heaviest red. It's fun to guess the type of wine, specific winery and which guest brought which bottle of wine. It's also fun just to sample. Be sure to provide plenty of cheese and crackers along with a pitcher of water to cleanse the palette in between tastings. You'll also need plenty of wine glasses if you're expecting a large group. Don't cut corners and serve out of plastic tumblers. A good wine deserves a decent wine glass. Hire a harpist or flutist, or play some nice jazz music in the background. Decorate with posters from the wine country, empty wine bottles filled with yellow roses, a picnic basket overflowing with fresh baguettes of bread and large rounds of imported cheeses. Gifts such as wine buckets, stemware, wine decanters, wine charms, decorative bottle stoppers and wine gift baskets complete this theme.

WHAT'S MY JOB?

As the bride, you are the center of all this wonderful attention, but you also have a few responsibilities of your own. The first is to provide the hostesses for the parties you are giving with guest lists. Keep the number at about fifteen to twenty guests. Some brides are given one shower for close friends or couples and another at the office. Next, although it is not mandatory to write a thank you note if you have personally thanked the gift giver at the shower, it is still a nice gesture. Thank you notes take very little time, are always appreciated and never go out of style.

Your final responsibility, as a couple, is to give gifts to the members of your wedding party. Select personal and meaningful gifts. Your bridesmaids might enjoy special pieces of jewelry that match their bridesmaids dresses, small evening bags, or heart-shaped jewelry boxes. Other good choices are charm bracelets, lipstick holders or compacts, silver or crystal picture frames, music boxes, key chains, silk pajamas or boxes of personalized monogrammed stationery. You might even consider a day at a spa, gift certificates for a manicure and pedicure or gift baskets holding their favorite things. For your fiancé's attendants, he might present them with pocket or standard men's watches, pens, money clips, key chains or business card cases. There are also valets, Swiss army knives, golf shoe bags, black leather or stainless steel flasks, cigar cases or humidors. Things Remembered offers most of these items, and the majority of them can be engraved or personalized. Another great place for gifts is redenvelope.com. If your children are part of your bridal party, you might select the Family Medallion or other piece of commemorative jewelry, a music box, photo album or picture frame to hold a picture of you together at the wedding reception. Even if your children decide not to participate in the bridal party, a small gift to express your love for them would be a good idea and help toward bonding as a new family.

Parties highlighting the bride are, as many have told me, special events for second-timers to remember and cherish.

Stacy's Story

"My first bridal shower, held at a friend's house, was a lingerie party with lots of red and black lace teddies, risqué garters, babydolls, satin slips and sheer camisoles. Some of the more subdued ones were bridal lingerie and silk gowns in cream or white. The shower for my second wedding was held at a nearby day spa. Though the guests brought gifts, the highlight was a special day spent with friends, relaxing and getting pampered. It was also a great opportunity to stop and relax in the midst of the hectic pace of the wedding plans."

Lindsay's Story

"The bridal shower I was given for my second marriage was at a restaurant and bar during karaoke night. It was totally wild. There were about fifteen of us, all female, and everyone had to sing a love song. It could be country western, an Elvis Presley tune, something by the Beatles, as long as the song had the word "love" in it. As some would say, "It was the best of times, it was the worst of times." The songs my friends picked were so funny and yet very appropriate. I knew they had spent some time thinking about what they would sing for me. One of my friends videotaped the entire night, and when I showed it to my fiancé later in the week, he just couldn't believe it. It was very personal, fun and a night I will never forget."

Amanda's Story

"Since my fiancé and I love to travel, our friends gave us an international themed bridal shower. My matron of honor produced the invitations on her computer. Each one carried the flag of the country each guest was representing. For example, the guest whose invitation had a Japanese flag on it was to bring a gift representative of that country, such as a wok, sushi plates or a Kama sutra kit. The guest who represented France brought a bread machine; the guest from Italy gave us a pasta machine and pasta bowls; and our Mexican representative brought a set of margarita glasses and matching pitcher. Our German friend presented us with beer steins and a twelve pack of specialty German beers, and from Switzerland came a fondue set with enough Swiss chocolate to feed an army. The round the world trip was completed by our Greek guest who brought us a shish kabob set and our Spanish friend who surprised us with a paella pan. (My fiancé and I love to make paella together.) My matron of honor decorated the room with international flags, travel posters from a local travel agency, a couple of globes, and an atlas on the coffee table. She bought several large maps, spread them out and used them as the tablecloth. She really outdid herself."

Fun bridal showers and thoughtful gifts add to a memorable time. Of course, the real center of the celebration is the wonderful, mature love you and your fiancé have found together.

Chapter Eight

Legalities

Look (and Sign) Before You Leap

*F*irst Wedding: Bride and groom sign the marriage license. Most do not sign pre-nuptial agreements, because they are young, have little prior emotional baggage and hope to spend a lifetime together. The majority haven't yet considered a will or life insurance because that's for "old" people. Usually the bride takes her husband's last name. Sometimes she keeps her maiden name or combines names.

Second Wedding: The majority of brides and grooms sign prenuptial agreements. They update their wills and life insurance policies. Some brides take the husband's last name, but others keep their previous names as well because they match their childrens' names. Often such women are already known in the business or professional world and don't want to disturb their identities.

A ROSE IS A ROSE BY ANY OTHER NAME

In my own life, I've utilized different names. Beth Nelson was my maiden name. Beth Reed was my first married name. Beth Ramirez is my second married name. Beth Reed Ramirez is the name I use in business. I continue to use either Reed Ramirez or Ramirez, depending on the circumstances. Since I have a young daughter and her last name is Reed, it is useful for me to write Reed Ramirez on all her school, medical and dental forms. When I started "Bride Again" magazine, I used Beth Reed Ramirez to show that I, too, was a second-time bride who was speaking from experience. The name Ramirez is of Hispanic origin and some people are shocked to meet a blonde-haired, blue-eyed Swede with that last name.

Whatever name or names you choose to use, there's a lot of paperwork that you will need to make this your legal name. The process varies from state to state, but the first choice usually must be made when obtaining a marriage license. You'll need to decide which name you are going to use when you apply; the name you write on the license becomes your legal name.

Within a few weeks of your wedding ceremony, you will receive a certificate of marriage in the mail. This is a legal document and can be used to change your name with all the agencies. If you have decided to retain your old name, do nothing. But, if you are taking your new husband's name or using some combination of both his and yours, then this information is required. As with your first marriage, some of the agencies that will need to be notified of your new name are the Social Security Administration, Department of Motor Vehicles, your bank, the mortgage company, and insurance and credit card companies. You'll also have to inform your employer, doctors, the telephone, gas, electric and cable companies, professional and social organizations, your gym and the post office. Remember to change your passport and voter registration as well.

One excellent name change kit is offered by bridekit.com. It is called "The Wedding Sense Name Change Guide and Kit for New Brides." Everything you need to know is in this kit. There's no software to install as the kit is formulated the old fashioned way—simply fill in the blanks of the preprinted forms. The kit contains over fifty forms, which are good in all fifty states, covering every imaginable situation. The kits costs about $25 and is worth every penny. All you have to do is decide which name you will use: your new name, your old name, or both.

PRE-NUPTIAL AGREEMENTS

When most couples decide to remarry, sooner or later the topic of a pre-nuptial agreement will come up for discussion. A lot of the times when this happens, tensions flare, suspicions surface and doubts develop. The question arises, "Does signing a pre-nuptial agreement express our lack of faith in this new marriage?"

According to Laura Morgan, a family law attorney in Charlottesville, Virginia, this is not the case. She reports that "not only do courts favor and support pre-nuptial agreements, but so do most couples entering a second marriage." She feels there are several reasons for this: almost one-half of all first marriages end in divorce, which means that remarrying couples have already been through the horror of dividing up assets and most are leery of going through this process again. This leads to the next reason. Over 60 percent of all second marriages end in divorce. The remarrying couple sees this statistic as validation that divorce could happen to them again. Another reason is that older couples who are remarrying tend to plan more carefully and realistically for their futures. Finally, Morgan says, the majority of couples also want to protect their assets for their children.

Having children may be the most important reason for a pre-nuptial agreement. By signing one you can provide for your children in the event of divorce or death. In most states, if you do not have a pre-nuptial agreement, anywhere from one-third to one-half of your assets will go to your surviving spouse in the event of your death or to your ex-husband in the event of a divorce. This means that your children will not receive the amount it might take to support them. Not only are we talking cash, but we're talking about other assets as well. It could be an object or collection of monetary or sentimental value. Without a pre-nup, your grandmother's diamond ring might go to your husband instead of your daughter. The same goes for that precious family heirloom, the piano you've had since you were a child or the painting you bought in Paris. It might be the savings you have set aside for your child's college education. Maybe it's the house you owned before you remarried and kept as rental property. You had always intended your son to have that house and the resulting rental income it generated. As a parent, you are responsible for your children. A pre-nup can help you protect them.

Other common reasons for a pre-nup are: if one or both of you have substantial assets, a high amount of debt, a possible future inheritance, a high income, a large discrepancy in your incomes, or a previous divorce settlement that was unjust. Perhaps you have accrued a substantial retirement fund. Maybe you will soon need to take care of your elderly parents. It's possible that you or your fiancé own your own business or are part of a family business or partnership. There are many good reasons for a pre-nup, so don't let guilt, fear or embarrassment keep you from considering one.

An added bonus of either signing a pre-nup or simply considering one is that it forces you and your fiancé to have a frank discussion about finances, spending, saving and expectations. Money is the number one cause of divorce, so it's best, especially in a remarriage, to start with full disclosure of each other's assets and debts. You may even want to review each other's divorce agreements from your previous marriages, just to avoid any future misunderstandings about what assets have already been promised and for how long. Better to have a discussion about finances take place now, before your wedding, rather than later on during a crisis. As Nancy Dunman, a New York financial advisor and author, says: "Marriage is not just an emotional and physical union—it's also a financial union. A pre-nup and the discussions that go with it can help ensure the financial well-being of the marriage."

When I remarried, one thing really worried me. I was concerned that when my husband died, I would have to sell our house to give his children their share of the inheritance. I had seen this happen to more than one person. Adult stepchildren may not be too concerned with where their stepparent is going to live after their dad or mother dies. Their parent left them an inheritance and they want it. My husband, understanding my fear, put stipulations into our pre-nup that would prevent this from happening. So not only did he protect certain assets for his children while I protected certain assets for mine, he protected me as well.

A pre-nup is a document that spells out what is "yours, mine and ours." You and your fiancé list what assets and debts you are bringing to the marriage and your wishes for them in the event of death or divorce. You then agree on what is to be done with any assets or debts that are accrued while you are married. For example, if you are expecting an inheritance, you may stipulate that it is solely yours and goes to your children upon your death. You can also stipulate that if this marriage ends in divorce, it will not be included in the division of assets.

If you choose to draft a pre-nup, each of you should hire your own attorney, and if possible, ask that all four of you sit down together to hash out the details. Then, let the attorneys handle the paperwork. I do not recommend preparing a pre-nup on your own with one of those do-it-yourself kits. You'll want to start the legal process about three months before your wedding date. If you sign a pre-nup in the last few days leading up to the wedding, a judge may rule that one of you signed under pressure or duress. Keep in mind that you can have your document include an expiration or renewal date and that you can change it, update it or cancel it at anytime. When my husband and I reviewed our agreement after about ten years, we realized a rather large mistake had been made. The plan had been to divide my husband's assets into thirds. One-third of the estate would be awarded to me and one-third would be awarded to each of his two children. That's when we discovered that because of incorrect wording, I would receive one-half, *plus* one-third of his children's portion. This is just one reason why it's good to have two separate attorneys, something we did not do. A pre-nup is meant to be flexible, provide for your children and protect each of you equally. Signing one doesn't mean you're expressing doubt about your marriage. It's almost like a spare tire. You don't plan to get a flat tire and you may never get a flat tire, but you carry a spare, just in case.

WILLS AND LIFE INSURANCE

Whether you choose to have a pre-nup or not, it is a good idea to update your will and life insurance policies before you remarry. If you don't have a will, make this a priority. Without a will, the state will decide what to do with your assets. If you are married with children and don't have a will, most states will award one-third to one-half of your estate to your spouse and the rest to your children. If you are married without children, most states will award the same amount to your spouse and the rest to your parents. If your parents are deceased, then it will go to your siblings. This means if you want your money and your assets to be distributed in any other way, you need a will.

Each state has different requirements for a will, but basically you must declare that the document you are signing is your will. It must be witnessed by at least two people who must sign in each other's presence. It should state that you are of sound mind and list the names, birth dates and birthplaces of your spouse and children. Most important, it should appoint a guardian for your children as well as an alternate. According to Dr. Margorie Engel, president of the Stepfamily Association of America, it is estimated that between 80 and 90 percent of parents with young children have no formal instructions specifying who will care for their children in the event of a parent's death. This is terrible! If you have children and don't yet have a will, make an appointment with your attorney now!

Should you die and there is a surviving parent (i.e. your ex-husband) and your children are under the age of eighteen, he would regain custody of them. This is not always what you desire. Make decisions of this magnitude now, when you can. Take the right steps to ensure your child's welfare.

Your will should also specify who should inherit what. Be very specific. If you want to leave things to your stepchildren, use the word "stepchildren" and name them as well. If you just write "all my children," the judge will assume you mean your biological children only. Last, the will should name the executor of your estate. This is the person who you want to be responsible for carrying out the directions listed in the will. This person will have to distribute the property, pay off any debts and handle the final taxes.

Your will should be kept in a safe place such as a safety deposit box or a fireproof safe in your home. We also keep copies at the office, with a family member and on our home computer. Do not stick this document in a drawer or file cabinet where it may not be found.

Anytime your circumstances change, you need to review

your life insurance policy. The beauty of life insurance is that the policy is not required to go through probate court. It pays the beneficiary directly and the proceeds are free of all taxes. As far as listing your beneficiary, you can list your new husband or perhaps your only child. If you or your fiancé's divorce agreements state that you must maintain your ex as the irrevocable beneficiary, you will need to purchase new separate policies naming each other as the beneficiaries. You may also need to adjust the amount of coverage. If you are taking on more financial responsibilities, such as a larger house and stepchildren, you will most likely need to increase your coverage. Consult with a financial planner or insurance professional to review your specific situation and goals to ensure you and your new family are properly covered.

Jeffrey Fuller, a financial advisor in California, says that in his experience, the following items are the most frequently overlooked details that should be addressed.

1. Group benefits: when you enroll in a retirement plan or for insurance at your workplace, you often identify your spouse as your beneficiary on those accounts. Fuller says it's a good idea to update your beneficiary to ensure your old spouse isn't the one benefiting from those accounts. The same concept applies to any personal savings, investment or insurance accounts.

2. If you have a will or trust: you'll want to review both the beneficiaries and the successor trustees on these documents. You may have certain people listed to administrate your estate that are no longer an important part of your life.

3. Investment accounts: if one partner enters into a new marriage with large debts, Fuller suggests that you consider separating investments between pre-marriage

and after-marriage accounts. By establishing new accounts for savings after marriage, you may protect the other's accumulated assets.

4. Account ownership: while this doesn't happen as often, some investment accounts continue to be owned jointly by a person and their ex-spouse.

Again, your financial advisor is in the best position to know your specific situation and understand how remarrying will impact your overall financial goals. When you double-check these areas, you'll be able to look forward to your new life, rather than rehash the old.

THE TAX MAN COMETH

I'm sure you've heard the saying before, "You can run, but you cannot hide." This is especially true of the Internal Revenue Service (IRS). I hate to be the bearer of bad news, but according to Dr. Engel, if you filed joint tax returns with your ex-husband when you were married to him, you may still liable for the accuracy of those returns. This means that if the IRS chooses to audit a tax return from 2001 when you were married to your ex and the agency finds a discrepancy, they can come to you and your new husband for payment. This is one reason, Dr. Engel states, why some remarried couples decide to file their taxes "married, filing separately." It may protect your new husband from possible tax liabilities from your first life. On the other hand, according to Todd Wester, a CPA in California, if you choose to file "Married, filing separately" you might miss out on tax credits such as the earned income credit and student loan deductions. It may also inhibit your ability to contribute to retirement accounts. His advice is to choose "Married, filing jointly" unless your fiancé is coming to this marriage with heavy financial burdens and problems.

Dr. Engel also notes that remarriage will affect your tax status. Unfortunately, you will no longer be able to file as "Head of Household." You can continue to claim your children as a deduction if they live with you more than six months out of the year, unless you did what I did. In my case, my first husband and I stipulated in our divorce agreement that we would claim our daughter in alternate years, in an attempt to share the benefit equally. However, if no stipulation was made in your divorce agreement, the exemption automatically goes to the custodial parent.

MIXED MARRIAGES:
ARE YOU A SPENDER OR A SAVER?

While you and your fiancé are talking about finances, have a frank discussion about your personal spending habits. Before I remarried, I had a job where I was making a fairly good income. I was quite accustomed to my spending habits and the average dollar amount of my monthly credit card bill. After I remarried, I continued my same habits and paid my own credit card bills. Eventually, my husband and I merged our separate checking accounts and he began to handle the payment of our monthly bills. I was surprised at the utter shock he expressed over my bills.

Sit down and talk with your fiancé now about your habits, expectations and feelings about money. Some people use money as a control factor, some don't think about it at all, and others continually worry there will never be enough. Some like to spend, others like to save. Some are generous and others very frugal. Since opposites tend to attract, it is very likely that you will marry your financial opposite. There's absolutely no problem with that. In fact, it's probably better that way. Your knack for saving will balance out his tendencies to splurge. Talking about it now will prevent problems later.

CHILD SUPPORT IN, SPOUSAL SUPPORT OUT

If you are receiving child support from your ex-husband or your husband is paying out child or spousal support to his ex-wife, these support payments may continue for many years to come. It is important that you discuss, now, how these monies will be handled after you remarry. Are you comfortable with placing your child support money in a joint account? Do you want a certain portion of it to go into your children's savings accounts? Some women choose to save some child support for college tuition. What does your fiancé expect you to do with these payments? On the other hand, how do you feel about his payments to his ex-wife coming out of your joint checking account? What if your fiancé loses his job and you have to make the payments for a month or two? Or maybe you make more money than he does. Will it feel like you're supporting his ex-wife? There are no right or wrong answers to these questions. However, it's critical that you address them head-on before you remarry. When you remarry, you come to the new relationship with emotional and financial baggage, and it's best to share it, talk about it and unload it before you tie the knot.

HIS, MINE AND OURS

Next on your "to discuss" list is how to handle everyday financial concerns. Decide whether you should have joint or separate checking accounts. Some remarried couples have both. They each have their own separate account for personal items and then a joint account for shared expenses such as mortgage, groceries and household items. Do you want one joint credit card, separate cards or both? To this day, I like to have one of my own credit cards for several reasons. First, if I'm buying my husband a gift, I don't want him to know how much I paid for it. And worse, if I'm going to splurge on that pair of shoes that I just have to have, I really don't want him to know how much I spent on them either! I also like to keep my own credit rating and don't want to lose my credit status should I ever become single again. If you choose to go with the three-pot method of his, mine and ours, Dr. Engel suggests you consider one of two variations on the theme:

1) Have small separate accounts and a large checking account
2) have large separate accounts and a minimal joint account.

Whichever you choose, she advises that you fund the joint account in proportion to how much each of you earn, rather than funding it equally.

CREDIT ISSUES

In the process of divorce and sometimes beforehand, finances are the most prevalent problem. Negative information remains on your credit report for seven years, and a bankruptcy can remain for up to ten years. In my own case, I had to work with an attorney to have my credit report corrected. This not only cost a lot of money, but was a hassle as well. Your good credit is one of your most important assets. You need to protect it. Many employers, lenders and companies use your credit rating to decide if they want to do business with you or not.

To avoid any nasty surprises, sometime between now and your wedding date, write to the top three credit reporting agencies (Experian, Equifax and Trans Union) and request a copy of your credit report. You'll need to supply them with your full name, maiden name, your current address (and former, if you've lived at your current address for less than two years), your birth date, place of birth, and a phone number in the event they need to contact you. Or, you can go online and access your information there. You are entitled to a free report if you've recently been denied credit. Otherwise, it is available for about $8.00.

Once you receive your report, review it carefully. Make sure your social security number is correct. Make sure other family names are not mixed in, and if you have a common name like Jane Smith, check each account number as well. Another surprise I had when I checked my report was that several accounts belonging to my ex-husband's new wife were on my credit report! And don't forget to call and make sure that the accounts that say closed really are closed. Ask that your name be removed from the accounts entirely. If you find inaccurate information, notify the reporting agency in writing and they will investigate your claim. It usually takes thirty to sixty days to complete the investigation—another reason why you want to start this process a few months prior to your wedding date.

Here are some pertinent experiences from women grappling with credit, financial and personal issues that you may also be going through.

Suzanne's Story

"I was married for the first time when I was just eighteen years old. The marriage lasted twenty years. This means I've had my married name longer than my maiden name. It's who I am. It's also the last name of my two children. I am really not looking forward to changing my name this late in the game. I'm fifty-one years old, for heaven's sake! The problem is I know it will hurt my fiancé's feelings if I don't take his last name. I'll probably compromise and use both, but I'm really not sure yet."

Janet's Story

"When my fiancé first asked me if I'd sign a pre-nup, I was stunned. I had to stop and ask myself, "Do I really want to marry this man if he doesn't trust me or have faith in this marriage?" But then, after we talked about it at length, I realized that he was just trying to be fair to his three kids from his first marriage, and I could hardly blame him for that. Frankly, that discussion led to an in-depth talk about money in general. While we share a lot of the same values, when it comes to money, we were brought up differently. I was taught to earn every penny, give 10 percent to the church and another 10 percent to my piggy bank. He, on the other hand, was given a hefty allowance, a credit card and the knowledge that his grandfather left him a small trust fund. So, I'm glad we talked about everything before we married. I felt like we started with a clean slate and that's hard to do with all the emotional baggage you bring to a second marriage."

As you can see from these stories and the topics we've discussed, when you remarry there are complex issues to consider and decide upon which the first-time bride usually doesn't have to deal with. However, by handling them before the wedding, with maturity, tact and love, you'll ensure smooth sailing later.

Chapter Nine

The Honeymoon

At Long Last...Again

*F*irst **Wedding:** Week in Pennsylvania's Poconos at a honeymoon hotel or a huge Florida hotel filled with other first-time brides and grooms.

Second Wedding: Ten days in Fiji on a small, remote island with plenty of privacy, gourmet meals and fine wines.

HONEYMOON ORIGINS

The practice of a bride and groom going on a honeymoon dates back to the days when a Scandinavian groom would abduct his bride from a neighboring village. He would take her to a secluded spot until her family gave up the search or she became pregnant and they no longer wanted her back. He would then take his bride back to his village. The word "honeymoon" comes from an ancient Northern European custom. Apparently, the bride and groom would drink mead, an alcoholic beverage made from honey, every day for the first moon (one month) of their married life. It was believed that the mead increased the bride's fertility. (I think it just increased the likelihood of sex!) Eventually, the honeymoon became the standard of every marriage. Lasting anywhere from a weekend to a full month, today's honeymoon is that special time when a new bride and groom can become accustomed to one another and discover the sweetness of married life.

YOUR HONEYMOON PERSONALITY

The plans for your encore wedding are in motion. The invitation has been selected, your dress is being altered, any kids are adjusting to their new roles and things are moving along smoothly. Then one day you ask your fiancé, "So, where should we going for our honeymoon?" Suddenly, everyone has suggestions. Your fiancé proposes a trip to the Adirondacks, complete with camping, hiking and fishing. Friends list their honeymoon sites from the Bahamas to Hawaii. And the kids who have Disney World on their minds start singing the theme song to "Mickey Mouse Club." Meanwhile, your idea of a romantic getaway seems to be slipping farther and farther away.

Before things go any further, make time to sit down with your fiancé to seriously discuss your honeymoon options. By asking yourselves the following questions, you can guarantee a memorable honeymoon for both of you.

What do each of you envision as the ideal honeymoon? Your honeymoon is meant to be the ultimate vacation, but what may be a dream come true for you may resemble ancient torture to your fiancé. For example, I love to shop and lie on the beach soaking up the sun's rays. My husband prefers to play golf and relax poolside. He hates sand and his idea of shopping is picking up a shirt in the pro shop after his game is over. One couple I know took a road trip across the United States for two weeks, stopping whenever and wherever the mood struck them. They didn't even make hotel reservations; wherever and whenever they wished, they spent the night. That type of trip would terrify me, but they were in heaven. So, start by talking about your expectations with your fiancé. This trip is for both of you. These will be your first days as man and wife, and you'll want to spend them doing things and in places you both want to be.

What are the things you enjoy doing as a couple? Do you like adventurous activities such as scuba diving, snowboarding or bungee jumping? Do you like sightseeing, browsing through museums or going to the theater? Do you enjoy the hustle and bustle walking in the big city streets or strolling on the boardwalk along the beach? Have you always dreamed of being on board one of those big luxury ocean cruise ships? Maybe you'd like to play golf on each and every island in Hawaii or play the famous links in Scotland? Make a list of your favorite activities. After prioritizing and reviewing the list, you both should have a pretty good idea of the type of honeymoon you would both enjoy.

Rule number one: Do not go to the same place you went on your first honeymoon. Remember, as I've said before this is a new marriage and a fresh start. Do not bring ghosts from the past. To build new memories you might want to go someplace completely new where neither of you has ever been before. One of the best ways to bond as a couple is to share a new experience. By exploring uncharted territory together, you create memories that will last a lifetime and are uniquely yours.

Take a good look at your budget to see how much you can comfortably afford, as well as how much time you will be able to spend away from work, home and kids. According to a *Bride Again* survey, about 35 percent spend under $3,000, while 60 percent spend between $3,000 and $7,500. Only 5 percent spend over $7,500. As for time spent, the majority of these couples honeymooned anywhere from seven to ten days.

TOP 10 HONEYMOON DESTINATIONS

According to *Modern Bride's* 2004 survey among travel agents nationwide, the top ten honeymoon locations for American newlyweds are:

1) Hawaii
2) Jamaica
3) Mexico
4) Tahiti
5) St. Lucia
6) Italy
7) United States Virgin Islands
8) Aruba
9) Las Vegas
10) Bermuda

Let's take a look at each of these hot spots and find out which one might be your ticket to paradise.

Hawaii

Two of Hawaii's most popular islands for honeymoons are Maui and Kauai. Boasting temperatures year-round of 80 to 85 degrees in the daytime and 65 to 70 degrees at night, Hawaii is an ideal destination for sun worshippers and fair weather fans. My favorite island in the chain has always been Maui. They have a proverb that says, "He mea'ai'ia kahi pilipili maunu kapae 'ia," which literally means, "The bit of bait set to one side is edible still." In other words, "A man or woman who has been the mate of another can still be a good mate to have."

Maui boasts miles and miles of white sandy beaches for walking, swimming or soaking up the sun's rays. You can board a boat and go whale watching where you will see humpback whales cavorting along Maui's shores. One of my best once-in-a-lifetime experiences in Maui was biking down the Haleakala volcano. Although you have to get up before the crack of dawn, it's well worth it. At about 4 a.m., you meet at the bike shop, select your bike, helmet and cold weather gear, jump in a van and reach the top of the 10,000-foot high volcano before dawn's first light. It's quiet up at the top and kind of surreal. There is nothing as magical as that moment when the sun comes up and shines on the volcano, producing a shadow on the Pacific Ocean behind you. It's an awesome sight to behold. Then comes the exciting bike ride down the volcano and back into town. There's a great little restaurant at the halfway point that serves a big, satisfying breakfast. If you have kids with you, you can skip the first half of the ride, which is full of winding switchbacks, and have the van drop you off at the restaurant. You can enjoy breakfast before the crowd arrives, and then it's smooth sailing all the way down to the bottom.

Then there's scuba diving, or snorkeling if you and your fiancé are not certified divers. On the other hand, if you want to get certified while in Maui, you can do that too, in just three or four days. Or choose the "resort dive" for non-certified divers. You'll go just fifteen to twenty feet below the surface and see an amazing array of fish, eels, coral and starfish.

There's plenty of shopping in Lahaina where you'll find Hawaiian wear, scrimshaw, art galleries, jewelry and numerous restaurants. I've always enjoyed Longhi's where the menu is spoken rather than in print. The wait staff literally recite the entire menu to you! At night take in a show at Warren & Annabelle's on Front Street for magic, comedy and cocktails.

A Hawaiian honeymoon is not complete without attending one of its famous Luaus. This traditional feast features a roasted pig, salmon, coconut pudding, poi, sweet potatoes and an endless array of tropical fruit. You'll receive a lei of fragrant plumeria flowers to wear around your neck and shoulders, watch hula dancers perform ancient traditional dances and see men perform the fire dance with torches ablaze.

Kauai, also known as Garden of the Gods, is one of the greenest islands you'll ever see. This is probably because with 486 inches of rainfall per year, it is considered the wettest spot on earth. Yet there are also miles upon miles of dry sand dunes as well. Waimea Canyon is 3,000 feet deep—rich in shades of rust, brown, amethyst and jade. It's as impressive as the Grand Canyon in Arizona.

Kauai is the oldest island in the chain. It has been the filming location for renowned cinematography in movies including *Jurassic Park* and *South Pacific.* This island is home to the Na Pali Coast, where sharp-edged cliffs force waterfalls to tumble 4,000 feet to the ocean below. You can experience Na Pali either by boat, catamaran or helicopter. I highly recommend the helicopter trip. It's exciting, spectacular and breathtaking. Kauai also has forty-three beaches, more beaches per mile of coastline than any other Hawaiian island. This island also has the only navigable rivers in all of Hawaii. The rivers are perfect for kayaking, and you will find lagoons leading to 100-foot waterfalls. The sunniest spot on the island is at the south end. It is called Poipu Beach and you can find plenty of resorts, beautiful beaches, shopping and restaurants.

Jamaica

Jamaica has given the world people like former Secretary of State Colin Powell, supermodel Naomi Campbell, entertainer Harry Belafonte and the legendary Bob Marley. This fifty-mile long and 140-mile wide bit of the Caribbean has sent a bobsled team to the Winter Olympics and a national soccer team to the World Cup. Jamaicans are artists, athletes, musicians and authors. A spirited human treasure chest, it is a beautiful place for a honeymoon.

If you choose to focus your honeymoon energy in just one

place on the island, consider Port Antonio. Located on the
northeast coast, it has long been a retreat for the world's rich and
famous. The movie *The Blue Lagoon* with Brooke Shields and
Cocktail with Tom Cruise were filmed in Port Antonio in
Jamaica. The Blue Lagoon is an actual place. At 178 feet, it's Port
Antonio's most famous attraction. While in Jamaica, you'll want
to try some Boston Jerk, the famous seasoned meat of the island,
and relax while you drift on a thirty-foot-long bamboo raft down
the Rio Grande.

For cliff diving, scuba diving among wrecks, hiking, golfing
and lighthouse touring, go to the seven-mile beach of Negril. Or
take a look at Ocho Rios and see where Christopher Columbus
first landed. Hike up the 7,000-foot Blue Mountain or better yet,
bike ride down the mountain. Waterfalls abound and include
famous Dunns River Falls, a dramatic 600-foot drop of cascading
water that's considered the Niagara Falls of the Caribbean. Don't
miss a visit to the shrine of reggae icon Bob Marley.

Another popular choice is Montego Bay. Here, you can tour
a rum distillery where every visitor receives a complimentary
bottle to take home or visit haunted Rose Hall, once a plantation
and home to a woman named Annie Palmer. Apparently, Annie
murdered several of her husbands as well as a few slave lovers.
Also called the White Witch, visitors still claim to catch glimpses
of her ghostly apparition. As an added bonus, if you plan to
honeymoon in Montego Bay in the summer, you can make it
coincide with their annual reggae festival.

Mexico

Among the wonderful spots are Cancun and Cozumel to the
east and Puerto Vallarta, Cabo San Lucas, Mazatlan and Acapulco
to the west. The best months weather-wise are November through
May. June and July are much too hot, and hurricane season runs
August through September.

Cancun and Cozumel are located in what is called the Mayan Riviera. Once the land of the Mayan Indians, you can still visit many of the ancient Mayan temples and ruins.

Cancun's most famous attraction is its stretch of beaches. The water is turquoise, pristine and calm with a year-round temperature of about 80 degrees. The air temperature is about 90 degrees year-round, making for a very temperate climate. Cancun has incredible scuba diving, snorkeling and sport fishing. You can also golf and play tennis.

At ten miles wide and thirty miles long, **Cozumel** is Mexico's largest island. With the largest coral reef in the world, it offers some of the best diving on earth. Divers come from across the globe to explore the limestone caverns, sea tunnels and rare black coral. If you're looking for sun, sand and crystal blue waters, Mexico's Mayan Riveria is for you.

Mexico's Pacific Coast offers a variety of resorts from the tip of Cabo San Lucas down to the shores of Acapulco. Enjoy grande margaritas, limitless seafood, brilliant bougainvillea and miles of soft sand and gentle surf.

Cabo San Lucas is a party town that's a bit wild (think spring break) and only a two-hour flight from Los Angeles. Situated on the Sea of Cortez, it is famous for its natural stone Arch and Lover's Beach where a small strand of beach unites the Pacific Ocean and the Sea of Cortez. Cabo offers tons of great restaurants and golf courses, as well as excellent shopping, marlin fishing, ATV riding, water sports and snorkeling. For nightlife, there's Cabo Wabo owned by Sammy Hagar, Squid Row where you can dance until dawn, and The Giggling Marlin where they string you up by your feet, feed you a shot of tequila and take your picture before releasing you. Like I said, this town is not for the faint of heart.

Mazatlan is located on a peninsula almost directly across from the tip of Baja. It is divided into two areas—the Zona

Dorada (Golden Zone), where the majority of hotels and restaurants are located, and El Centro (downtown), the heart of the city. Mazatlan has the charm of old Mexico and the excitement of city life. In addition to the usual water sports and activities, you can tour a tequila distillery, watch a bullfight or picnic on one of the three nearby islands.

Puerta Vallarta is where Elizabeth Taylor and Richard Burton filmed the famous movie *The Night of the Iguana*. In fact, you can even tour their seven-story, nine-bedroom, twelve-bathroom former home, which is currently a bed and breakfast. Once a sleepy little fishing village, Puerta Vallarta is now a world-class resort. Bordered by the Sierra Madre Mountains, the city overlooks Banderas Bay, the largest bay in Mexico.

Here, honeymooners can enjoy boating, parasailing, scuba diving, snorkeling and deep-sea fishing. Or try the Dolphin Adventure where you swim with the dolphins. They'll even let you be a dolphin trainer for a day, allowing you to work side by side with an experienced dolphin trainer. You might enjoy a day of whale watching or the thrilling experience of a Jeep safari trekking through forgotten villages. You can ride horseback, swim in waterfalls, hike, bungee jump or ride in a hot air balloon. And if you're really adventurous, you'll want to try the canopy tour. This eco-adventure takes place in the tropical forest where you rappel from platform to platform on zip lines ninety feet above the forest floor. Yes, you heard me right, ninety feet in the air above the canopy of the trees. On the more sedate side, there's great shopping downtown or at the Mercado Municipal, the traditional market with flowers, fresh produce, piñatas, crafts, clothing and local artwork.

Acapulco touts itself as the most exciting city in the world. It is famous for its nightlife, beautiful beaches and luxury hotels. Situated on the warm Acapulco Bay, it is ideal for water sports such as scuba diving and snorkeling. It has long been known for its sport fishing, with marlin, sail fish and dorado being very popular. Take a bay cruise, stroll through a botanical garden, or experience the rush of adrenaline on a jet boat ride. Or go all out and skydive with a tandem instructor, freefalling for forty-five seconds from an altitude of 10,000 feet until the parachute pops open and you drift gently down to the warm, sandy beach.

Tahiti

Also known as the French Polynesian, this collection of 118 islands is divided into five groups. One, called the Society Islands, is home to Tahiti, Moorea and Bora Bora, the most popular islands for honeymooners and vacationers. It's no wonder, since many of the resorts feature bungalows that jut out over the crystal clear blue water. The living rooms have glass windows in the floor where you can watch hundreds of colored tropical fish swim by.

Tahiti, the largest of the islands, offers black beaches, turquoise waters and pink coral reefs. It's easy to see why Paul Gauguin loved to paint here. The port city of Papeete is also the capital. The island is known for its black pearls, so a visit to the Pearl Museum is a must, as well as to Le Marche, the open-air market for fresh flowers, produce, fish and souvenirs.

On the island of **Moorea** you can take a Land Rover through the mountains, vanilla plantations and ancient sacrificial sites, swim with dolphins at Dolphin Quest, or glide on an outrigger canoe to a secluded spot where you will snorkel with gentle sting rays. Yes, sting rays are extremely docile and very friendly. They love to be petted and even kissed! End your evening at the Tiki Village with a traditional Tahitian dinner and stage show complete with fire dancers.

Bora Bora, perhaps the most famous island, was inspiration for the musical *South Pacific,* and is only twenty-three square miles in size. Here, you can board a helicopter for an awesome view of the islands, lagoon and Mount Otemana, an extinct volcano. Take a romantic sunset cruise on a catamaran or snorkel among coral gardens in a private lagoon. The best time of year to fully enjoy the beauty of the Tahitian Islands is May through October. The remaining months can be wet and humid, and cyclones are possible.

St. Lucia

This lush, tropical island in the Caribbean is twenty-seven miles long and fourteen miles wide. It has the beauty of the Atlantic Ocean on its Eastern shoreline and the calm Caribbean Sea on its West. There are rainforests filled with wild orchids, giant ferns and tropical birds. Orchards of mango, coconut, papaya and banana abound.

In addition to the usual water sports such as scuba diving, sailing, windsurfing and deep-sea fishing, there are also golf, tennis, squash, horseback riding and duty-free shopping. There is reggae dancing (called "jump ups") in the streets of Gros Islet, a tiny fishing village that turns into a carnival every Friday night. Not to be missed is Sulfur Springs, which boasts a seven-mile wide volcano where you can actually drive up to the rim. You can also swim and soak in the natural hot springs. You can also go turtle watching from mid-March to the end of July, take a helicopter tour or visit a banana, coffee or cocoa plantation. Temperatures vary from 65 to 85 degrees December through May and 75 to 95 degrees June through November, making it a year-round honeymoon paradise.

Italy

Italy is filled with romantic places. The hardest part will be deciding on the city or cities that you want to visit. If you're honeymooning in the capital city of **Rome,** start with Vatican City where you can see the Sistine Chapel, visit the Pope for a papal blessing, take a trip through one of the many Vatican museums, or take part in a group tour of the Vatican Gardens. Then there's classical Rome with Trevi Fountain, the Pantheon and Via Venetto. Imperial Rome includes the Colosseum, the Forum and St. Paul's Basillica. If traveling on to **Florence,** you will have the opportunity to see Botticelli's "Birth of Venus," Michelangelo's "David" and the famous Pont Vecchio Bridge.

Venice is the city for lovers. What could be more romantic than a gondola ride through the canals of Venice? You can sip champagne and kiss under each bridge while being serenaded by the gondolier. There's Piazzo San Marcos, also known as St. Mark's Square, and Murano, the glass island. After watching the famous glass blowers, walk next door to the Church of Santa Maria e San Donato to see the beautiful floor inlaid with marble in mosaic, completed long ago in 1140. You'll also want to shop at the nine-hundred-year-old Rialto Food Market where over twenty million visitors come to shop each year. And if you'll be in Venice during the eight days before Lent, you won't want to miss Carnival and its abundance of masquerades, balls and concerts.

United States Virgin Islands

I have a friend who is fearful of traveling outside the United States. When she became engaged to be remarried, she and her fiancé started the search for the perfect honeymoon destination. Knowing she had honeymooned in Hawaii the first time, I had already warned her not to repeat the past. So, where could she find a sun-drenched United States locale with white sandy beaches, pristine waters, warm weather and an ethnically diverse culture? Well, the U.S. Virgin Islands, of course! Made up of three main islands, St. Croix, St. John and St. Thomas, these islands are located between the Atlantic Ocean and the Caribbean Sea. Because it is an American territory, purchased by the United States in 1917, a passport is not required, although you will need your driver's license for identification upon leaving the islands. USVI is governed by US laws. Those born there are American citizens; the currency is the US dollar and the US Postal Service delivers your postcards to your friends and family back home. Here, you will feel the security of being in the United States, while enjoying the warmth and beauty of the gentle Caribbean.

St. Croix, at eighty-two square miles, is the largest of the three main islands. It has a diverse landscape with lush green tropical hills that cascade to meet both the sea and barren desert. This island was once the land of looting pirates, sugar plantations and rumrunners. Today, it is a mix of European eighteenth century architecture, nineteenth century churches and twentieth century Victorian houses. This mix of rich cultural diversity and fabulous beaches makes for a sensational honeymoon. A stay here would not be complete without a tour of the Cruzan Rum Distillery, a trip to Buck Island Reef and a stroll through the Estate St. George Botanical Garden.

St. Thomas is known for its shopping in downtown Charlotte Amalie, a favorite stop for cruise ship passengers. In fact, over 1 million visitors shop this mecca of unique stores and boutiques each year. You will also find elegant dining and exciting nightlife in this bayside town. Not to be missed on St. Thomas is a trip to Mountain Top. At 1,500 feet above sea level, the view is breathtaking and it is the perfect place to indulge in the island's famous daiquiri made with local rum, sugar cane and bananas.

St. John is the smallest of these islands and the most non-commercial and low key. Accessible only by boat or ferry, it is a forty-five-minute ride from St. Thomas. Often described as serene, untouched and unspoiled, seventy-five percent of the island is a preserved national park. A favorite among nature lovers, this island offers hiking, camping, rest and relaxation. It also boasts forty beaches. Trunk Bay, at one time voted one of the top ten most beautiful beaches in the world, offers some of the best snorkeling in the Caribbean. There is an easy-to-follow underwater trail, complete with markers, making it a great underwater experience for both the first-time and experienced diver.

Aruba

This Caribbean island of Dutch heritage is just two and a half hours by plane from Miami and offers over twenty-five luxury hotels. Its average nighttime temperature of 79 degrees is not much less than the daytime average of 82. Although the island experiences constant trade winds of ten to twenty miles per hour, it is located outside of the hurricane belt, so you can honeymoon there anytime of the year. A passport is not required, although you will need your birth certificate and photo identification.

The island is a study in extremes. The Southern and Western shores lie on the calm and tranquil Caribbean, offering beautiful white sandy beaches, palm trees and water that is so clear the visibility in some areas is over one hundred feet. Yet, on the north side of the island, the waves of the Atlantic Ocean crash against the rugged shore. In between these two opposites lies a desert landscaped with cactus, aloe and large rock formations.

Activities on the island include visits to the Archaeological, Numismatic and Historical Museums; a cruise on a glass bottom boat; or a trip 150 feet below the ocean's surface onboard the forty-six-passenger Atlantis Submarine. There's also the Guadirikiri Cave, which features a one-hundred-foot-long tunnel and hundreds of harmless bats. For honeymooners, Huliba Cave is a must-see. Known as the Tunnel of Love, the entrance is heart shaped and an ideal spot for what will be one of your favorite honeymoon photos.

Las Vegas

This sprawling, diverse city is synonymous not only with gambling but with weddings and honeymoons. Las Vegas is a wonderland of activity. You can visit King Tut's tomb at the Luxor, ride a roller coaster at the Stratosphere or take a romantic gondola ride at the Venetian. Maybe you'd like to ride up the Eiffel Tower at 340 feet per minute at the Paris Hotel where you can then dine at the posh restaurant at the top. You could also visit the shark reef at Mandalay Bay, watch as a volcano erupts one hundred feet into the air at the Mirage, or experience a Klingon attack aboard Star Trek's USS Enterprise at the Hilton. Or maybe you'd rather view the fountain show at the Bellagio or watch as divers feed the fish and sharks in the 50,000-gallon saltwater aquarium at the Atlantis. If all that's not enough, you can take in one of the hot shows, including *Mamma Mia!*, the Blue Man Group, Celine Dion or "Mystere." There are also tons of great day trips to places such as the Hoover Dam, the Grand Canyon, Lake Mead and the Colorado River. All can be toured by land, water or via helicopter.

Don't miss the Freemont Street experience. With its $70 million light canopy positioned ninety feet above Fremont Street, the attraction stretches 1,400 feet and is capable of producing millions of color combinations, animations and video feeds. It is the most amazing sound and light show you will ever see. Shows range from six to nine minutes, and best of all, they're free. Last, but not least, there's the gambling. Lots and lots of gambling. Don't say I didn't warn you.

Bermuda

This is the perfect honeymoon spot if you're looking to escape close to home. With its pink sand, clear turquoise sea and laid-back style, Bermuda seems worlds away. Yet, this tropical island is only 600 miles off the coast of North Carolina and less than two hours by plane from most major East Coast cities. With a year-round average temperature of 70 degrees, you'll want to pack accordingly. Shorts are the order of the day—every day. In fact, Bermuda shorts are considered to be professional business attire for men!

Bermuda was made for beach lovers. In addition to ocean swimming, honeymooners can enjoy snorkeling, sailing, water skiing, parasailing, sport fishing and glass bottom boat cruises. For scuba divers, you can explore the Constellation, a 200-foot, four-masted schooner that now lies in thirty feet of water. This ship was the inspiration for Peter Benchley's book *The Deep*. Other popular activities on the island are golf, tennis, croquet, horseback riding and shuffleboard. To really see Bermuda, hire a horse and carriage. Up until the first cars arrived in 1946, it was the only way to get around.

Due to the high limestone content in Bermuda, the island is rich with underground caverns. The Crystal Caves are magnificent. Here, you will walk on a wooden pontoon bridge across an underground lake into a vast cavern of stalactite and stalagmite formations 120 feet underground. Other attractions include the Devil's Hole Aquarium, the thirty-six-acre Botanical Garden and Gibb's Hill Lighthouse. There's also the Bermuda Railway Train, which runs on a secluded eighteen-mile trail the length of the island. If you're honeymooning in January or February, take advantage of the seven-week Bermuda Festival of Performing Arts which features classical, jazz and pop artists, theatre, and dance. And don't forget to visit the Moongate at Palm Grove Garden. Legend states that if a couple kisses under the Moongate (a wedding band shaped archway made of coral and stone), they will be assured of good fortune and a lifetime of happiness.

CRUISE SHIPS

I have always felt the lure of the cruise honeymoon. The ships are cities unto themselves and places where passengers can be pampered, entertained, wined and dined. You can travel to ports of call all over the world including Alaska, Hawaii, Mexico, the Caribbean, the Mediterranean, South America and Central America. You can cruise in Europe, Africa, Japan and Southeast Asia. You can choose from cruises that sail anywhere from three days to weeks on end. There's actually a world cruise that takes you to thirty ports of call in twenty-four nations around the globe. It's a 108-day experience of a lifetime, although you can select a portion of the trip from fourteen to eighty days if that fits your schedule better.

There are cruises for the young, the young at heart and the more mature traveler. You can travel economically or splurge on full luxury with no expenses spared. You can take the kids or leave them at home. You can even get married on a cruise.

Some cruises offer sports themes, Italian themes or educational themes. Cabins are filled with plush pillow-top mattresses, fluffy pillows and 300-thread count Egyptian cotton sheets. They have flat-screened televisions, DVD and CD players. You can enjoy a massage at the spa, indulge in an hour-long pedicure, dine on filet mignon and sip a perfectly aged glass of merlot. You could dance on deck under the stars or worship the sun poolside. All you have to do is pick the area of the world you wish to explore, decide how many days you'd like to be on the high seas and start packing.

DREAM HONEYMOONS

You've checked out the top ten most popular honeymoon locations and you've taken a look at cruises, but still nothing interests you and your fiancé. Sure, they all sound like great vacations, but not that once-in-a-lifetime trip you want for your honeymoon. If this describes your situation, you may be a prime candidate for a dream vacation. Just imagine a cruise down the Nile, an African Safari, a sailing trip along the turquoise coast of Turkey or perhaps a visit to some far off unknown spot like Mauritius.

JUST LIKE CLEOPATRA

Envision you and your new husband floating down the Nile in faraway Egypt, just like Anthony and Cleopatra did thousands of years ago. Begin your cruise in the modern city of Luxor at the north section of the Nile. This city boasts two temples, Luxor and Karnak. The Luxor Temple, which once served as a focal point for the Opet Festival back in the days when pharaohs ruled the land, is well preserved and spectacularly beautiful at night. Strangely, it sits among modern hotels and office buildings. About one and a half miles away is Karnak Temple, the largest compilation of religious buildings in the world. Built over 1,500 years ago, this site has the largest surviving obelisk in Egypt, two temples, the Great Hypostyle Hall and a fabulous sound and light show in the evening.

Across the river is the Valley of the Kings where you'll find the Tomb of Tutankhamen, the boy king. All of his treasures are at the Cairo National Museum, but you will still be able to see the actual tomb. You will then continue along the river about sixty-five miles to the West Bank where the Edfu Temple is located. Edfu was built by Cleopatra's father around the first century B.C. and is the most preserved temple along the Nile. It is dedicated to the god Horus and includes two black granite statues of him that guard the inner chapel.

The next port of call is Kom Ombo where there are two temples combined as one dedicated to Horus and Sobek, the crocodile god of the Nile and the god of fertility. Apparently, this area was once home to hundreds of crocodiles. There is even a small display of mummified crocodiles in the small chapel at the temple!

After all these temples, you will be happy to dock at Aswan, a large city that was once the border-trading city for Egypt and Nubia. You'll enjoy shopping at the bazaar, riding in a horse drawn carriage, and visiting the Old Cataract Hotel where Agatha Christie wrote her famous book *Death on the Nile*. This can be your last stop on the Nile or you can chose to go by air from Aswan to Abu Simbel. I have heard from many travelers that this was the highlight of their trip.

Ramses II built Abu Simbel, which marks the border between Egypt and Nubia, about 3,000 years ago. There are two temples here. The Great Temple, at over 100 feet high and 120 feet wide, is dedicated to the sun god Ra. It has four sixty-six-foot imposing statues of Ramses II cut out of the face of the cliff guarding its entrance. The temple is aligned so that every year on February 22 and October 22 the sunlight penetrates the length of the temple. Each night there are three sound and light shows performed in seven different languages. The smaller temple is dedicated to cow goddess Hathor and Nefertari, Ramses' most favored wife. Here you will see Nefertari carved in both sides of the entrance, standing between two statues of Ramses II. This was the first time that a queen was depicted on the front of a temple next to her husband, equal in size to him.

If you are considering a cruise along the Nile for your honeymoon, October through March is the best season, with temperatures at about 77 degrees. Also, keep in mind the region's three favorite sayings: "If it is the will of God," "Tomorrow," and "It doesn't matter." Together, they describe the laidback feeling of a Nile cruise. There is no rush and nothing happens fast, so sit back, relax and enjoy the ride.

AN AWESOME AFRICAN SAFARI

The word "safari" in the Swahili language means "journey." What better way to start your life's journey as husband and wife than on an African Safari? Whether your budget is tight or limitless, whether you will opt for turn-of-the-century European luxury or are open to the adventure of camping on the savannah, your only challenge will be to decide where to take your safari. You can choose from Kenya, Tanzania or Uganda.

Kenya is the most popular safari destination. There is a classic seven-day tour that takes you through the three most stunning regions in Kenya. You will see the open plains of Masai Mara where you'll watch wildebeest migrate and zebra roam. You'll then go on to Lake Nakuru, home to hundreds of flamingos and lions. Last stop is the swamps of Amboseli where you'll see enormous elephants and the awesome view of Mount Kilimanjaro.

If you choose a **Tanzania** safari, you will see the sweeping Serengeti filled with every type of wild game, the stunning sight of Mount Kilimanjaro, and the 2,000-foot-deep Ngorongoro Crater. For both a wild and romantic safari honeymoon, consider combining the Tanzania safari with several days spent on the lazy beaches of Zanzibar.

Uganda, known as the Pearl of Africa, is famous for Africa's great mountain gorillas. These are the rarest of all apes with only about 600 left in the region. They grow up to six feet tall, weigh between 300 and 425 pounds and can live to be forty years old. You must have a permit to track them, which can take hours, but I hear it is well worth the time and effort. Imagine staring into the face of a 350-pound silverback gorilla! Now that's a Kodak moment.

THE TURQUOISE COAST

In the Turquoise Coast of Turkey, Bathsheba seduced David. Cleopatra chose to spend her honeymoon here. Also, it is the land of Noah, the Virgin Mary and the legendary King Midas. You may sail aboard a private boat which begins its trip in the ancient seaside city of Marmaris. This quaint town is like a small French Riviera with tiny streets filled with shops, boutiques and family run restaurants. There are the famous Turkish rugs of wool and silk, traditional ceramics in cobalt blue, white and orange porcelain and numerous leather goods.

Just a day's sail away, where the Dalyan River meets the open sea, is the town of Ekincik. Ekinicik is famous for its tasty blue crabs, even tastier when served on the boat deck with a glass of chilled champagne. I've taken this dream trip, and it is incredible. Each day you sail to another small town, and each night you anchor in another deep lagoon. The Mediterranean Sea is so salty that you can dive into the water and float without treading water. Visibility is about one hundred feet, and the water temperature is just perfect. At night, the Milky Way can be seen clearly in all its glory. A highlight of your trip will be a visit to Gemiler Island, once a monastery amid a village of ruins.

INDIAN OCEAN PARADISE

Mauritius, a small island in the Indian Ocean just off the coast of Madagascar, is literally halfway around the world. Known for its beautiful, pristine beaches, it is the land of the now extinct dodo bird. It has been governed by the French, British and Portugeuese and became independent in the early 1960s. Its exotic mix of cultures—Creole, Chinese, French and Indian—makes for an amazing experience. Luckily, English is the official language, although you will still hear plenty of French being spoken there.

Mark Twain, during his varied travels, was so attracted to Mauritius that he stayed for many months and discovered, to his utter delight, the sugar fields and their resulting product—white rum. Today, his endorsement remains printed on the label of Mauritius Green Island Rum.

Mauritius combines the best of two worlds. There are cities and resorts for socializing and nightlife and isolated beaches and mountains for intimate moments filled with natural beauty. You can spend the day surfing, waterskiing, diving, snorkeling, deep-sea fishing, hiking or caving. There are ruins to explore, waterfalls to admire and vanilla plantations to tour. The capital city of Port Louis boasts numerous restaurants, shops, museums and casinos.

FAMILY TIME

Thinking of bringing the kids with you on your honeymoon? You are not alone. Many second timers choose to take their kids along for all or part of the honeymoon. Blending families can be challenging, and in some ways, including them in the honeymoon is a great way to start out on the right foot—as a family. As soon-to-be second-time bride Shannon said, "I can't even imagine going away for seven days without the kids. It's not an option. My fiancé and I knew we were all in this together. So together, as a new family, we'll be going to Walt Disney World, and we couldn't be happier."

If you're planning to take the kids, there are some fabulous destinations and resorts that cater to families. These kid-friendly places will allow you to spend time as a family, as well as time alone while the children are being safely entertained.

The Atlantis Resort on Paradise Island in the Bahamas ranks at the top of the list of kid-friendly spots. Its Discovery Channel Kids' Camp is specially designed for children ages four to twelve. The club offers day and evening programs where your kids can search for buried treasure, star gaze through a high powered-telescope or explore a replica of an Old Spanish galleon. The sails of this galleon are also used as a giant movie screen at night. There are arts and crafts, a science outpost with live animals, aquariums and fossils. The kids' camp also has eleven exhibit lagoons with over 50,000 sea animals where your kids can participate in fish feeding. And if that's not enough, they can swim or kayak in the protected Paradise Lagoon.

As for you and your new husband, you'll have fun in the casino playing craps, roulette, blackjack or baccarat. You can choose from seventeen restaurants for dining and eighteen lounges and clubs for entertainment. There's also diving, sailing, windsurfing, waterskiing, golf, tennis and horseback riding. It's pure heaven. You will need to bring your passports and your children's birth certificates.

Camp Hyatt is another good choice. There are over fifteen Hyatts that offer a Camp Hyatt for children ages three to twelve. For the camps in Maui and Kauai, the minimum age is five. Other locations include Lake Tahoe, Lake Las Vegas, Florida, Grand Cayman and Aruba. While you and your honey enjoy your time together, the kids can participate in a sandcastle-building contest, visit a turtle farm, go on a scavenger hunt, explore a butterfly farm, build a kite or race down a water slide.

Maui Loves Kids is a program developed by the Maui Visitors Bureau with sites on Maui, Molokai and Lanai. With an emphasis on family, area attractions include the Hawaiian Nature Center, Maui Ocean Center, Whalers Village Museum and the Sugar Cane Train. There are over sixty hotels and over one hundred condominiums participating in the program to ensure a wide variety of accommodations and budget options.

Club Med has about one hundred villages worldwide that offer children's programs for kids four to seventeen. They even have a Baby Club for babies four to twenty-three months and a Petit Club for tiny tots who are just two and three years old. About half the villages offer nannies as well. With villages in France, Greece, Italy, Spain, Mexico, the United States and more, there's certainly one to fit your honeymoon personality. If you're a snow ski buff, take a look at Crested Butte in Colorado. Its kids' program is for children ages four to seventeen. For the young ones, they offer a circus school, mini gym, in-line skating, video games and hip hop dancing. For the older kids, there are skiing lessons, snowmobiling, horseback riding, sleigh rides and dog sledding. Or try Club Med Sandpiper in Florida. It offers the same children's programs, as well as a Discover Florida package that includes admission to Universal Studios, Sea World, the Kennedy Space Center and Walt Disney World. Now that's a family vacation!

The Four Season's children's program, called Kids For All Seasons, includes indoor and outdoor activities for children ages four to twelve. Activities at most locations include arts and crafts, horseback riding, sandcastle building, beach and board games, swimming and shell collecting. Some even have teen game rooms and a dinner club with themed events on Friday and Saturday nights. Upon check-in, your child will receive a welcome gift, child-size bathrobe and complimentary baby or children's toiletries. The special children's menu includes items such as grilled cheese sandwiches, macaroni and cheese, pizza, fish sticks, spaghetti and peanut butter and jelly sandwiches. At your request, they will also childproof your guest room, supply a crib, and provide a complimentary video game unit.

The Franklin D. Resort on Runaway Bay in Jamaica is an all-suite, all-inclusive family resort. Children under sixteen years of age stay, play and eat for free. The best part is that the resort provides each family with its very own personal nanny from morning until late afternoon. If you require the nanny's services in the evening, she is available at an hourly fee paid directly to her, in cash.

The children's program includes a toddler's playroom, movie room and an arts and crafts room. There are lessons in photography, napkin folding, cooking, scuba, snorkeling, sailing, reggae dancing and aerobics. Kids can swim, collect shells, ride a donkey, play volleyball and float on a glass bottom boat. All this while you and your husband play a round of golf at the on-site course, take in a game of tennis, lay around the pool or take a romantic walk along the beach.

The Keystone Resort, about ninety miles west of Denver,

Colorado, is the perfect year-round resort. In the summer, there's hiking and biking on more than 100 miles of mountain trails; kayaking, canoeing and paddle boating on Keystone Lake; and gondola rides to the summit of Keystone Mountain. During the winter months, there's skiing, snowboarding, ice skating, sleigh rides, tubing and sledding. Stargazing, fireside storytelling and marshmallow roasts make for fun and memorable nights.

The children's program for ages three and up includes snowman-building, nature hikes, panning for gold and pony rides. For the parents, there's golf, tennis and a spa for massages, as well as the usual snow sports. For a bit of romance, enjoy a six-course dinner at the Alpenglow Stube Restaurant at the top of the 11,444-foot North Peak.

The Tyler Place Family Resort on Lake Champlain in Vermont is one of the most amazing family vacation resorts in the United States. In business since 1933, it is a family run all-inclusive resort designed specifically for families. There are eight programs for toddlers to teens. They boast an unbeatable fun-filled adventure vacation, with time and space for you and your husband to fully enjoy yourselves. The resort offers a mile of undeveloped lakeshore, 165 acres of woods and meadows and 500 acres of mountain bike trails.

There are so many activities for your kids that it's hard to know where to start. Some of the most interesting are cookouts and campfires, treasure hunts, wall climbing, waterskiing, woodworking, overnight camping trips, windsurfing and a pool party complete with a disc jockey.

As a family, you can enjoy a hayride, ice cream social, bonfire or nature hike. You might like a game of volleyball, basketball, tennis, or horseshoes. The resort carries over 250 bikes, including children's bikes and child seats. Of course, there's the lake with Hobie Cat sailboats, paddleboats and banana boats, plus instruction for wakeboarding, sailing and windsurfing.

There are thirty fireplace family cottages and family suites that have bedrooms where you and your new husband will feel spoiled and pampered and one to four bedrooms for your kids. They will provide you with a candlelight dinner for two while your kids are off being entertained for the evening.

For those of you who like to cruise, there's nothing better for families than a **Disney Cruise.** You can combine it with a trip to Walt Disney World, although there are so many activities aboard the ship that you may want to remain on board.

The kids can dance with Snow White, attend a "Lion King" pajama party or camp out under the stars. They can learn to draw Mickey Mouse, be a detective or attend a Peter Pan party. Older kids can engage in a game of music trivia, listen to ghost stories or solve an age-old mystery.

You and your husband can attend a cooking demonstration or wine tasting with the cellar master, participate in a game show, display your musical talents with karaoke or simply enjoy the entertainment at one of the many lounges or theaters onboard. One of the best ports of call is Castaway Cay in the Bahamas, reserved exclusively for Disney Cruise Line guests. There is Serenity Bay for adults only, a family beach, a special teen beach and a separate small cove for kids ages three to twelve.

DESTINATION WEDDINGS

Looking to combine your wedding with your honeymoon? This type of wedding, called a destination wedding, is one where you go to a far off location, get married and then stay for a few days or weeks for your honeymoon. This type of wedding is gaining in popularity among encore brides. They are usually less expensive, since you are combining the two events and there are fewer guests. Most destination weddings include just the bride and groom, their kids and closest friends and family. They can be less stressful because your travel agent, an on-site hotel wedding coordinator or a hired local wedding planner handles most of the details.

If you are considering a destination wedding, plan early. Apply for a passport if you don't already have one. Go online and research destinations. Find out the legal requirements for getting married in those countries. They vary substantially, although most will require you provide your passport, a certified copy of your birth certificate and proof of divorce or death of spouse. Some will also require a health certificate and blood test. Most countries also have a waiting period that can vary from twenty-four hours to a full month. If you are Catholic or Jewish, there can be additional requirements. Costs for all these details can run from $25 to over $600 and cover things such as a notary, judge, registrar, and your marriage license and certificate.

Are you looking for an exotic location? Do you want to marry next to a waterfall in Kauai? Maybe on a gondola on the canals of Venice? Or perhaps you'd like to experience a traditional Tahitian wedding. You can watch as your fiancé arrives at the beach on an outrigger canoe, listen as local musicians serenade you with love songs, be baptized with Tahitian names, exchange your vows before a Tahitian High Priest and then be wrapped in a traditional, handmade wedding quilt.

Of course, you don't have to travel far to get the feel of distant lands. You might choose Las Vegas and get married at the top of the Eiffel Tower at the Paris Hotel. If you've dreamed of Venice, get married on the gondola at the Venetian Hotel. Then there's the Luxor Hotel for a wedding in the shadow of the great pyramid.

Your destination need not even be exotic. You may want to have your destination wedding at your favorite winery in Napa and then spend the week enjoying the many wine tours. Maybe you'd like to marry on the slopes of your nearest mountain resort and then enjoy a week of skiing, sledding and ice skating. A destination wedding can be as simple as a weekend at a nearby resort where you can be married in the resort's garden gazebo and then indulge in spa treatments, enjoy a sunset harbor cruise or play a round of golf.

Once you have settled on a location, talk with a travel agent and hire a destination wedding professional. You want to work with someone who lives and works at the destination rather than someone in your hometown. They will know more about the area you're going to visit and its customs. They will also be aware of the current requirements and can assist you with all the necessary paperwork. Many of the hotels and resorts will have a wedding coordinator on staff at no extra charge. Most resorts have special wedding packages, and some will even provide a complimentary wedding ceremony, discounts on room rates for you and your guests, and even a nice bottle of champagne upon arrival.

If you plan on taking some wedding guests with you, send out "Save the Date" cards at least six months in advance. This will give your guests time to decide if they can take the time to join you, as well as budget for the trip. Talk with your family members and friends to see how many will be able to join you. This will give you an idea of the type and size of resort you will need. It is your responsibility to pay for your wedding party's hotel accommodations but not their airfare. If you can pick up the cost of your other guest's hotel accommodations, that is wonderful, but it's not necessary. You will also need to cover the costs of related wedding events, such as the rehearsal dinner and breakfast or brunch the morning after the wedding.

A last pearl of wisdom if you are planning a destination wedding: carry your wedding gown and your fiancé's tuxedo (or whatever the two of you are planning to wear for your ceremony) onboard the plane with you. You don't want to take the chance of having your luggage lost or your wedding dress damaged.

25 Tips For a Great Honeymoon

1) Use a travel agent.

2) Ask friends where they went for their honeymoons or recent vacations and get their opinions.

3) Know your honeymoon personality.

4) Don't repeat the past and honeymoon at the same place you honeymooned with your first husband.

5) Go someplace neither of you have ever been before.

6) Go during the off-season for the best hotel and travel rates.

7) Think outside the box. Sometimes it's cheaper to fly to London than to San Francisco.

8) Fly non-stop. Too many connections will zap your energy.

9) Wait a day or two after the wedding, if possible. This will give you time to recuperate from the wedding festivities.

10) Photocopy your passports and travel tickets. You never know what can happen when you're out of the country.

11) Use the ATM rather than traveler's checks. You can get cash daily, and if you're in a foreign country, it dispenses the local currency at the best conversion rate.

12) Don't pack valuables such as cash, glasses, medicines and keys. Pack these items in your carry-on luggage for safekeeping.

13) Reconfirm international flights forty-eight hours prior to departure. In most cases, this means the day before your wedding.

14) Bring Imodium. It sounds terrible, but Montezuma's Revenge can strike in Japan as easily as in Mexico.

15) If traveling to a small island, pack lightly. The planes can be as small as a four seater. They will actually weigh you and your luggage—and every pound counts.

16) If traveling to a tropical locale, pack insect repellant. It's hard to be romantic when you're covered in mosquito bites from head to toe.

17) When traveling in Italy, ask for your dinner bill. They don't bring it to you automatically after coffee and dessert.
18) Use a credit card for most purchases. Again, your credit card will obtain the best possible conversion rate.
19) Bring extra prescriptions, just in case.
20) Consider package deals. Although they may offer less flexibility, they often combine the best rate with the best quality.
21) If going to an all-inclusive resort, clarify exactly what is included. Wine at dinner may be included, while your two cocktails poolside may not be.
22) Don't take advantage of "last minute" airfares. Generally speaking, the closer to departure you book, the higher the odds are that you'll encounter some type of glitch.
23) Don't wear a fanny pack. It screams TOURIST.
24) Watch the dress code. Many areas of the world are much more conservative than the United States. Some will even deny you admittance if you aren't respectfully attired.
25) When planning your honeymoon, be aware of local and international holidays, events such as spring break and weather that can adversely affect your first days together as man and wife.

NO TIME?

Perhaps you barely have time to get married, let alone go away on a honeymoon for a week. Maybe you just started a new job and don't have any vacation time accrued yet. Perhaps you just can't leave the kids, but you really don't want to take them with you either. Or maybe you're saving up for a dream vacation next summer and simply can't afford a big honeymoon right now. Whatever your reason for skipping a honeymoon, don't. Even if you spend only one night in a nearby hotel or bed and breakfast, the memory will be well worth it. Kathleen, a friend of mine, was unable to take a honeymoon vacation due to both time and money. As a wedding gift, her sister Ann switched houses with her. When Kathleen and her new husband arrived at Ann's house after the reception, they found the house lit with candles and rose petals strewn on the floor from the door to the master bedroom. Inside the bedroom, the quilt on the bed was turned back, complete with a Godiva chocolate on each pillow. Soft music was playing in the background and a bottle of chilled champagne with two flutes was placed on the nightstand. Needless to say, Kathleen and her new husband enjoyed every moment of their "honeymoon."

Here are a group of honeymoon experiences which, I hope, will inspire you to create your own memorable time.

Joan's Story

"We were married on a Saturday. On Sunday evening, we met thirty people at the airport. They were our closest friends and immediate family. We all boarded the plane and took off to Tahiti, the place where my husband proposed to me. He rented an entire pier of bungalows that sit over the water, the ones where you can dive into the water from the porch or look through the glass bottom window in the living room floor. Our kids (we had four between the two of us) came with us as well. Our group stayed for a full week and we all had so much fun. When the group flew home, my husband and I boarded a plane for our two-week excursion to New Zealand and Australia. If ever there was a dream honeymoon, ours was one come true."

Jennifer's Story

"We went to the Body Holiday in St. Lucia. It was the best vacation I have ever had. Body Holiday is an all-inclusive resort that is listed as one of the top one hundred in the world. The spa is rated as one of the ten best in the world. One spa treatment per day per person is included in the rate. I had a shiatsu massage, a honeymoon massage where they teach you to massage each other, a body scrub, hydrotherapy, oasis bathing, a body wrap, a facial, an acupuncture session, and a pedicure and manicure! My husband indulged in all the same treatments, except for the pedicure and manicure. He opted for the ayurvedic massage instead. The resort also offered about forty different daily activities. There was so much to do that we only left once in the week we were there. We tried a lot of new things we'd never done before, including pilates, yoga, aqua-fitness and tai chi. We went parasailing and participated in the daily morning walks. It was truly heaven on earth. I had tears in my eyes as we left the resort."

Amy's Story
"I wanted to go to Tahiti and stay in a bungalow over the water and go to a black pearl farm. My husband thought that Tahiti would be too crowded and decided on a tiny island called Yasawa in Fiji. It contained only a dozen bures, or cottages, which meant at any given time there would be no more than twenty-four guests on the entire island. I was worried that with so few people, there wouldn't be anyone interesting to meet. My husband, on the other hand, wasn't interested in meeting other people. He wanted privacy and a high level of service. Well, we both got what we wanted. We had tons of privacy, miles of untouched beaches, excellent service, a very friendly staff and we thoroughly enjoyed the company of the other couples we met. All were there for a honeymoon, vow renewal, anniversary or birthday. We even met one couple from Europe who were married on the very same day that we were married.

Another couple married on the beach while we were there and invited everyone to attend the ceremony. I was worried upon arrival when our small, four-seat prop plane landed on the small soccer field they called an airport, but after that Fiji was paradise."

Your honeymoon, no matter how modest or lavish, can be a very special entry into your new life as husband and wife. Discuss what you both dream of and make it come true.

Chapter Ten

Parenting 101

*Blending, Combining and Mixing
Your Two Families*

First Wedding: The newlyweds welcome their first baby one year after their dream wedding. Now they begin learning parenting skills.

Second Wedding: Bride has two kids, groom has three. Nine months later they have a "mutual" child. They've created their version of "The Brady Bunch" and they settle into blending, combining and mixing.

Getting along in stepfamilies, or in any family for that matter, can be difficult at times. Although the term "blended family" is most commonly used to describe stepfamilies, according to Ron L. Deal, a licensed marriage and family therapist and author of *The Smart Stepfamily*, it's actually inaccurate in its description. Blending is the cooking process by which you combine ingredients into one mixture. Rarely does a stepfamily become "one." In fact, Deal stresses that biological parents and children will always have a stronger bond than stepparents and stepchildren. The preferred term used by most therapists, researchers and educators is "combined family." After all, this is what really happens in a stepfamily. Your children, if you have kids by a prior marriage, and his will combine. There is no actual blending, upon which the original ingredients are made into something new. Instead, combining occurs, where everyone maintains his or her own individuality, contributing to a new family dynamic. And, like synergy, the sum can be greater than its parts.

Basically a stepfamily combines children from a previous union. They live together under one roof some, or most, of the time, following the same rules, sharing some or hopefully most of the same common goals, eating together, playing together and growing together. It may not be a nuclear family or your first family, but it can be a real family nonetheless.

According to the Stepfamily Association of America, 65 percent of all remarriages include children from a previous union, thus forming a stepfamily. Furthermore, about one-third of all children in the U.S. are expected to live in a stepfamily before they reach the age of eighteen.

Children in a stepfamily can consist of siblings, half-siblings and mutual children. They can be considered residential or non-residential stepchildren depending on whether they live with you most of the time or come for bi-weekly visitations. Your child might be a member of your stepfamily as well as a member of her father's stepfamily if he also has remarried. Yes, it can get quite confusing.

Stepfamilies differ from nuclear families in several ways, according to the Stepfamily Association of America.First, your stepfamily is formed out of loss. It came about after divorce or the death of a spouse. This relationship formed after you all experienced much turmoil and unhappiness. It's not your first family; it's your second. Furthermore, you and your children have a longer history together than you and your new husband. In most nuclear families, children come after marriage and time spent as a couple. In a stepfamily, your bond with your own child will always be years longer than the bond you will have with your new mate.

The fact that there may be a parent in another location is another major difference between many nuclear families and stepfamilies. Although you have cut the ties that bind between you and your ex, your child has not and should not. In fact, it's best that you help nurture their relationship by encouraging your child to hang photos of her father (and possibly his new wife if he has one) on her bedroom walls, talk with you about the fun she had at his house last weekend and even help her select and purchase his Christmas and birthday presents with. I know from personal experience that this can be hard to do, especially if there is acrimony between you and your ex. However, make every attempt. Research shows that kids who have easy access to both parents adjust the best.

Additionally, your child may actually be a member of two households. He or she might have to adjust and fit into two completely different families. That's two sets of rules, two types of discipline and two sets of parental expectations. Another difference is that you or your new husband may have to take on a parenting role before you've even had a chance to connect emotionally with your stepchild. If one of you has no children of your own, it's pretty difficult and challenging immediately to step in and fill that role, especially when the stepchild is wary and uncertain of you. Even if you have children of your own, it is not an easy thing to take on another's child. Always keep in mind, while you may be taking on a parenting role, you are not replacing the biological parent.

Finally, the Stepfamily Association of America reminds us that there is no legal relationship between you and your stepchildren. This is also known as having responsibility without authority. You are responsible for getting your stepchild to school, but you aren't authorized to sign his permission slip for a field trip. You can take him to the pediatrician, but you can't admit him to the hospital for emergency treatment without written consent from his biological parent.

Here is one final word of caution about what a stepfamily is *not*. It is not a re-creation of a nuclear family where everyone pretends the first family didn't exist. You can't and shouldn't try to erase memories of your first family or pretend that your stepchild is your biological child and that you are one perfectly happy little family. If you go into this new relationship thinking this will be the case, you are doomed for failure right from the start. One of my friends, Sheila, tried to explain to her five-year-old daughter, Sara, that her stepmother was not her "real" mommy. Sheila even went so far as to show Sara pictures of herself when she was pregnant with her and giving birth. Unfortunately, Sara's stepmother tried to convince her that she was the "mommy," encouraging her to call her by that name and trying to instill in her the belief that the stepfamily was really a nuclear family. She wanted her family to be a re-creation of a nuclear family, rather than accepting and celebrating her new stepfamily. Needless to say, this was one of those second marriages that didn't make it.

This brings me to the "The Brady Bunch" myth. In each episode they sang: "Then one day when this lady met this fellow, they knew that it was much more than a hunch; that this group should somehow form a family...that's the way we all became "The Brady Bunch." Many second-time brides envision their new families will be this way when they remarry. In their minds, they see themselves, a divorced woman with kids meeting a divorced man with kids. They fall in love, get married, form one big family, and of course, live happily ever after. Oh yes, "The

Brady Bunch" had their various problems and issues, but every one of them was solved and handled in a half-hour, complete with smiles and hugs at the conclusion of each show. But in real life what happens when the vision fades? What happens when the dreams of being just like "The Brady Bunch" turn into the nightmare of being more like "The Osbournes"?

The reality is that stepfamilies take years to reach the point where everyone feels comfortable with each other and their role in the new family. Most statistics indicate that it takes about four to eight years to reach a true comfort level in a stepfamily. From my own experience, I'd have to say that's about right. It took us about four or five years to reach equilibrium, with each subsequent year getting better and better. Face the facts; it's difficult and stressful to adjust to a newly formed stepfamily. Much of the adjustment period will depend on the ages of your children. Most times, the younger they are, the easier the adjustment. Therapist Deal says that a child under the age of five will usually bond with the stepparent within one to two years. Pre-teens may have the hardest time adjusting, since that age group simply tends to be opposed to change and their hormones are just beginning to rage. Deal also cautions that it may take as many years as they are old to completely forge a connection. That could mean that if your stepchild is nine years old, it could take nine years to truly bond. But don't let that scare you. Just be aware that building strong relationships take time-lots of it. On the brighter side, older teens usually fare better, because they are more interested in their own relationships and have already begun the natural process of separating from their parents.

OTHER MYTHS

The Stepfamily Association of America says that in addition to "The Brady Bunch" myth there are several other prevalent myths about stepfamilies, none of which are true.

1) Instant love. As a newly remarried woman, you may be under the impression that because you love your new spouse, you will automatically love his children and they will love you. Sorry, this just isn't the case. It will take time to get to know his kids and for them to know you. You may or may not grow to love them. They may never love you. And that's okay. Really. But you can respect them, and they should be expected to respect you.

2) Children of divorce and remarriage are forever doomed and damaged. You may feel that you have emotionally harmed your child when you divorced or that the remarriage is yet another nail in the coffin. It seems we are always hearing doom and gloom stories about the negative effects of divorce. However, research shows that after about five to ten years, the majority of children are no different than kids from nuclear families.

3) The evil stepmother. Blame it on Cinderella, but stepmothers have always gotten a bad rap. Not to mention it was also Snow White's stepmother who put her to sleep and Hansel and Gretel's stepmother who left them alone in the forest. Just the word "stepmother" has a negative connotation. Early in my remarriage, when I had to introduce myself to one of my stepchildren's friends, I'd laughingly refer to myself as the "evil stepmother." It usually loosened the tension. The truth is stepmothers can be nice people too.

4) Part-time stepfamilies are easier to adjust to. If your stepchildren visit every other weekend or only occasionally, it seems like it would be easier. However, the fact that you get to spend so little time with them means you have less time to build a relationship. And as I mentioned earlier, relationships take lots and lots of time. Stepfamilies go through several stages of development, so the process may actually take even longer with a part-time stepfamily.

WHERE WILL YOU LIVE?

One of the first decisions you'll be making as a new couple is where you will live. Most have several choices. You can live in his house; you can live in your house or you can purchase a new home together. The best-case scenario may be a new home where there are no ghosts from the past, but that just might not be an option for you when you marry.

So, let's discuss living at his house. What if he lived there with his ex-wife when they were still married? How will you feel about sleeping in their bedroom? Cooking in her kitchen? Will it mean uprooting your children to a new school district? What if it means another thirty minutes added to your commute back and forth from work each day? Will selling your house right now mean a financial loss? What about your child's best friend who lives conveniently right next door? There are many things to be considered.

Let's discuss living at your house. Will his kids have to be uprooted? Will they be leaving behind their doting grandparents? How will his kids feel about moving into your house? Will they have to share a room with one of your kids? Will their church now be an hour away? What about their friends, school and sports activities?

As you can see, settling on a place for you and your new husband to live together may be the hardest decision you'll have to make. Calmly discuss the pros and cons of each of your homes. Review the logistics. Whose house is bigger? Which one is the most centrally located to both your places of work? Does one have a pool, nearby park or sports center that the children can take advantage of? Which one would sell for a higher profit? Should you retain one as rental property? Which house is in the best school district? Whose children are the most flexible and amenable to change?

Whatever decision you make, it will require compromises from all parties. Use the experience as a lesson for your children. It's good for them to see how compromise works, where everyone gets a little and gives a little, with the goal being what works best for the entire family.

There are also things you can do to ease the move. Let each child select his or her own room, choose the color paint or wallpaper and decorate it with posters or wall prints. Help each of them pick out a new comforter or beanbag chair. Let them plant flowers in the yard, hang up their basketball hoop and have all their friends over for a slumber party. If they will be changing schools, try to wait until the end of the year, even if it means driving them clear across town from now until school is out. Then, during the summer get the children involved in activities at the new school or a nearby YMCA so they'll get a chance to meet and make new friends.

DISCIPLINE IN A STEPFAMILY

There will be times when disciplining your stepchildren will require more patience and skill than disciplining your biological children. Part of the difficulty is that a stepparent may feel uncomfortable disciplining children that are not his or her own. You may feel as if you lack the necessary authority to do so, especially when they yell, "I don't have to—you're not my real mom!"

Talk with your new spouse and come up with a game plan for disciplining your kids and his kids. You need to agree on your methods and philosophy. The discipline for his kids and your kids should be consistent and fair for all the children combined, but at the beginning you each may want to take on the primary role of disciplinarian for your own children. The biological parent should set the limits, enforce the rules and carry out the consequences. Later, you can gradually release the reins to each other. It will take awhile to earn your stepchildren's trust and respect, and you'll need both of those things before you can expect to effectively discipline them.

Be specific about your expectations. When I was newly remarried, my husband told my daughter to "be good" when we were out to dinner at a restaurant. Eventually, as the night wore on, she became bored. Then she began to slide in her seat very slowly until her head disappeared under the table and she was on the floor at our feet. Later, she struck up a friendly conversation with the folks at the adjacent table. Then she asked to go to the bathroom for the third time. This upset my husband. During a visit to our therapist (yes, we went several times during those first few years), we were asked, "What does 'be good' mean?" That's when we learned to say to my daughter, "Stay in your seat, do not interrupt the people at the neighboring tables and use the bathroom before we are seated." Guess what? It worked.

Another learning experience came when my husband became exasperated with my daughter's refusal to obey him. At the therapist's he said, "She never does what I tell her to do. I tell her again and again, but she continues to ignore me." The therapist's first question to my husband was, "Why do you keep doing the same thing over and over again if it's not working?" The lesson here: If a discipline technique is not working, then try something else. In our case, my daughter wanted to know why she had to do it and when it had to be done. It wasn't about obeying; she simply needed more information from my husband. Once he started giving her the information, what he was asking made sense to her. For example, instead of demanding, "Clean your room," my husband explained, "Please clean your room, because we have company arriving in two hours." Before he learned that technique, he did what many parents are guilty of doing—he thought that because he was the parent, the child should obey immediately with no questions asked. In the real world, "because I'm the parent and I said so" has never been a successful discipline technique.

It's also wise to pick your battles. Some things simply are not worth arguing or fighting about. Save your time and energy for the big stuff. Rather than focusing on strict discipline and obedience, think about ways you can encourage your children and stepchildren to be independent, make good decisions, be responsible and feel good about themselves in the process.

DEALING WITH TEENS

The teenage years are challenging at best. But combining two families with teens can be downright intimidating. Luckily, there are several things you and your husband can do to help your teens bond and grow into the responsible adults that you want them to be.

Peer into their peer groups. You've heard the saying "birds of a feather flock together," right? Well, this is never truer than in the case of your children and stepchildren's peer groups. In fact, the influence of their peers may be one of the most important factors in your children's success. Essentially, kids model themselves after the kids with whom they hang out. They look to these friends for ideas on how to dress, what music to listen to, how to talk and how to behave in any number of given situations.

Therefore, one of the best things you can do is to quietly influence whom your children and stepchildren's friends are *most likely* to be. Do this by encouraging certain friendships and discouraging others. Be selective about the type of schools your children attend and the kind of clubs or organizations to which they belong. Encourage after-school sports or other extra-curricular activities where they can meet and form friendships with kids of like mind. Statistics show that most kids get "in with the wrong crowd" and "into trouble" during the after-school hours of 3:00 p.m. to 5:00 p.m. when parents are least likely to be around. So, fill this time with activities that interest your children and stepchildren—something that helps them develop into mature and responsible adults.

Know their personalities. Personality traits also affect who your children and stepchildren will be as adults. Studies show that we are born with specific personality traits that determine our temperament, character and the way we see the world around us. Sure, our environment, including our home life (whether it is with a nuclear or stepfamily), can enhance or hinder these basic traits, but it cannot change them. Accept that you cannot change your children or stepchildren's basic personality traits. However, you can do things to accentuate the positives and diminish the negatives. Encourage their interests, allow them room to just be kids, give them clear-cut expectations and be available to them.

Be accepting. One of the basic needs of kids of all ages is to be accepted by the adults in their lives. This is why it is so important that, as parents and stepparents, we interact with our kids in positive and encouraging ways. This means accepting them just the way they are and not comparing them with their siblings or you when you were growing up.

Accepting the differences in family members teaches kids not only to accept themselves and each other, but also encourages them to have greater empathy and tolerance for others in the world around them.

Communicate. Speaking with a teenager is like speaking a foreign language. They know it all and don't want to hear what you have to say. Remember the saying "Talk to your teenager today while he knows all of the answers"? Well, it's good advice. Teens can be very trying, but insist on keeping the lines of communication open at all times. As a parent, when I am talking to my daughter and she's telling me things about her friends, a boy at school or a situation that occurred that day, I sometimes want to interrupt her and say: "What in the heck are you thinking? Are you crazy?" But instead, I calmly respond: "So, what happened next? What did he say? How does that make you feel?" Inside I'm cringing at the details (everything in high school is drama, drama, drama), but outside I try to appear unruffled, because I don't want to say anything that will keep her from confiding in me in the future. Keep the lines of communication open, which most of the time means simply listening.

THE MUTUAL CHILD

Almost every remarried couple of childbearing age inevitably discusses having a child together—a baby who is the product of your union—a mutual child. Sure, you may each have children from a previous union, but won't having a child together bring you closer, unite your combined family and cement your new marriage? Maybe. Possibly.

There are many reasons for having a mutual child. Maybe you've always wanted a larger family and want to hear the pitter patter of two more little feet. Perhaps only one of you is bringing a child into this remarriage and the childless partner wants to experience having a child of his or her own. Maybe you're older and more mature now, and feel more ready for the demands of parenting. You may feel that having an "ours" child will cement your marriage and unite your combined family. These are all valid reasons for having a mutual child.

However, if combining a stepfamily is already difficult, you may be wondering if your remarriage can handle the addition of another child. You may wonder if that might be even more disruptive to the adjustment process. In a first marriage, a child may reduce the chances of divorce, but at the same time, it may negatively affect the quality of the marriage. After all, children are a joy and bring us much happiness, but they are also quite challenging and require much of our time, money and attention.

Even if you've agreed to have a mutual child, there's the timing. Should you wait until your stepfamily is comfortable with each other before adding to the mix? If you wait the four to eight years for that to happen, will you feel or be too old? Will you want start over again nursing a newborn at two in the morning? Or will waiting result in too wide of an age gap between your children? It's hard to be twelve years younger than your siblings. There are some professionals who believe that having a mutual child in the first five years will lower your risk of a divorce, but after about ten years, the child no longer has such an effect. This may be because, as parents, we are most fearful of divorce when our children are very small, but when they are older, we tend to feel they will adjust more easily. There's also the worry that this marriage may too end in divorce, and then you'll have children with different fathers on different visitation schedules.

In addition, there's the pressure that can be put on the mutual child. Since that child is seen as the single bond between all the family members, he often feels pressured to be the mediator or center of attention. He may also get special attention, causing jealousy in the ranks. These are all reasons not to have a mutual child.

Having a mutual child can be a joy and the essential ingredient needed to make your new combined family complete. But then again, it might be adding more dissension. If you are considering having a mutual child, I would highly suggest you read the book *Yours, Mine and Ours* by Anne C. Bernstein. As a family therapist, mother and stepmother she draws on her own background as well as the experience of fifty other couples grappling with having mutual children and gives in depth questions and information to consider.

THE OTHER STEPS—STEP PETS

More than 60 percent of households with children have pets, and of those, more than 40 percent have more than one pet. This means it's fairly likely that you own a cat and your fiancé owns a dog. Like most people, you probably feel that pets are family. You and your children are just as emotionally attached to Fluffy as his kids are attached to Fido. This means you are going to have a step pet, whether you like it or not. And if Fluffy and Fido don't like each other, trouble may occur.

Even if you both have dogs, it's not always easy. I had two dogs coming into my second marriage, and at first my husband had none. His family dog, Freckles, lived with his kids and ex-wife after their divorce. However, one day we came home to a message on the answering machine. "Mom's gonna take Freckles to the pound! She'll die there! Please take her, just until I can find a home for her." Three months later my husband remarked, "You know, she never did find a home for Freckles." I replied, "Honey, yes she did, and it's our home." Unfortunately, Freckles enjoyed chasing my two dogs. She nipped at their tails, ate their food and with just a look, sent them running. Luckily, Freckles and my father became fast friends, and she went to live with him and my mom. My dogs could once again relax and eat in peace.

Be prepared for fights and arguments concerning where the pets of your combined family will live, if they will be allowed on the couch or the beds and who will feed them, walk them and keep them separated if they don't get along. Some families allow their pets on the couch, while others would never dream of letting it happen. Some feed their pets table scraps, while others are quite strict about allowing them pet food only. You may find that while you are fine with dogs, you are highly allergic to cat hair. It happens. Then what? Have a family meeting and talk about the pets, their habits, their dispositions and each family member's expectations. Decide upon and delegate duties, discuss acceptable pet behavior and determine what's allowed and what's not. Declare one area of the house pet-free.

If you're marrying a man who doesn't have pets, never had pets and hates pets, this can be just as bad as you both having pets, perhaps worse. He won't understand why the veterinary bills are so high or why you have to hire a "babysitter" for your Labrador retriever when you go way for the weekend. A man I know said, "What? You paid $800 to save Spot's life? For $25 you could have had him put to sleep!" Clearly not a dog lover and not a very good stepdad to his new step pet.

Step pets can be a sore spot in your new marriage and just as difficult to deal with as stepchildren, so beware, forewarned and forearmed. Here are a few helpful hints for combining you and your husband's furry friends with each other and with your family.

1) If you each have a dog, introduce them slowly. Take them to a neutral territory, without leashes. Let them do their sniff test. If you have more than two dogs, introduce them one at a time, so two don't gang up against one. If they aren't spayed or neutered, you may want to consider this as it will help lessen aggressive behavior. Allow the dogs to establish their own hierarchy. One will be the dominant alpha dog and the other or others will follow as the subordinate members of the "pack".

2) For cats, try putting each one in a separate cage and setting the cages side by side for the initial meeting. At the next meeting, let the cats out of the cages and give them a toy to play with to encourage interaction.

3) If you have a cat and your future husband has a dog, they will most likely learn to get along over time. Just make sure that the cat has a safe place to escape where the dog can't find him.

4) If a step pet is your child's first pet, go over some ground rules such as no poking the animal's face, no pulling the animal's tail and no playing too rough.

5) If a member of the household has allergies, vacuum daily and consider purchasing an air filtration system. You could also have the person go to a physician who treats allergies.

THE WIFE- OR HUSBAND-IN-LAW

When my ex-husband remarried, I got a wife-in-law. When I remarried a year later, I got another wife-in-law. And yes, you guessed it, I, too am a wife-in-law. Confusing, isn't it? You see, when a remarriage takes place where one or both partners has children, the new mate gets more than stepkids and stepfamilies. He or she is now connected to the new spouse's ex-wife or ex-husband. Notice I say "connected' and not "related." Whether you both like it or not, you will come into contact with ex-spouses, especially if kids are involved. Ann Cryster wrote a book called *The Wife-in-Law Trap,* in which she coined the term "wife-in-law." I'll try to explain how it works from my own personal wife-in-law relationships.

I have a wife-in-law on my new husband's side. She is actually quite a joy. Although it was rough at first, we now enjoy a fairly easy relationship. We've agreed on, and play by, some simple rules. Unless it's an emergency, she calls my husband only at work, between 9:00 a.m. and 5:00 p.m., and only to discuss the kids or child support. She gets dibs on all major holidays, the kids' birthdays and vacations. This is okay with us, as we all consider her "the mom"—and she's great at it. She doesn't need me at all, though I have to admit, I'm pretty darn good as support staff. Since we all put the kids first, we are able to celebrate the big events (like graduations) under the same roof without batting an eyelash.

Wife-in-law situations are not always easy. Sometimes there is jealousy or ill-will. Do what you can to cause as few problems as possible. I, too, am a wife-in-law. I take this role very seriously and try to do my best. I attempt to get along, stay out of the way, be supportive of the children and behave in a courteous, polite and respectful manner. In short, I try to treat my wife-in-laws the way I like to be treated.

Like all relationships, being a wife-in-law can be quite confusing. It has its own ups and downs, good days and bad days. It's a relationship that you didn't choose or ask for, and yet it's one that is highly charged and very intense. It's one that affects millions of women every day: women like me and women like you. Welcome to the club.

BECOMING A STEPFAMILY

My second husband and I were a couple for several years before we married. This meant that I had plenty of time to get to know his two teenage kids, bond with them, and they had time to become comfortable with me. Or so I thought.

A couple of months before our wedding, I thought it might be a good idea to have a photo taken of all of us together to use as that year's Christmas card. When my fiancé mentioned my plan to his kids, they quickly responded with: "No way! She's not part of our family!" I was shocked, then hurt, then disappointed. I thought we had come a long way in the process of combining our two families, but I quickly learned differently. I had been trying so hard, maybe too hard. I wanted them to like me. Well, okay, maybe even love me. I felt that I was supposed to love them, too. I mean, we were going to be a family, and families love each other, right? Isn't love supposed to conquer all? Another side of my brain played the devil's advocate and asked if it was really necessary for me to love them.

That's when I decided to implement plan B. For me, this meant getting some counseling. While in counseling, I learned that it wasn't my job to love my stepchildren, nor should it have been my goal. At the same time, when I married their father, I did take on a certain responsibility for them. That responsibility was to interact with them in a way that helped them grow up and become responsible and productive adults. That's it.

This meant my interactions needed to be positive and consistent. It meant that I needed to respect them as individuals, have consideration for their feelings, show an interest in their pursuits and be sincerely concerned for their well-being. But I did not have to love them to be successful as a stepparent. Let me repeat that. I did not have to love them to be a good stepparent.

What a relief! No more guilt. No more carrying that heavy burden. Now I had a clear vision of what I needed to do, or rather not do. I quit trying so hard. Actually, I quit trying— period. I was tired of going out of my way to please these kids, do the right thing, and make them like me. I decided to take love out of the equation and handle them just as I would any other child in my house.

In doing so, I treated them with kindness. I was respectful. I showed concern for their well being, and I was considerate of their feelings. Basically, I was polite. I didn't ask anything of them, leaving that to their dad. I didn't expect anything from them, which meant I could not be disappointed. I respected them as individuals and went on about the business of being me. I took the emphasis off of them and put it on my husband and I, figuring that they could fit around us. I stopped making special accommodations for them. I gave up the idea that if I did things right, they would love me, and in return I would love them. I aimed for mutual respect rather than love.

I also brought a daughter to my new marriage. As a parent, it was impossible to believe that anyone could resist loving my precious little girl. However, I learned to accept that the rules of stepparenting applied to my husband, too. Chances were good that he wouldn't automatically love my daughter, just as I wouldn't necessarily love his children. I could only ask that he treat my daughter with the same respect and kindness I showed his children.

The road to wedded bliss was somewhat rocky at times. Living under one roof with children is challenging in and of itself. When you're a stepparent, it can be overwhelming. Sure, there were disagreements, but every family encounters problems along the way. There were instances when my husband disagreed about the way I approached his children. There were also times when I disagreed with how he treated my daughter. For the most part, however, we stood united and worked through our challenges together.

What finally happened, you wonder? Well, years went by. Then a few more. One Mother's Day I received my first card that read, "To My Stepmother on Mother's Day." It was such a small thing, and yet it was a big moment for me.

As more years went by, the kids grew and ventured out on their own. So, you can imagine my surprise the day the mailman delivered another card to me. It wasn't Mother's Day or Valentine's Day or even my birthday. It was just a day like any other one so I was taken back. This time my stepdaughter wrote: "I've been thinking of you a lot lately and about how much you have done for me. I realized that I probably never told you how much I appreciate all you have done, not just for me, but for my dad, too. I just wanted to write and say thanks for everything." Did she sign it "With Love" or "Love"? No. But in that moment, I knew that I mattered to her and she mattered to me.

How did we get to this place? Did I have to love her to get here? No, but somehow along the way, a mutual respect and fondness grew. These can grow in your stepfamily, too. Combining two families may not be as easy as sitcoms make it seem, but difficulty often breeds understanding and acceptance. There are many ways to help you successfully combine your two families. Try some and soon your new family will be humming its own theme song.

SUGGESTIONS TO UNITE STEPFAMILIES

Create a united front. The strength of a stepfamily is derived from the strength of your marriage. Kids will gain comfort and trust from the stability of your marriage, so it is imperative for you and your husband to agree on rules and practices. At the beginning, it may seem natural for each of you to assume responsibility for your own children, but eventually you will want to work as a team in a shared effort. Parents who unite early on and form a parenting partnership will avoid many of the conflicts that are the direct result of the "divide and conquer" technique used by most every child at one time or another. In fact, I'm sure you tried it on your own parents, right? You and your new husband must back each other at all times. Sometimes this can be very difficult, especially if you have different approaches to parenting. Perhaps your new husband will think you are too lenient with your kids. You might think he's too hard on them. You may feel that he's being a "Disney Dad" with his own kids, while he may feel you're not being nice enough to them. Discuss all situations in private, work out your game plan and then stand united.

Know your role. Although you can never *replace* your stepchild's biological parent, you can add to your stepchild's well-being by knowing your role and responsibilities. As a stepparent, your responsibility is not to learn to love that child but to help that child grow into a mature, responsible and productive adult. If you are emphatically told, "You are not my mother," you may want to quietly respond: "You're right, but I do care about you. I am not here to replace your mom, but I am here to help you." Your role is more like that of an aunt, babysitter, caregiver or teacher. You are an adult with sufficient authority to parent and discipline without being the actual "mom."

Allow plenty of time. When two families combine, each child will learn to find his or her new place—where he or she fits in the new pecking order. The oldest may now be the middle child and the only child may now be one of many. There may also be a new house, new school and new set of family rules, in addition to a new stepparent and stepsiblings. Sometimes you will take three steps forward just to take two steps back. That's okay. Allow plenty of time for each member of your combined family to adapt, letting relationships grow and develop at their own pace. If you bring a child from a previous marriage to your new one, allow your husband and your child to get to know each other at their own pace. I know, your child is so sweet and adorable, how could he not love and bond with her or him instantly? Maybe he has two sons and has never been to a ballet recital. It may take you husband and child a while to find common ground. Remember, it took you months, if not years, to really know your fiancé. Allow your children that kind of time as well.

Don't try too hard. I know you feel as if you should do everything you can to make your stepchildren like you. But when you try that hard, you set yourself up for failure and continued disappointment. It's a cycle. The harder you try, the more the child backs off. So, take the emphasis off of him or her, and put it on your new marriage.

Focus first and foremost on your relationship with your husband. Nurture your relationship. Go out on a weekly date. Take time for each other. Communicate. The stability of your marriage will be the rock for your children and stepchildren. They have already been through one divorce. They have seen one marriage disintegrate before their eyes. One of their fears is that it will happen again. Let the children see your love for each other. Let them watch as you solve problems together. Let them see that this is a marriage that will last.

Be consistent. By the time you have become a stepfamily, every member of your household has been through the turmoil, stress, grief and upheaval caused by divorce, remarriage and all that happens in between. Your stepfamily is yearning for stability. Consistency will help provide that for them.

Aim for mutual respect rather than love. Just because you love their dad doesn't mean your stepchildren will love you or you will love them. Don't be disappointed by their lack of affection for you and don't take it personally. However, expect and demand mutual respect. It's a good place to start.

Interact with your stepchildren in ways that help them to become responsible and mature adults. Help them make good, solid decisions. Be a good role model.

Accept your stepchildren for who they are as individuals. Do not compare them to your own children. Your stepchild might be a sports jock and your child might be highly uncoordinated. Don't push your child to compete against his stepbrother or stepsister. Accept each child's differences and praise each one for his or her uniqueness and strengths.

Be true to yourself. As a new stepmother you may feel the need to exert yourself and do things you wouldn't normally do, just to keep the peace. Please don't do that. Do what you know is best.

Be a source of support and encouragement. Kids need to hear that they did a good job. They like being cheered on. Let them know that they can come to you and discuss whatever is going on in their lives.

Spend time together as a family. Keep in mind that just as it took time to get to know your new husband, it will take time to get to know his kids. Remember, it can take years for stepfamilies to bond. So relax. Get to know your stepkids gradually. There's no rush. Remember, love and trust grow slowly over a period of time.

Discover their interests, their strengths and their dreams. Be interested in who they are, what sports they like to play, what books they like to read and what they want to be when they grow up. If your stepdaughter is interested in the stars, get her a book on the constellations and learn about them together. If your stepson loves to play baseball, pitch to him in the park on the weekends or watch a ballgame with him. If he wants to be a firefighter when he grows up, take him to your local firehouse. I think you get the idea.

Spend time alone with your biological children, one-on-one. This is equally as important as spending time with the entire family. Sometimes, in the eagerness to form a connection with your new stepfamily, the special time you had with your child when you were a single mom can get lost. Set aside time to spend with your child when your stepchildren are busy with other activities. This also means making sure your new husband spends time alone with his kids, without you in the mix.

Expect chaos. Families are messy. Stepfamilies can be even more so. You may have kids moving back and forth on a weekly basis between separate households. There might be more than one set of parents at each parent-teacher conference. Maybe it will require higher math to keep up with the visitation schedules and who needs to be picked up when. If you expect chaos, you'll be able to deal with it much more easily and calmly.

Set household rules. Your child may be a member of two households. A clear set of expectations will help them transition from home to home. Agree on bedtimes, chores, curfews and allowances. Make sure that your children know that either you or your new husband will enforce those rules and that they must obey their stepparents. You may even want to post the rules on the bedroom or kitchen wall as a reminder.

Listen. Really listen, without interrupting. Set aside time each day to spend one-on-one with each child and give them what they love most—your complete and undivided attention. It's amazing what kids will tell you when they know you're really listening to them.

Be considerate of feelings. It is perfectly normal for members of a stepfamily to have feelings of insecurity, jealousy and uncertainty. Your child will now have to share you with a new mate and his kids. Your child and his may have mixed feelings about where they fit into this new life.

Keep your promises, be dependable and be on time. Do what you say and say what you mean. Kids need to know they can count on you. I can't tell you the disappointment and hurt one friend's daughter experienced when she took a plane to see her dad and no one met her at the airport. Be on time. If you say you'll be there at 4:05 p.m. to pick the children up after school activities, be there. If you promise to be at the school play, arrive before the play begins, not during intermission. Again, your children have been through the uncertainty that comes with divorce or death, and they need to know they can count on what you say to them. This means don't promise things when you can't deliver.

Create new family rituals and traditions. Part of being a family is having a shared history and creating memories together that can be reflected upon for strength or just a smile. They bring a sense of identity and closeness to a family. Creating new family rituals can be as simple as "game night on Mondays" or "pizza and a video on Fridays." It can be an activity such as camping or waterskiing. Anything that is done together as a family on a regular basis can become a family tradition. What you do on each holiday and how you celebrate these days are rituals. Even small things like "every Sunday after church we get an ice cream cone" can become a lasting and rewarding family ritual. If you try something new as a family and everyone "has the best time ever," then continue doing that activity and make it a tradition. And if you have a family ritual from your days as a single mom, keep it going as well. For example, I have a friend who always took a summer vacation with her daughter and mother. It was a three-generational "girls only" vacation. They'd done it for years. When she remarried, her new husband encouraged her to keep up the tradition, even though it meant he'd be staying home alone. He didn't even insist his wife take his own daughter, because he knew how important the mother-daughter-granddaughter trip was to them.

Keep your eye on the big picture. Some days will be good and other days you'll wish you could stay in bed and hide under the covers. Some days will be calm. Some days you'll want to scream. Don't focus on the things that make you upset. Keep your eye on the goals you have for your new family. Remember, you can lose a few battles and still win the war.

Respect your stepchildren's privacy. Make sure that each child has his own space, whether that's his own room, one-half of a shared room or the den. This is particularly important if the child is only living with you every other weekend. He needs to know that no one is going to ride his bike, sleep in his bed or play with his toys while he is gone. One child I know hated going to her dad's house because she never knew what to expect when she got there. Once, her favorite toy had been broken and another time they took her bedroom and turned it into a guest room! Children need stability. Also, don't eavesdrop or pry for information about life at the "other house." And always remember to knock on his bedroom door before entering.

Respect all your children's biological parents. This means respecting your ex as well as your husband's ex-wife, even when your ex fails to pick up the kids on Friday after school or his ex calls you in the middle of the night. Be pleasant and respectful. I find it's helpful to think of my ex-husband as "my daughter's father." The prefix "ex" is negative, whereas the word "father" is positive and reminds me that my daughter's relationship is the one to focus upon.

Find a common interest with your stepchild. For some, this will be easy. If not, try experimenting with different things. Visit a museum, go to a sporting event or bake a cake together. Find something that you both enjoy. It can be as simple as a love of reading. You can share favorite books, talk about the latest bestseller or exchange books as gifts on birthdays and holidays.

Be flexible. In a stepfamily, things change often and they change quickly. You might buy all the ingredients for a big family dinner, just to find out that your stepkids are sick and won't be coming that weekend. Maybe you were planning a romantic night out when suddenly your child is home because your ex decided at the last minute that he or she can't take the child that night. Be flexible and go with the flow.

Treat all kids equally. If your son gets to play club soccer, your stepdaughter should be able to do the same if she wishes. If you spend $100 on your daughter's birthday present, spend a similar amount on your stepdaughter's. On the other hand, if you discipline your own child by restricting computer time, do the same with your stepchildren. It works both ways. In addition, ask that your parents do the same. It's important that when your child receives a Valentine's Day card from Grandma, your stepson receives one as well.

Encourage your stepchildren to bring their friends home. If your child spends time at your house and her dad's house, your place might be two towns away. Make it a point to drive to her old friend's house, pick her up and have a sleepover. Offer to drive your child and her friends to the mall on the weekend or have them over after school. If there's a birthday party, make sure your child gets to attend it, even if it's forty-five minutes away. Ensuring that your child keeps up with his or her own friendships may take effort, but it's well worth it.

Don't make excuses for being a stepfamily. Remember that there are some bad or difficult things all families go through, whether they are a stepfamily or a nuclear family. One night my daughter came home after a sleepover at a friend's house. They were the typical nuclear family and one that she somewhat envied. This time she said, "Mom, they are even weirder than our family. They argue more and her sister even locked us out of her room!" She had been under the impression that nuclear families were somehow better than stepfamilies. After seeing that all families had problems, she felt more relaxed about being a member of a stepfamily.

Have a weekly family meeting. Let everyone talk, one at a time. It's a great way to air feelings and clear up any misunderstandings.

When children know that they will be listened to and that there is a special time set aside for talking about how they feel, they are much more comfortable speaking up, rather than burying their feelings. It's also a good way for them to learn that it's okay to have problems.

Don't insist on being called mom. This is a highly emotionally charged issue. For some children, the name mom or dad can and will be reserved for one person only—their biological parent. Asking a stepchild to call you mom may make them feel resentful, uncomfortable and disloyal to their mother. On the other hand, some children will automatically call you mom just because their stepsiblings do and it feels natural to them. Let them choose the name for you, whether it is your first name or mom. Believe it or not, my husband and my daughter both share the name Kelly. And yes, it's even spelled the same. When she was a little girl, he affectionately referred to her as Little One, while she called him Big Kelly. Now a teen, she simply calls him B.K. and refers to him as "dad" when talking with her friends.

Write notes of encouragement. Slip them into your stepchildren's backpacks or under their pillows. Do little things that say, "I'm thinking of you." Everybody likes to feel special and know that someone cares.

When you have an errand to run, take along one of the kids. Take a different one each time, so they all get some one-on-one time with you. Kids often have to vie for an adult's attention and this gives them a chance to have you all to themselves.

Go to family counseling. Go now, before you are in a crisis. Learn the tools for dealing with problems before they arise. There are many simple parenting techniques that you'll use again and again.

Parenting is hard. Parenting other people's children is even harder. Go alone, with your husband or with the kids. Sometimes children are bothered by a problem, but have a difficult time expressing and sorting through their feelings. A few sessions with a family therapist can help bring the problem out and mutually resolve it.

Be flexible about celebrating holidays the day or week before or after the actual holiday. We have celebrated Christmas on the 25, the 23 and the 30. At first, it was very difficult not to be with my daughter on Christmas Day. It felt pretty lonely. Eventually, I came to learn that what is most important is the time we spend together, not the actual day.

Worship together as a family. If you're of the same faith, you're fortunate. If you and your new husband are of different religions, take turns worshipping at each other's church. Much strength can be gained from the foundation of faith.

Let the kids work out their differences on their own. Nine times out of ten, they don't want or need you to referee. If you are continually rescuing them, they'll never learn the fine art of negotiation.

Don't talk negatively about your ex-spouse in front of your child. Again, remember, this is your child's parent. As my mother always told me, if you don't have anything nice to say, don't say anything at all.

Treat your stepchildren like family, not guests, even if they only stay with you every other weekend. Guests get special attention and special privileges. Guests get waited on. Family members make themselves at home. They set the table, do the dishes, take out the trash and make their own beds.

Allow each parent to take on the role of primary disciplinarian for his or her biological children, at least at the beginning. Support each other's parenting decisions in front of the children. If you disagree about strategy, discuss it in private.

If you don't have children of your own, educate yourself. Read books on raising toddlers, handling teens and helping with homework. Take a parenting class. Talk with other parents and ask for their advice.

Think carefully before you and your new husband decide to have a mutual child. Adding to the mix can help or hinder an already tenuous family situation. If you decide to have a mutual child, make sure that all your children understand that both you and your new husband planned for and want this child.

Be nice to your husband's ex-wife. Of course, this is easier if your husband has a good relationship with her as well. But even if he doesn't, do your best to be polite, friendly and accommodating. Remember, she is entrusting you with the care of her children.

Take a vacation with your children and stepchildren. Sometimes getting away from it all, being on neutral turf and sharing a new experience together can help build and strengthen family bonds.

Educate yourself about stepfamilies. Check out the Stepfamily Association of America at www.ssafamilies.org. Better yet, join for only $40 per year and receive the association's monthly newsletter and access to local support groups. The organization offers tons of information about stepfamilies, advice on combining families and a resource list that you'll want to refer to again and again. Read Ron L. Deal's book, *The Smart Stepfamily*, and *Parenting the Other Chick's Eggs* by Ruth-Ann Clurman. Go online for support and chat with other stepmoms at www.secondwivesclub.com.

Don't hesitate to admit your mistakes and say you're sorry. This also goes for your husband, your kids and your stepchildren. Everyone makes mistakes, and your children need to know that adults make mistakes, too. They also need to learn that when they make a mistake, they should apologize, try to correct the mistake and then move on without holding a grudge or feeling embarrassed.

Don't use children as messengers between two households. If you need to tell your ex-husband something, pick up the phone or e-mail him. Do not send a child with a message or even a note. It's not the child's job, and it puts him or her in the uncomfortable position of mediating situations between parents.

Celebrate being a stepfamily. You've found love again, remarried and are blessed with children. You are not a nuclear family, nor are you a first family, but you are a real family. Celebrate it.

Chapter Eleven

Vow Renewals

Still In Love After All These Years

First **Wedding:** You married the man of your dreams. You promised each other that you would love, care for and support each other all the days of your lives.

Vow Renewal: He continues to be the man of your dreams. For twenty-five years you have loved, cared and supported each other, just as you promised.

You married for the first—or second time—many years ago. During that time, you have been through numerous experiences together. You've bought and sold houses, raised kids—yours, his and the two you had together—and have seen them off to college or seen them get married. You've lost jobs, made it through chemotherapy or maybe even the betrayal of an affair. Your love has not only endured it all, it has matured, grown and become stronger through the years. You and your husband are more in love with each other now than ever before. You are looking forward to the next twenty-five years together and want to express and reaffirm your love for each other. There is no better way to celebrate that love and commitment than with a vow renewal ceremony.

Like a wedding, your vow renewal can be large or small. It can be held in a church, at home or on the beach in Hawaii. You can celebrate it on a milestone anniversary, such as your tenth, fifteenth, twentieth or twenty-fifth. You can even combine it with a vacation, much like a destination wedding. You can do it on the spur of the moment or make it a well-planned event. It is not a legally binding ceremony, but an affair of the heart. You may have a clergy member, friend or relative officiate, or you can do without one and exchange your vows on your own. Most couples choose to have a small, intimate affair unless they eloped or had a very small ceremony the first time around. They tend to hold them in their own backyards, much like a garden party, at their churches with receptions at home, at nearby restaurants, or at tropical destinations, such as Hawaii or Jamaica.

Unlike a wedding, there is no gift registration, bridal shower, wedding veil or gown with a long train. You'll rarely see a bouquet or garter toss either. Ditto for a receiving line and cute little party favors.

To get started, first decide on an appropriate budget. Then, think about where you'd like to have the ceremony. Decide if it will be formal or casual. Your invitation should follow the formality or informality of the event, generally using words such as, "Mr. Michael Smith and Mrs. Jane Smith request the honor of your presence as they renew their marriage vows." If your children are hosting the event for you, it might read, "The children of Michael and Jane Smith ask you to join them as their parents renew their wedding vows." You might select a traditional wedding invitation, casual party invitation or personalize one with a photo of the two of you from your first wedding.

Based on the style and tone of the ceremony, it will be easy to decide what to wear. While some women wear their original wedding gowns, most choose cocktail dresses, evening gowns or suits. If you chose not to wear your wedding gown, you may want to display it at the reception alongside a photograph from your original nuptials. Your dress can be any color you like. You can carry a floral bouquet or place fresh flowers in your hair. Some women have their original bouquets re-created. Your husband could wear a suit and boutonniere or slacks and dinner jacket. If you plan to renew your vows in a tropical location, a simple sundress for you and shorts and shirt for him will be the order of the day.

Although you will not need attendants, you may want to invite your original maid of honor and best man to stand with you as you exchange your vows. You could have them recite special readings or simply be in attendance. Some couples ask their children to act as attendants. They can recite poems, sing songs or share special family memories. They may also want to offer a toast at the reception.

There are a few great songs with lyrics especially appropriate for vow renewals that you might want to play at your reception. One of my favorites is "Through the Years" by Kenny Rogers. A portion goes like this:

> *"I can't remember when you weren't there.*
> *When I didn't care for anyone but you.*
> *I swear, we've been through everything there is*
> *Can't imagine anything we've missed*
> *Can't imagine anything the two of us can't do."*

Another all-time favorite is "You're Still the One" by Shania Twain. Perhaps these lines will speak to you:

"When I first saw you, I saw love.
And the first time you touched me,
I felt love.
And after all this time, you're still the one I love."

Of course, there's the timeless song "Evergreen" by Barbara Streisand and Paul Williams:

"Love, soft as an easy chair,
love, fresh as the morning air.
One love that is shared by two,
I have found with you.
Like a rose under the April snow
I was always certain love would grow.
Love, ageless and evergreen
seldom seen by two."

Don't forget to include the song from your first dance at your original wedding, as well as favorite songs from that year or decade.

You may want to exchange new rings or have your old rings cleaned and polished. Some couples are very sentimental and retain their original rings, while others see it as a good opportunity to "trade up." If you currently wear a wedding band, you might want to have it engraved or add a diamond ring to complement the band.

The essential part of a vow renewal ceremony is the actual vows. While some couples recite their original vows, the majority spend much of their time and focus writing new, customized vows. They want to use this opportunity to express the depth of their love and how much it has meant to them to have been blessed with a great marriage.

When writing your own renewal vows, sit down alone or together and think back over the years. Recall the highlights, the major life events and special memories. Write down specific feelings that these memories bring and how you felt about your spouse at that time. For example, you may recall how you finally got that big job offer that meant you would have to move to another town, and your husband believed in you so much that he took the leap of faith and moved so that you could continue in your career path. Or maybe you'll recall a certain vacation, a special Christmas or the birth of your first child.

A trip down memory lane will also bring more traumatic events to mind—maybe a devastating illness, the rough teenage years when your son landed in jail or an unfortunate miscarriage. Those were the times you stood by each other, supported each other and shared your heavy burdens. You'll want to express those feelings of gratitude for helping each other through the inevitable rough times. Ask yourself: "What is it that I love most about my husband? How has he made me a better person? How has our love grown?" Think about the kind of father he has been to your kids, the baseball games he never missed and the science projects he helped complete.

After all this reflection, your feelings may be overwhelming. Jot them down as best you can. Later you can go over the list and turn these thoughts, feelings and memories into vows and expressions of love. Last, think about the years to come and write down new promises that will see you through the weddings of your children, the addition of grandbabies, retirement and the golden years.

Following your vow renewal ceremony, you may want a reception to celebrate the occasion with your friends and family. Most couples include a cake, often replicating their original cake from old wedding photos. Many even use the same cake topper. Speaking of photos, you may also want to display your wedding album, posters bearing a collage of photographs of you, your husband and family throughout the years and even your original guest book. You might want to put together a video of your photos. You could have it play in the background, or let it be one of the highlights of the reception. I have seen this done, and it's very heartwarming to watch a couple's love grow through the years.

After the ceremony and reception, you may want to go on a second honeymoon. Often times, a couple will choose to return to the site of their first honeymoon, even staying at the same hotel and requesting the same room. If you didn't have the chance for a honeymoon the first time around, this could be your opportunity to splurge. At the very least, plan an overnight stay at a nearby hotel, complete with champagne and breakfast in bed.

Most couples say that their vow renewal ceremonies were even more romantic and meaningful than their original wedding vows. Their love has been tested, and it has beaten the odds. After all they have been through on the road of life, they still want to travel that road together. As Linda Pasadava of A Vow Exchange in Hawaii says, "Vow renewals are especially joyful. These couples have passed the test of time. They are much more relaxed than couples marrying for the first or even second time. I always encourage couples to bring their children, even adult children. What better lesson than to see your parents so much in love that they are willing to marry all over again?"

Here's a heartwarming story about couples renewing their vows:

Nicole's Story
    "My husband and I had been married for fourteen years. We'd always talked about returning to Kauai, where we honeymooned, for a vow renewal ceremony when we hit the twenty-year mark. Then 9/11 hit, and we realized that life is uncertain. We didn't want to wait, so we moved up the date and returned to Kauai for our fifteenth anniversary.

We invited our best friends, a couple we've known for most of our married lives. Our children were happy to join us as well. We exchanged vows on a bluff overlooking the ocean on a spectacularly beautiful day. We wrote our own vows and exchanged leis rather than rings. My husband and I are very sentimental and couldn't stand the thought of giving each other new rings when our old ones had seen us through so much. Just looking at my scratched wedding band is like proof of all we have been through together. The ceremony was simple, heartfelt and romantic. Everyone stayed for five days, and then my husband and I stayed on for an additional three days. Let me tell you, there's nothing like a second honeymoon!"

Chapter Twelve

Your Story...

*T*his chapter belongs to you. Use it to record the first page of your story. My best wishes and congratulations to you and your new family as you embark on this exciting journey. Bon voyage!

Epilogue

Planning a first wedding and getting married when you're in your twenties is a piece of cake. Planning a second wedding and getting remarried, no matter what your age, can be a bit overwhelming. Add children from a previous union and this just might be the most challenging feat you have ever undertaken.

You are, however, already a step ahead of the game by having read this book now, while you are just beginning the planning process of your wedding. You are going in with your eyes wide open, you have added some new tools to your belt and you're armed with a few more tricks up your sleeve.

You now know to make that date with your therapist to hone those relationship skills and clear the air for a fresh start. You'll set aside time to talk with your fiancé about how and when to make the big announcement of your engagement to your kids. You'll make a point to discuss finances, budgets, pre-nuptial agreements, wills and life insurance sooner rather than later—getting all your ducks in a row now, before the thrill of the wedding plans begins.

So go ahead, have the wedding of your dreams. Wear white. Register for gifts. Choose the one invitation that gives your guests a glimpse of the wedding to come. Dance the night away and celebrate this second chance at love, topping it all off with a honeymoon in paradise. Even if it's just for the weekend. Last, you'll come home, knowing you have dozens of ways to start the process of blending and combining your two families together. That's when your own story truly beings. Congratulations! My best wishes to you and your new family as you embark on the exciting journey of a second marriage. Hopefully, this journey will last a lifetime.

Index